Basic Citation Forms: Law Review Footnotes

This table gives examples of commonly used citation forms printed in the typefaces used in law review footnotes. The facing page presents these same examples in the typefaces used in briefs and legal memoranda. For a fuller explanation of different typeface conventio

cases (rule 10)	
reporter (rule 10.3)	Jackson v. Metropoli 58 (M.D. Pa. 1972) *aff'd,* 419 U.S. 34
	Herrick v. Lindley, 5 729, 731 (1979)
	Willis v. Thomas, 600 P.2d 1079, 1083 (Alaska 1979)
looseleaf service (rule 18)	Lake v. Kidder, Peabody & Co., [1978 Transfer Binder] FED. SEC. L. REP. (CCH) ¶ 96,509, at 93,971 (N.D. Ind. May 22, 1978)
slip opinion (rule 10.8.1)	Jackson v. Virginia, No. 77-1205, slip op. at 3 (4th Cir. Aug. 3, 1978) (per curiam), *aff'd,* 443 U.S. 307 (1979)
constitutions (rule 11)	N.M. CONST. art. IV, § 7
statutes (rule 12)	
code (rule 12.3)	Administrative Procedure Act § 6, 5 U.S.C. § 555 (1976)
	22 U.S.C. § 2347 (Supp. III 1979)
session laws (rule 12.4)	Department of Transportation Act, Pub. L. No. 89-670, § 9, 80 Stat. 931, 944–47 (1966)
legislative materials (rule 13)	
unenacted bill (rule 13.2)	H.R. 3055, 94th Cong., 2d Sess. § 2, 122 CONG. REC. 16,870 (1976)
hearing (rule 13.3)	*Toxic Substances Control Act: Hearings on S. 776 Before the Subcomm. on the Environment of the Senate Comm. on Commerce,* 94th Cong., 1st Sess. 343 (1975)
report (rule 13.4)	S. REP. NO. 910, 89th Cong., 1st Sess. 4 (1965)
books (rule 15)	2 F. POLLOCK & F. MAITLAND, THE HISTORY OF ENGLISH LAW 201–14 (1895)
works not formally printed (rule 15.5.2)	H. Wechsler, Remarks at the Meeting of the Bar of the Supreme Court of the United States in Memory of Chief Justice Stone 5 (Nov. 12, 1947) (available in Columbia Law School Library)
periodicals (rule 16)	Reese, *Legislative Jurisdiction,* 78 COLUM. L. REV. 1587, 1591–94 (1978)
	Note, *The Logic of Secession,* 89 YALE L.J. 802, 809–12 (1980)
newspapers (rule 17)	Boston Globe, Oct. 14, 1954, at 6, col. 1
treaties (rule 19.2)	Parcel Post Agreement, June 3–14, 1951, United States-Gold Coast Colony, art. IV, 2 U.S.T. 1859, 1862, T.I.A.S. No. 2322, at 4

Many of the above examples include pinpoint cites, which are used to direct the reader to particular pages. Citations to an entire authority need not contain pinpoint cites. *See generally* rule 3.3.

Published and Distributed by
The Harvard Law Review Association
Gannett House
Cambridge, Massachusetts 02138
U.S.A.

First Printing 1981
Second Printing 1982
Third Printing 1983
Fourth Printing 1983
Fifth Printing 1984
Sixth Printing 1984
Seventh Printing 1985

Printings are updated as appropriate.

Book design by
Jack Schwartz Graphics, Boston, Massachusetts

Typesetting by
DEKR Corporation, Woburn, Massachusetts

Printing by
Lorell Press, Avon, Massachusetts

A Uniform System of Citation

Thirteenth Edition

How to Use This Book

This book has three basic parts. The first (rules 1–9) includes general rules of citation and style. It is intended to serve as a self-contained introduction to principles of legal citation. A reader familiar with these principles will find it easy to remember and use the citation forms prescribed in this book. The second part (rules 10–19) collects technical rules of citation relating to cases, statutes, periodicals, and other specific forms of authority. Although the reader will soon become familiar with many of these technical rules, this part's arrangement by type of authority also makes it a valuable reference. The final part (tables) contains lists—divided by country and state—of reporters, codes, session laws, and other sources, and their abbreviations. It is intended as a reference.

Legal citations should (1) *identify* the source being cited, (2) *distinguish* it from other sources, and (3) help the reader *locate* the source. The forms prescribed by this uniform system of citation will generally meet these goals. However, when unusual circumstances make these forms confusing or otherwise inadequate, a different citation form should be substituted.

Because of the ever-increasing range of authorities cited in legal writing, neither this nor any other system of citation can be comprehensive. When citing material not referred to in this book, be sure to list information that will make it possible for the reader to find the source quickly and reliably. In deciding what information to include and how to arrange it, citation forms prescribed by this book for similar types of authorities can serve as a useful guide. In citing sources that are not printed (such as microfiche, film, computer tape, and computer data bases), parenthetically give information that aids in their location.

The editors recommend use of the following reference works: for punctuation, capitalization, compounding, and other matters of style, *U.S. Government Printing Office Style Manual* (rev. ed. 1973); and for grammar, H.W. Fowler's *Modern English Usage* (E. Gowers 2d ed. 1965).

The editors are grateful for the suggestions for revisions offered by all segments of the legal community. We also wish to thank all those who directly participated in preparation of this edition. In particular, we thank the members of the *Columbia Journal of Transnational Law,* who assisted in revising the rules and tables governing foreign and international law materials. Special thanks are due to Louis Touton of the *Columbia Law Review*, without whose continuing involvement this project could not have been brought to completion.

Finally, the editors request that any errors or omissions be reported and that suggestions for revisions be sent to the Harvard Law Review, Gannett House, Cambridge, Massachusetts 02138.

Changes from the Twelfth Edition

Although this edition of *A Uniform System of Citation* retains the basic approach to legal citation established by its predecessors, it contains important revisions and additions. Users familiar with previous editions should review this edition for changes. Here are a few particularly noteworthy ones:

The inside front cover and facing page give examples of the proper form for citations in briefs, memoranda, and typewritten materials as well as in law review footnotes. In addition, rule 1 gives a detailed description of typeface conventions used in various contexts (pp. 3–6).

The meaning of the signal "*see also*" has been changed: it now indicates specific support. In string citations, it follows "*see*" and precedes "*cf.*" (Pp. 8–9, 10).

Explanatory parenthetical phrases are strongly encouraged after authorities introduced by the signals "*see also*," "*compare*," and "*see generally*." (Pp. 8–10).

The rule specifying the order of authorities within a given signal is more detailed and slightly revised. (Pp. 10–13).

Volume numbers are always given in Arabic numerals. (P. 15).

Square brackets should not be placed around the year used as a volume number, unless the volume designation contains words (e.g., [1967–1968 Transfer Binder]) or has a separate volume number (e.g., [1943] 2 K.B. 154). (Pp. 15–16).

Cross-references in briefs must specify the page(s) to which the reader is referred. (P. 21).

Rule 4, which governs short citation forms, has been extensively revised. (Pp. 21–25).

Numbers containing five or more digits should be separated by commas into groups of three digits. (P. 30).

Common expressions such as "i.e.," "e.g.," and "sic" are no longer italicized for stylistic purposes; when used as a signal, however, "*e.g.*," is still italicized. (Pp. 6, 31).

The treatment of case names containing business firm or union names has been changed. (Pp. 40–41).

All cases cited to periodicals or looseleaf services now require an exact date. (P. 48).

Citations to the Internal Revenue Code now require the date of the edition of *United States Code* being cited. (Pp. 66–67).

This edition gives detailed instructions for citing uniform acts, model codes, restatements, standards, and ABA materials (pp. 67–70) and formal advisory opinions (p. 77).

The tables of periodical abbreviations have been expanded and reorganized into a single table. (Pp. 92–103).

Material in bound services should be cited by paragraph or topic number wherever possible. (Pp. 108, 109–14).

Changes from the Twelfth Edition

[illegible]

Contents

How to Use This Book iv
Changes from the Twelfth Edition v

General Rules of Citation and Style

1 Introduction and Typefaces 3
1.1 Typeface Conventions for Briefs and Legal Memoranda 3
1.2 Typeface Conventions for Law Review Text 5
1.3 Typeface Conventions for Law Review Footnotes 5
1.4 Textual Footnote Material 6

2 Structure and Use of Citations 7
2.1 Citation Sentences and Clauses 7
2.2 Introductory Signals 8
2.3 Order of Signals 10
2.4 Order of Authorities Within Each Signal 10
2.5 Parenthetical Information 13
2.6 Related Authority 13

3 Subdivisions 14
3.1 Subdivision Abbreviations 14
3.2 Volumes, Parts, and Supplements 15
3.3 Pages and Footnotes 16
3.4 Sections and Paragraphs 18
3.5 Appendices, Notes, and Other Addenda 20
3.6 Cross-References 21

4 Short Citation Forms 21
4.1 "*Id.*" 21
4.2 "*Supra*" and "Hereinafter" 22
4.3 Short Forms for Cases and Statutes 23

5 Quotations 25
5.1 Indentation, Quotation Marks, Citation, and Punctuation 25
5.2 Alterations 26
5.3 Omissions 26
5.4 Paragraph Structure 27

6 Abbreviations, Numerals, and Symbols 28
6.1 Abbreviations 28
6.2 Abbreviations in Languages Other Than English 29
6.3 Numerals and Symbols 30

7 Italicization for Stylistic Purposes 31

8 Capitalization 31

9 Titles of Judges, Officials, and Terms of Court 33

Citation Forms for Specific Types of Authority

10 Cases 35
10.1 Basic Citation Forms 35
10.2 Case Names 36
10.2.1 Case Names in Text 36
10.2.2 Case Names in Footnotes 41
10.2.3 Names of Administrative Cases and Arbitrations 42
10.3 Reporters and Other Sources 43
10.3.1 Which Source(s) to Cite 43
10.3.2 Reporters 44
10.4 Court and Jurisdiction 44
10.5 Date or Year 48
10.6 Parenthetical Information Regarding Cases 49
10.7 Prior and Subsequent History 50
10.7.1 Explanatory Phrases 50
10.7.2 Different Case Name on Appeal 51
10.8 Special Citation Forms 52
10.8.1 Pending and Unreported Cases 52
10.8.2 Briefs, Records, Motions, and Memoranda 53
10.8.3 Civil Law and Other Non-Common-Law Cases 53

11 Constitutions 57

12 Statutes 57
12.1 Basic Citation Forms 57
12.2 Choosing the Proper Citation Form 58
12.2.1 General Rule 58
12.2.2 Exceptions 59
12.3 Current Official and Unofficial Codes 60
12.3.1 Year of Code 62
12.4 Session Laws 63
12.5 Secondary Sources 64
12.6 Repeal, Amendment, and Prior History 65
12.6.1 Repeal 65
12.6.2 Amendment 65
12.6.3 Prior History 65
12.7 Explanatory Parenthetical Phrases 66
12.8 Special Citation Forms 66
12.8.1 Internal Revenue Code 66
12.8.2 Ordinances 67
12.8.3 Rules of Evidence and Procedure 67
12.8.4 Uniform Acts 67
12.8.5 Model Codes, Restatements, and Standards 68

12.8.6 ABA Code of Professional Responsibility and Opinions on Ethics 69
12.8.7 Commonwealth Statutes 70
12.8.8 Civil Law and Other Non-Common-Law Statutes 71

13 Legislative Materials 71
13.1 Basic Citation Forms 71
13.2 Bills and Resolutions 72
13.3 Hearings 73
13.4 Reports, Documents, and Committee Prints 73
13.5 Debates 74
13.6 Separately Bound Legislative Histories 75

14 Administrative and Executive Materials 75
14.1 Basic Citation Forms 75
14.2 Rules, Regulations, and Other Publications 76
14.3 Adjudications and Advisory Opinions 77
14.4 Federal Taxation Materials 77
14.5 Presidential Papers and Executive Orders 78
14.5.1 Executive Orders, Presidential Proclamations, and Reorganization Plans 78
14.5.2 Other Presidential Papers 79
14.6 Court Administrative Orders 79

15 Books, Pamphlets, and Unpublished Materials 81
15.1 Author 81
15.2 Title 82
15.3 Serial Number 83
15.4 Edition and Date 83
15.5 Special Citation Forms 85
15.5.1 Essays in Collection 85
15.5.2 Letters, Interviews, Speeches, Unpublished Works, and Other Materials of Limited Circulation 85
15.5.3 Other Special Citation Forms 86

16 Periodicals 87
16.1 Authors and Titles 88
16.1.1 Articles 88
16.1.2 Student-Written Law Review Materials 89
16.1.3 Book Reviews 89
16.1.4 Annotations 90
16.1.5 Miscellaneous Matters 90
16.2 Periodical Abbreviations 91
16.2.1 Periodicals with English-Language Titles 91
16.2.2 Periodicals with Foreign-Language Titles 103

17 Newspapers **104**

18 Services **107**
18.1 Citation Form for Services 107
18.2 Service Abbreviations 108

19 International Materials **117**
19.1 Basic Citation Forms 117
19.2 Treaties and Other International Agreements 118
19.2.1 Name of the Agreement 118
19.2.2 Date of Signing 119
19.2.3 Parties to the Agreement 119
19.2.4 Treaty Series and Other Sources 120
19.3 International Law Cases and Arbitrations 121
19.4 United Nations Materials 124
19.4.1 Basic Citation Forms 124
19.4.2 Specific Types of Materials 126
19.5 Materials of Other International Organizations 128
19.5.1 League of Nations Materials 128
19.5.2 European Community Materials 129
19.5.3 Council of Europe Materials 130
19.6 Yearbooks 130

Tables

United States **132**
Federal 133
Alabama 136
Alaska 137
American Samoa 137
Arizona 137
Arkansas 138
California 138
Canal Zone 140
Colorado 140
Connecticut 141
Delaware 142
District of Columbia 143
Florida 143
Georgia 144
Guam 145
Hawaii 145
Idaho 145
Illinois 146
Indiana 146
Iowa 147
Kansas 147

Kentucky ... 148
Louisiana ... 149
Maine ... 150
Maryland ... 150
Massachusetts ... 152
Michigan ... 153
Minnesota ... 153
Mississippi ... 154
Missouri ... 154
Montana ... 155
Nebraska ... 155
Nevada ... 155
New Hampshire ... 156
New Jersey ... 156
New Mexico ... 157
New York ... 157
North Carolina ... 161
North Dakota ... 162
Ohio ... 163
Oklahoma ... 164
Oregon ... 165
Pennsylvania ... 165
Puerto Rico ... 167
Rhode Island ... 167
South Carolina ... 167
South Dakota ... 169
Tennessee ... 169
Texas ... 170
Utah ... 172
Vermont ... 172
Virgin Islands ... 173
Virginia ... 173
Washington ... 174
West Virginia ... 175
Wisconsin ... 175
Wyoming ... 176

Foreign: Common Law Jurisdictions ... 179
Australia ... 179
Australian States and Territories ... 179
Canada ... 181
Canadian Provinces and Territories ... 182
India ... 184
New Zealand ... 184
United Kingdom ... 185
England and Wales ... 186

Northern Ireland (and Ireland until 1924) ... 189
Scotland ... 190

Foreign: Other Jurisdictions ... 190
Argentina ... 190
Brazil ... 191
France ... 191
German Democratic Republic (East Germany) ... 193
Germany, Federal Republic of (West Germany) ... 194
Länder (West German States) ... 195
Italy ... 196
Japan ... 197
Mexico ... 198
Netherlands, Kingdom of the ... 198
Roman Law ... 198
Switzerland ... 199
Swiss Cantons ... 200

Index ... 203

A Uniform System of Citation

General Rules of Citation and Style

Rule 1: Introduction and Typefaces 3

Rule 2: Structure and Use of Citations 7

Rule 3: Subdivisions 14

Rule 4: Short Citation Forms 21

Rule 5: Quotations 25

Rule 6: Abbreviations, Numerals, and Symbols 28

Rule 7: Italicization for Stylistic Purposes 31

Rule 8: Capitalization 31

Rule 9: Titles of Judges, Officials, and Terms of Court 33

Introduction and Typefaces 1

A

The citation forms in this book have been designed for use in all types of legal writing. The typefaces in which the forms are printed, however, may be varied to suit the needs of the writer. This rule outlines the typeface conventions commonly used in briefs and legal memoranda (rule 1.1), law review text (rule 1.2), and law review footnotes (rules 1.3 and 1.4). Because the typeface conventions for law review footnotes are more complex than those for briefs, memoranda, and law review text, most of the examples in this book appear as they would in law review footnotes. Except for typeface differences, however, all rules in this book are directly applicable to citation in briefs and memoranda: simply apply the typeface rules in rule 1.1 to the examples given in this book. The tables on the inside front cover and facing page show how the most common citation forms should appear in both law review footnotes and typewritten briefs or memoranda.

Typeface Conventions for Briefs and Legal Memoranda 1.1

Only two typefaces are used in briefs, memoranda, and similar materials:

> Ordinary Roman and *Italics* (indicated in typewritten materials by Underscoring)

To distinguish citations from text in briefs and legal memoranda, this book recommends the following usage of typefaces:

(a) Introductory signals (rule 2.2), **phrases introducing related authority** (rule 2.6), **and explanatory phrases** introducing prior or subsequent authority (rules 2.6, 10.7.1, 12.2.2(c), and 12.6) should be underscored or appear in italics.

(b) Cases (rule 10). Italicize or underscore all case names, including the "v." and any procedural phrases:

> In re Winship, 397 U.S. 358 (1970).
>
> NAACP v. Alabama ex rel. Patterson, 357 U.S. 449 (1956).
>
> United States v. Reynolds, 449 F.2d 1347 (9th Cir. 1971), cert. denied, 408 U.S. 924 (1972).

(c) Publications (rules 13, 15, 16, and 17). In citations, italicize or underscore book titles and the titles of articles that appear in periodicals or newspapers. Authors' names and periodical or newspaper titles appear in ordinary roman type. Thus:

O.W. Holmes, The Common Law 1 (1881).

T. Plucknett, A Concise History of the Common Law (5th ed. 1956).

Comment, Reconstructing the Independent Evidence Requirement of the Coconspirator Hearsay Exception, 127 U. Pa. L. Rev. 1439 (1979).

Baker, The Beer Culture, N.Y. Times, May 27, 1980, at A27, col. 2.

SEC Ends Inquiry of Auto-Train Corp. Without Any Actions, Wall St. J., May 27, 1980, at 12, col. 2.

Treat congressional publications (such as hearings, documents, and committee prints) as books; italicize or underscore titles and print authors' names (if given) in ordinary roman type:

Corporate Rights and Responsibilities: Hearings Before the Senate Comm. on Commerce, 94th Cong., 2d Sess. 47 (1976).

C. Davenport, Report on Administrative Procedures of the Internal Revenue Service, S. Doc. No. 226, 94th Cong., 2d Sess. 619–726 (1975).

Where reports or documents are cited without author or title, print in ordinary roman:

S. Rep. No. 1319, 89th Cong., 2d Sess. (1966).

H.R. Rep. No. 98, 92d Cong., 1st Sess. 4, reprinted in 1971 U.S. Code Cong. & Ad. News 1017, 1017.

When referring to a publication rather than citing to it, italicize or underscore the publication's full name:

The library receives both the Yale Law Journal and the Federal Reporter.

(d) Cross-references and short forms (rules 3.6 and 4). Italicize or underscore "supra," "infra," and "id.," but not "hereinafter."

(e) Style. Italicize or underscore words for emphasis or other stylistic purposes (rule 7) and words italicized in quotations (rule 5).

(f) Everything else. Print everything else—including reporters, services, constitutions, all statutory material, restatements, model acts, rules, executive orders, administrative materials, unpublished sources, and treaties—in ordinary roman type.

A

Typeface Conventions for Law Review Text 1.2

Law review text contains no citations. Most material appears in ordinary roman type. Only the following are italicized:

(a) Case names, including the "*v.*" and all procedural phrases ("*In re*," "*ex parte*," and "*ex rel.*").

(b) Titles of publications, speeches, or articles. Thus:

> The library has copies of the *Wall Street Journal, Harvard Law Review,* and *Federal Supplement*. It does not have a copy of *Hearings on S. 776* or other congressional hearings.

(c) Style. Italicize words for emphasis or other stylistic purposes (rule 7) and words italicized in quotations (rule 5).

Typeface Conventions for Law Review Footnotes 1.3

Law reviews use various typeface conventions with the forms given in this book for citation in footnotes. Most law reviews use three different typefaces in footnotes:

> Ordinary Roman, *Italics*, and LARGE AND SMALL CAPITALS

Some replace large and small capitals with ordinary roman type. Thus:

> Note, *Conditional Guilty Pleas*, 93 HARV. L. REV. 564 (1980)

becomes:

> Note, *Conditional Guilty Pleas,* 93 Harv. L. Rev. 564 (1980).

Other law reviews replace some italics, as well as all large and small capitals, with ordinary roman type:

> Note, Conditional Guilty Pleas, 93 Harv. L. Rev. 564 (1980).

Regardless of which typeface convention is used, authorities discussed textually in footnotes should be italicized according to rule 1.4.

The examples in this book follow the first convention, using all three typefaces, unless the context indicates otherwise. The rules concerning typefaces for citation in law review footnotes are incorporated into the examples throughout this book. The following list describes a few of the typeface conventions used in law review footnotes:

(a) Case names (rule 10.2). Use ordinary roman type for case names, except for procedural phrases, which are italicized:

State *ex rel.* Scott v. Zinn, 74 N.M. 224, 392 P.2d 417 (1964).

(b) Books (rule 15). Both author and title should appear in large and small capitals:

R. KLUGER, SIMPLE JUSTICE (1976).

(c) Periodicals (rule 16). Italicize article titles, and use large and small capitals for the name of the periodical; the author's name appears in roman:

Berger, *Man's Trial, Women's Tribulation: Rape Cases in the Courtroom,* 77 COLUM. L. REV. 1 (1977).

(d) Introductory signals (rule 2.2). Italicize all introductory signals, including "*e.g.*":

See, e.g., Clyde v. Hodge, 460 F.2d 532 (3d Cir. 1972).

(e) Explanatory phrases (rules 2.6, 10.7.1, 12.2.2(c), and 12.6). Italicize all explanatory phrases:

Oreck Corp. v. Whirlpool Corp., 579 F.2d 126, 131 (2d Cir.), *cert. denied,* 439 U.S. 946 (1978).

1.4 Textual Footnote Material

Regardless of the typeface conventions used, italicize case names in footnotes whenever only one of the two adversary parties is named or no citation is given. Thus:

Prior to *Spinelli v. United States,* the Court had addressed the issue in *Aguilar,* 378 U.S. at 114.

But:

the issue in Aguilar v. Texas, 378 U.S. at 114.

When a footnote refers to any other kind of authority without giving either the full citation or a citation shortened according to rule 4, follow the typeface conventions for law review text (rule 1.2). Thus:

Judge Hand explained his philosophy of judicial review in *The Bill of Rights.*

But:

A different view is expressed in L. HAND, THE BILL OF RIGHTS (1958), and O.W. HOLMES, *supra* note 2.

Structure and Use of Citations 2

Citations are made in citation sentences and clauses (rule 2.1) and are introduced by signals, which indicate the purposes for which the citations are made and the degree of support the citations give (rule 2.2). Citation sentences and clauses may contain more than one signal. Signals are ordered according to rule 2.3. Individual citations following each signal are ordered according to rule 2.4. Additional information about an authority may be given parenthetically (rule 2.5), and related authority may be appended according to rule 2.6.

Citation Sentences and Clauses 2.1

Citations may be made in either of two ways: in citation sentences or in citation clauses. (i) Authorities that support (or contradict) an entire sentence or that are appended as footnotes are given in separate citation sentences that begin with capitalized letters and end with periods. (ii) Authorities that support (or contradict) only part of a sentence and that are not appended as footnotes are cited in clauses, set off by commas, that immediately follow the proposition they support. In both citation sentences and clauses, multiple citations are separated with semicolons. Thus a discussion in a brief or memorandum would appear:

> Some American jurisdictions place the burden of sustaining criminal defenses on the accused. See Jeffries & Stephan, Defenses, Presumptions, and the Burden of Proof in the Criminal Law, 88 Yale L.J. 1325, 1329–30 (1979). States have required defendants to prove both insanity, e.g., State v. Caryl, 168 Mont. 414, 543 P.2d 389 (1975); State v. Hinson, 253 S.C. 607, 172 S.E.2d 548 (1970), and self-defense, see, e.g., Quillen v. State, 49 Del. 114, 121, 110 A.2d 445, 449 (1955); State v. Skinner, 32 Nev. 70, 74, 104 P. 223, 224 (1909). See generally W. LaFave & A. Scott, Handbook on Criminal Law § 8, at 46–51 (1972). In several jurisdictions the defendant must even establish that a homicide was accidental. See, e.g., Chandle v. State, 230 Ga. 574, 198 S.E.2d 289 (1973); State v. Enlow, 536 S.W.2d 533 (Mo. Ct. App. 1976).

The same discussion in law review text and footnotes would appear:

Some American jurisdictions place the burden of sustaining criminal defenses on the accused.[1] States have required defendants to prove both insanity[2] and self-defense.[3] In several jurisdictions the defendant must even establish that a homicide was accidental.[4]

[1] *See* Jeffries & Stephan, *Defenses, Presumptions, and the Burden of Proof in the Criminal Law*, 88 YALE L.J. 1325, 1329–30 (1979).

[2] *E.g.*, State v. Caryl, 168 Mont. 414, 543 P.2d 389 (1975); State v. Hinson, 253 S.C. 607, 172 S.E.2d 548 (1970).

[3] *See, e.g.*, Quillen v. State, 49 Del. 114, 121, 110 A.2d 445, 449 (1955); State v. Skinner, 32 Nev. 70, 74, 104 P. 223, 224 (1909). *See generally* W. LAFAVE & A. SCOTT, HANDBOOK ON CRIMINAL LAW § 8, at 46–51 (1972).

[4] *See, e.g.*, Chandle v. State, 230 Ga. 574, 198 S.E.2d 289 (1973); State v. Enlow, 536 S.W.2d 533 (Mo. Ct. App. 1976).

2.2 Introductory Signals

(a) Signals that indicate support.

[no signal] — Cited authority (i) states the proposition, (ii) identifies the source of a quotation, or (iii) identifies an authority referred to in text.

E.g., — Cited authority states the proposition; other authorities also state the proposition, but citation to them would not be helpful. "*E.g.*," may also be used in combination with other signals, preceded by a comma:

See, e.g.,

But see, e.g.,

Accord — Cited authority directly supports the proposition, but in a slightly different way than the authority(ies) first cited. "*Accord*" is commonly used when two or more cases are on point but the text refers to only one; the others are then introduced by "*accord*." Similarly, the law of one jurisdiction may be cited as in accord with that of another.

See — Cited authority directly supports the proposition. "*See*" is used instead of "[no signal]" when the proposition is not stated by the cited authority but follows from it.

See also — Cited authority constitutes additional source material that supports the proposition. "*See also*" is commonly used to cite an authority supporting a proposition when authorities that state or directly support the proposition have already been cited or discussed. The use of a parenthetical explanation of the source material's relevance (rule 2.5) following a citation introduced by "*see also*" is encouraged.

Cf. — Cited authority supports a proposition different from the main proposition but sufficiently analogous to lend support. Literally, "*cf.*" means "compare." The citation's relevance will usually be clear to the reader only if it is explained. Parenthetical explanations (rule 2.5), however brief, are therefore strongly recommended.

(b) Signal that suggests a profitable comparison.

Compare . . . [and] . . . with . . . [and] . . . — Comparison of the authorities cited will offer support for or illustrate the proposition. The comparison's relevance will usually be clear to the reader only if it is explained. Parenthetical explanations (rule 2.5) following each authority are therefore strongly recommended.

(c) Signals that indicate contradiction.

Contra — Cited authority states the contrary of the proposition. "*Contra*" is used where "[no signal]" would be used for support.

But see — Cited authority directly contradicts the proposition. "*But see*" is used where "*see*" would be used for support.

But cf. — Cited authority supports a proposition analogous to the contrary of the main proposition. The use of a parenthetical explanation of the source material's relevance (rule 2.5) following a citation introduced by "*but cf.*" is strongly recommended.

"*But*" should be omitted from "*but see*" and "*but cf.*" whenever the signal follows another negative signal:

> *Contra* Blake v. Kline, 612 F.2d 718, 723–24 (3d Cir. 1979); *see* C. WRIGHT, LAW OF FEDERAL COURTS § 48 (3d ed. 1976).

(d) Signal that indicates background material.

See generally — Cited authority presents helpful background material related to the proposition. The use of a parenthetical explanation of the source material's relevance (rule 2.5) following each authority introduced by "*see generally*" is encouraged.

(e) Signals as verbs. When "*see*," "*compare*," "*see generally*," or another signal word is used as the verb of an English sentence, the word should be printed in ordinary roman type:

> For a discussion of limits on the property power, see Note, *The Property Power, Federalism, and the Equal Footing Doctrine*, 80 COLUM. L. REV. 817 (1980).
>
> For a related view, compare Note, *The Rights of Sources*, 88 YALE L.J. 1202 (1979), which discusses the rights of reporters' sources.

2.3 Order of Signals

When more than one signal is used, the signals (together with the authorities they introduce) should appear in the order in which they are listed in rule 2.2. Signals of the same basic type—supportive, comparative, contradictory, or background (rule 2.2)—must be strung together within a single citation sentence. Signals of different types, however, must be grouped in different citation sentences. Thus:

> *See* Massachusetts Bd. of Retirement v. Murgia, 427 U.S. 307 (1976); *cf.* Palmer v. Ticcione, 433 F. Supp. 653 (E.D.N.Y. 1977) (upholding mandatory retirement age for kindergarten teachers). *But see* Gault v. Garrison, 569 F.2d 993 (7th Cir. 1977), *cert. denied*, 440 U.S. 945 (1979). *See generally* Comment, O'Neil v. Baine: *Application of Middle-Level Scrutiny to Old-Age Classifications*, 127 U. PA. L. REV. 798 (1979) (advocating new constitutional approach to old-age classifications).

Within a citation clause (rule 2.1(ii)), however, citation strings may contain signals of more than one type.

2.4 Order of Authorities Within Each Signal

If one authority is considerably more helpful or authoritative than the other authorities cited within a signal, it should precede the others. Absent a similar reason for placing one authority before another, cite authorities in the following order:

(a) Cases are arranged within a signal according to the courts issuing the cited opinions; subsequent and prior history is irrelevant to the order of citation. Cases decided by the same court

are arranged in reverse chronological order; for this purpose the several United States courts of appeals are treated as one court and all federal district courts are treated as one court. The ordering system is as follows:

Federal	(1) Supreme Court
	(2) courts of appeals, Emergency Court of Appeals, Temporary Emergency Court of Appeals
	(3) district courts
	(4) Court of Claims
	(5) Court of Customs and Patent Appeals, Court of International Trade, Court of Military Appeals, Customs Court, Railroad Reorganization Court, Tax Court (including Board of Tax Appeals)
	(6) bankruptcy appellate panels and judges
	(7) administrative agencies (alphabetically by agency)
State	(8) courts (alphabetically by state and then by rank within each state)
	(9) agencies (alphabetically by state and then alphabetically by agency within each state)
Foreign	(10) common law jurisdictions (as for states)
	(11) civil law jurisdictions (as for states)

(b) Constitutions are cited in the following order:

(1) federal
(2) state (alphabetically by state)
(3) foreign (alphabetically by jurisdiction)

Constitutions of the same jurisdiction are cited in reverse chronological order.

(c) Statutes are cited according to jurisdiction in the following order:

Federal	(1) statutes in U.S.C., U.S.C.A., or U.S.C.S. (by progressive order of U.S.C. title)
	(2) statutes currently in force but not in U.S.C., U.S.C.A., or U.S.C.S. (by reverse chronological order of enactment)
	(3) rules of evidence and procedure
	(4) repealed statutes (by reverse chronological order of enactment)
State (alphabetically by state)	(5) statutes in the current codification (by order in the codification)
	(6) statutes currently in force but not in the cur-

rent codification (by reverse chronological order of enactment)
(7) rules of evidence and procedure
(8) repealed statutes (by reverse chronological order of enactment)

Foreign (alphabetically by jurisdiction)	(9) statutes currently in force (10) repealed statutes

(d) Treaties and other international agreements are cited in reverse chronological order.

(e) Legislative materials are cited in the following order:

(1) bills and resolutions
(2) committee hearings
(3) reports, documents, and committee prints
(4) floor debates

Cite materials within each classification in reverse chronological order.

(f) Administrative and executive materials are cited in the following order:

Federal administrative rules, regulations, and rulings	(1) Executive Orders (2) current Treasury Regulations, proposed Treasury Regulations (3) all others currently in force (by progressive order of C.F.R. title) (4) all repealed (by reverse chronological order of promulgation)
Other administrative rules, regulations, and rulings	(5) state (alphabetically by state), currently in force, then repealed (6) foreign (alphabetically by jurisdiction), currently in force, then repealed

(g) Records, briefs, and petitions are cited in that order, and within each classification by order of the court in which filed.

(h) Secondary materials are cited in the following order:

(1) books, and essays in a collection of a single author's essays (alphabetically by author; if none, by first word of title)
(2) articles, and essays in a collection of various authors' essays (alphabetically by author)
(3) student-written law review materials—special student projects, then long works such as notes, then short commentary on recent de-

velopments (alphabetically in each category by periodical as abbreviated in citation)
(4) signed book reviews (alphabetically by reviewer)
(5) student-written book notes (alphabetically by periodical as abbreviated in citation)
(6) newspapers (in reverse chronological order)
(7) annotations (in reverse chronological order)
(8) unpublished materials and other materials of limited circulation (alphabetically by author; if none, by first word of title)

Parenthetical Information 2.5

Information may be enclosed in parentheses and added to the basic citation:

> 3 *Consequences of Changing U.S. Population: Hearings Before the House Select Comm. on Population,* 95th Cong., 2d Sess. 52 (1978) (statement of Dr. David Birch) ("[T]here are more mayors of Rockville, Md., than there are mayors of Detroit.").

These explanatory parenthetical phrases should precede any citation of subsequent history or other related authority (rule 2.6):

> Atlantic Richfield Co. v. Federal Energy Admin., 429 F. Supp. 1052, 1061–62 (N.D. Cal. 1976) (stating that "not every person aggrieved by administrative action is necessarily entitled to due process"), *aff'd,* 556 F.2d 542 (Temp. Emer. Ct. App. 1977).

See also rule 10.6 (parenthetical information for cases); rule 12.7 (parenthetical information for statutes).

Related Authority 2.6

Related authority may be appended to a citation with an italicized explanatory phrase (in the following order, if more than one type of related authority is used). In italicized explanatory phrases and elsewhere, discussion is located "in" a work, "at" given pages or sections. Other prepositions may be used as appropriate.

(a) *"Reprinted In."* A work that conveniently reprints the primary authority but would not ordinarily be cited as a source for that authority may be introduced by "*reprinted in*":

> H.R. 3020, 80th Cong., 1st Sess. § 301 (1947), *reprinted in* 1 NLRB, LEGISLATIVE HISTORY OF THE LABOR MANAGEMENT RELATIONS ACT, 1947, at 92–94 (1948).
>
> Proposed Tenant Equality Act: An Amendment to the

New York Real Property Tax Law, *reprinted in* Kee & Moan, *The Property Tax and Tenant Equality,* 89 HARV. L. REV. 531, 548 app. (1976).

Rule 3.5 discusses the appropriate citation forms for appendices, notes, and other addenda.

(b) Relevant history. The prior or subsequent history of a case (rule 10.7) or of a statute (rule 12.6) may be appended to the main citation. See rules 10.7 and 12.6 for circumstances in which the subsequent history of a case or statute *must* be indicated.

(c) Commentary. Works that discuss or quote the primary authority may also be appended to the citation. Use phrases such as *"noted in," "construed in," "quoted in," "reviewed by," "cited with approval in," "questioned in."* Works that the primary authority discusses, cites, or otherwise mentions, however, should be indicated parenthetically. Thus:

Filled Milk Act § 1, 21 U.S.C. § 61 (1976), *construed in* Milnot Co. v. Richardson, 350 F. Supp. 221 (S.D. Ill. 1972).

But:

Milnot Co. v. Richardson, 350 F. Supp. 221 (S.D. Ill. 1972) (construing Filled Milk Act § 1, 21 U.S.C. § 61 (1976)).

Capron, *Tort Liability in Genetic Counseling,* 79 COLUM. L. REV. 618, 643 (1979) ("[I]n Judge Cardozo's classic statement, '[t]he risk reasonably to be perceived defines the duty to be obeyed'. . . .") (quoting Palsgraf v. Long Island R.R., 248 N.Y. 339, 344, 162 N.E. 99, 100 (1928)).

S. REP. NO. 181, 95th Cong., 1st Sess. 14 (1977) (citing Bituminous Coal Operators' Ass'n v. Secretary of the Interior, 547 F.2d 240 (4th Cir. 1977)), *reprinted in* 1977 U.S. CODE CONG. & AD. NEWS 3401, 3414.

3 Subdivisions

3.1 Subdivision Abbreviations

Subdivisions may be abbreviated as follows:

Subdivision	Abbreviation	Rule
amendment [s]	amend., amends.	8
appendi[x, ces]	app., apps.	3.5
article [s]	art., arts.	8

book [s]	bk., bks.	
chapter [s]	ch., chs.	
clause [s]	cl., cls.	
column [s]	col., cols.	
decision [s]	dec., decs.	
folio [s]	fol., fols.	
footnote [s]		
in cross-references	note, notes	3.6
other references	n., nn.	3.3
number [s]	No., Nos.	
page [s]		
in cross-references	p., pp.	3.6
other references	[at]	3.3
paragraph [s]		
if so in source	¶, ¶¶	3.4
otherwise	para., paras.	3.4
part [s]	pt., pts.	3.2
schedule [s]	sched., scheds.	
section [s]		
in amending act	sec., secs.	3.4
all other contexts	§, §§	3.4
series, serial [s]	ser.	
title [s]	tit., tits.	
volume [s]	vol., vols.	3.2

Volumes, Parts, and Supplements 3.2

A single work often appears in separately paginated (or sectioned or paragraphed) volumes, parts, or supplements. A citation to material that appears in one such volume, part, or supplement must identify the separately paginated subdivision in which the material appears.

(a) Volumes. When the volumes are numbered, cite the volume number in Arabic numerals. If the author of the entire volume is cited, the volume number precedes the author's name:

> 2 F. POLLOCK & F. MAITLAND, THE HISTORY OF ENGLISH LAW 205–06 (1895).
>
> 2 SUBCOMM. ON LABOR OF THE SENATE COMM. ON LABOR AND PUBLIC WELFARE, 92D CONG., 2D SESS., LEGISLATIVE HISTORY OF THE EQUAL EMPLOYMENT OPPORTUNITY ACT OF 1972, at 1007 (1972).

Otherwise the volume number precedes the volume's title:

> Zeigler, *Young Adults as a Cognizable Group in Jury Selection,* 76 MICH. L. REV. 1045, 1047 (1978).
>
> Standard Oil Co. v. FTC, 1979-2 Trade Cas. ¶ 62,776 (N.D. Ind. 1979).

If no volume number is given but the volume is readily identifiable by year, use the year of the volume instead:

1966 SUP. CT. U.S. J. 106

Black, *What is a Court?*, 1978 N.Z.L.J. 81.

If the volume designation includes words, use brackets to avoid confusion:

[1977–1978 Transfer Binder] BANKR. L. REP. (CCH) ¶ 66,472

If volumes are numbered in a new series each year, give both the year and volume number, bracketing the year to avoid confusion:

[1943] 2 K.B. 154

(b) Separately paginated numbered parts. Where works are divided into separately paginated (or sectioned or paragraphed) series, books, chapters, or other parts, include the relevant subdivisions in the citation:

26 CONG. REC. app. at 156 (1894) (statement of Rep. Hicks).

ser. 14, pt. 2, at 150

pt. 3, § 4, at 15

(c) Supplements. When citing a separately paginated, sectioned, or paragraphed supplement, identify the supplement and its date in parentheses:

HAWAII REV. STAT. § 296-46.1 (Supp. 1979).

G. BOGERT, THE LAW OF TRUSTS AND ESTATES § 496 (rev. 2d ed. Supp. 1979).

To cite both the main volume and the supplement, use the form:

42 U.S.C. § 1396a (1976 & Supp. III 1979).

3.3 Pages and Footnotes

(a) Pages. Give the page number after the full citation, but before any parenthetical phrase, without any introductory abbreviation:

A. SUTHERLAND, CONSTITUTIONALISM IN AMERICA 45 (1965).

H.R. REP. NO. 353, 82d Cong., 1st Sess. 5 (1951).

Never use "p." except for cross-references (rule 3.6); use "at" if the page number may be confused with another part of the citation:

BIOGRAPHICAL DIRECTORY OF THE GOVERNORS OF THE

UNITED STATES 1789–1978, at 629 (R. Sobel & J. Raimo eds. 1978).

Davis, *Foreword* to F. WEINER, EFFECTIVE APPELLATE ADVOCACY at v (1950).

If the article, case, or other source is not separately paginated, cite the page on which the item begins:

Diamond, *The Psychiatric Prediction of Dangerousness,* 123 U. PA. L. REV. 439 (1974).

United States v. Bruno, 144 F. Supp. 593 (N.D. Ill. 1955).

Government Employees Training Act, Pub. L. No. 85-507, 72 Stat. 507 (1958).

When referring to specific material within such a source, include both the page on which the source begins and the page on which the specific material appears, separated by commas:

Note, *Municipal Bankruptcy,* 84 YALE L.J. 918, 996 (1974).

When referring to the first page, repeat the page number:

Note, *Beyond* Marvin: *A Proposal for Quasi-Spousal Support,* 30 STAN. L. REV. 358, 358 (1978).

In citing material within a concurring or dissenting opinion, give only the initial page of the case and the page on which the specific material appears, not the initial page of the concurring or dissenting opinion:

Baker v. Carr, 369 U.S. 186, 297 (1962) (Frankfurter, J., dissenting).

(b) Footnotes. To cite to a footnote, give the page on which the footnote appears, "n.," and the footnote number:

20 B.C.L. REV. 601, 613 n.97 (1979).

To cite all of a footnote that spans several pages, cite only the page on which the footnote *begins,* "n.," and the footnote number:

20 B.C.L. REV. 601, 613 n.100 (1979).

When referring only to specific pages of a multipage footnote, cite only those specific pages, rather than the page on which the footnote begins:

20 B.C.L. REV. 601, 614 n.100 (1979).

(c) Multiple pages and footnotes. When citing material that spans more than one page, give the inclusive page numbers, separated by a hyphen or, in printed materials, an en dash.

Always retain the last two digits, but drop other repetitious digits:

Note, *Fairness, Flexibility, and the Waiver of Remedial Rights by Contract,* 87 YALE L.J. 1057, 1065–69 (1978).

Cite nonconsecutive pages by giving the individual page numbers separated by commas:

Kleppe v. New Mexico, 426 U.S. 529, 531, 546 (1976).

When a point is often repeated throughout the entire source, use "*passim*":

Mandel Corp., 47 B.T.A. 68 *passim* (1942).

Cite multiple footnotes "nn.":

141 nn.180–86

Treat nonconsecutive footnotes like nonconsecutive pages, but substitute an ampersand for the last comma:

291 nn.14 & 18, 316 nn.4, 6 & 8–10

To refer to a page in text as well as a footnote which begins on that page, cite:

Note, *Believers and Freedom,* 44 DICK. L. REV. 31, 33 & n.7 (1939).

3.4 Sections and Paragraphs

If an authority is organized by sections (§) or paragraphs (¶), cite to these and give a page number only if necessary for further identification:

15 U.S.C. § 18 (1976).

6 J. MOORE, W. TAGGART & J. WICKER, MOORE'S FEDERAL PRACTICE ¶ 56.07 (2d ed. 1981).

L. TRIBE, AMERICAN CONSTITUTIONAL LAW § 15-4, at 898 (1978).

Session laws amending prior acts are often divided into sections within sections. The session law is divided into sections; these sections, in turn, contain sections of the amended act. Cite the *bill's* sections by abbreviation (sec.) and the *amended act's* sections by symbol (§):

Labor-Management Relations Act, ch. 120, sec. 101, § 8(a)(3), 61 Stat. 136, 140–41 (1947).

If an authority is organized in part by indented paragraphs not introduced by paragraph symbols (¶), cite such paragraphs with the written abbreviation (para.), not the symbol:

The Declaration of Independence para. 2 (U.S. 1776).

Do not cite to indented paragraphs if the authority is ordinarily cited by page or column:

N.Y. Times, May 23, 1980, at A1, col. 8.

(a) Subsections. Use the original punctuation separating sections from subsections unless the source contains no such separating punctuation, in which case place the subsection designation in parentheses. Thus, place "1." and "a)" in parentheses ("(1)" and "(a)"), but not ".01" or "-32."

N.M. STAT. ANN. § 4-44-7(G) (1978).

Not: N.M. STAT. ANN. § 4-44-7 G. (1978).

(b) Multiple sections and subsections. When citing consecutive sections or subsections, give inclusive numbers; do not use "*et seq.*" Identical digits or letters preceding a punctuation mark may be omitted, unless doing so would create confusion. Otherwise retain all digits.

WASH. REV. CODE ANN. §§ 18.51.005–.52.900 (1978).

DEL. CODE ANN. tit. 9, §§ 817–819 (Supp. 1978).

Not: §§ 817–19

42 U.S.C. §§ 1396a–1396d (1976 & Supp. III 1979).

Not: §§ 1396a–d

If a hyphen or en dash would be ambiguous, use the word "to":

MONT. CODE ANN. §§ 75-1-301 to -324 (1979).

When citing scattered sections, separate the sections with commas:

N.J. STAT. ANN. §§ 18A:54-1, -3, -6 (West 1968).

Repeat digits if necessary to avoid confusion:

N.J. STAT. ANN. §§ 18A:58-17, :58-25, :64A-22.1, :64A-22.6 (West 1968).

When citing multiple subsections within a single section, use only one section symbol:

28 U.S.C. § 105(a)(3)–(b)(1) (1976).

19 U.S.C. § 1485(a)(1)–(3) (1976).

DEL. CODE ANN. tit. 9, § 6919(a)–(c) (1974).

DEL. CODE ANN. tit. 9, § 6910(a), (c) (1974).

Multiple subsections within *different* sections are cited:

19 U.S.C. §§ 1485(a), 1486(b) (1976).

Note that letters are sometimes used to designate sections, rather than subsections, and that section designations may contain punctuation within them:

42 U.S.C. §§ 1396a–1396d (1976 & Supp. III 1979).

42 U.S.C. §§ 1973aa-2 to -4 (1976).

(c) Multiple paragraphs. Multiple paragraphs should be treated like multiple sections, following rule 3.4(b):

1 BLUE SKY L. REP. (CCH) ¶¶ 4471–4474

6 J. MOORE, W. TAGGART & J. WICKER, MOORE'S FEDERAL PRACTICE ¶¶ 54.32–.35 (2d ed. 1981).

3.5 Appendices, Notes, and Other Addenda

Indicate an appendix or appended note by placing the appropriate designation (e.g., "app.," "note," "annot.," "reporter's note," "comment") after the citation to the largest full subdivision to which the item is appended, whether page, section, paragraph, chapter, title, or volume:

Kee & Moan, *The Property Tax and Tenant Equality*, 89 HARV. L. REV. 531, 548 app. (1976).

24 U.S.C. § 168 note (1976).

Cite to a particular page, section, or other subdivision in an appendix thus:

50 U.S.C. app. § 454 (1976 & Supp. III 1979).

RESTATEMENT (SECOND) OF TORTS § 623A comment a (1977).

Appended material that serves as a commentary on the material to which it is appended, or that further discusses a point related to the textual discussion, should be cited simply as a note or appendix to that material, as indicated above:

N.Y. BUS. CORP. LAW § 624 note on legislative studies and reports (McKinney 1963).

FED. R. EVID. 702 advisory committee note.

RESTATEMENT (SECOND) OF PROPERTY § 2.1 comment c, illustration 2 (1977).

Further information necessary to identify which of several named notes is meant may be added parenthetically:

24 U.S.C. § 168 note (1976) (Transfer of Functions).

Appendices that reprint materials normally cited to another source should be cited according to rule 2.6(a).

A

Cross-References 3.6

Groups of authorities and textual materials within the piece in which the citation is being made may be referred to by use of "*supra*" or "*infra*":

See infra p. 41.

See infra p. 50 & note 100.

See supra text accompanying notes 305–07.

See supra notes 12–15 and accompanying text.

But see cases cited *supra* note 22.

See generally Jones & Merritt, *supra* note 27, at 543.

In briefs a cross-reference to material on another page should give the page of the brief to which the cross-reference refers. For example, if a full citation to:

G. Haugen, <u>The Psychiatrist as a Witness</u> (1966)

appears on page ten of a brief, a reference on a subsequent page should read:

G. Haugen, <u>supra</u> p. 10, at 400.

Short Citation Forms 4

"*Id.*" 4.1

"*Id.*" may be used in citation sentences and clauses for any kind of authority. In briefs, legal memoranda, and similar materials, use "*id.*" when citing to the immediately preceding authority. In law review footnotes, use "*id.*" when citing to the immediately preceding authority within the same footnote or within the immediately preceding footnote *when the preceding footnote contains only one authority*. Indicate any particular in which the subsequent citation varies from the former. If the first citation is to only part of an authority, do not use "*id.*" for a subsequent citation to the entire authority. The following examples illustrate the use of "*id.*" with parallel citations (nn.1 & 2), without parallel citations (nn.3 & 4), when references are by sections (n.5), when references are by numbered paragraphs (nn.6 & 7), and when references are to pages of a book or similar source (nn.8–11):

[1] Chalfin v. Specter, 426 Pa. 464, 233 A.2d 562 (1967).

[2] *Id.* at 465, 233 A.2d at 563.

[3] Moore v. Illinois, 434 U.S. 220 (1977).

[4] *See id.* at 221.

[5] U.C.C. § 3-302(2)(1977); *see also id.* § 3-303(a).

[6] Dupey v. Dupey, [1977–1978 Transfer Binder] FED. SEC.

L. REP. (CCH) ¶ 96,048, at 91,701 (5th Cir. May 9, 1977).

[7] *Id.* at 91,705.

[8] A. SOLMSSEN, THE COMFORT LETTER (1975).

[9] *See generally id.* at 38.

[10] 3 W. HOLDSWORTH, A HISTORY OF ENGLISH LAW 255 (3d ed. 1927).

[11] 1 *id.* at 5–17 (2d ed. 1914).

The following example is **incorrect** because "*id.*" may not be used to refer to one authority in a preceding footnote if that footnote contains more than one source:

[12] Moore v. Illinois, 434 U.S. 220 (1977); Reich, *Toward a New Consumer Protection,* 128 U. PA. L. REV. 1 (1979).

[13] *Id.* at 4.

4.2 "*Supra*" and "Hereinafter"

"*Supra*" and "hereinafter" may be used to refer to legislative materials, administrative and executive materials, books, pamphlets, unpublished materials, periodicals, services, newspapers, and international materials. "*Supra*" and "hereinafter" should not be used to refer to cases, statutes, or constitutions except in extraordinary circumstances, such as when the name of the authority is extremely long:

In re Multidistrict Private Civil Treble Damage Antitrust Litigation Involving Motor Vehicle Air Pollution Control Equipment, 52 F.R.D. 398 (C.D. Cal. 1970) [hereinafter cited as Air Pollution Control Antitrust Case].

(a) "*Supra.*" When an authority has been fully cited previously, the "*supra*" form may be used (unless "*id.*" is appropriate). The "*supra*" form consists of the author of the work followed by a comma and the word "*supra.*" If no author is cited, use the title; for student-written law review materials, use the designation (*see* rule 16.1.2). Volume, paragraph, or section numbers may be added to refer to specific material:

5 R. POUND, *supra,* at 61.

If an authority is fully cited in another footnote or (in a brief) on another page of text, indicate that fact:

Reich, *supra* note 10, at 4.

Note, *supra* note 3, at 258.

In a brief:

4 J. Wigmore, <u>supra</u> p. 6, § 1302, at 721.

A

(b) "Hereinafter." For authority that would be cumbersome to cite with the simple *"supra"* form, a special shortened form may be established. After the first citation of the authority, place the phrase "hereinafter cited as" and the special shortened form in brackets. Thereafter, use the shortened form followed by a comma and the word *"supra."* Indicate the footnote (or, in a brief, the page) where the full citation can be found, unless the full citation is in the same footnote (or on the same page of the brief), in which case *"supra"* should be used without cross-reference. The shortened form should appear in the same typeface as it would were it a part of the full citation. Thus:

[14] *Proposed Amendments to the Federal Rules of Criminal Procedure: Hearings Before the Subcomm. on Criminal Justice of the House Comm. on the Judiciary,* 95th Cong., 1st Sess. 92–93 (1977) (testimony of Prof. Wayne LaFave) [hereinafter cited as *Hearings*].

[15] P. BATOR, P. MISHKIN, D. SHAPIRO & H. WECHSLER, HART AND WECHSLER'S THE FEDERAL COURTS AND THE FEDERAL SYSTEM 330 (2d ed. 1973) [hereinafter cited as HART & WECHSLER].

[16] *Hearings, supra* note 14, at 33 (testimony of Hon. Edward Becker).

[17] HART & WECHSLER, *supra* note 15, at 614.

Do not use the "hereinafter" form where a simple *"supra"* form is adequate:

[18] 2 W. HOLDSWORTH, *supra* note 10, at 35.

The "hereinafter" form, however, may be used to distinguish two authorities appearing in the same footnote if the simple *"supra"* form would be confusing:

[19] *See* Note, *The Right to Attend Criminal Hearings,* 78 COLUM. L. REV. 1308 (1978) [hereinafter cited as Note, *The Right to Attend*]; Note, *Trial Secrecy and the First Amendment Right of Public Access to Judicial Proceedings,* 91 HARV. L. REV. 1899 (1978) [hereinafter cited as Note, *Trial Secrecy*].

[20] *See* Note, *The Right to Attend, supra* note 19, at 1323; Note, *Trial Secrecy, supra* note 19, at 1906–09.

Short Forms for Cases and Statutes 4.3

(a) Cases. In briefs, legal memoranda, and similar materials, citations to a case that has already been cited in full in the same general discussion may be shortened to any of the following forms that clearly identifies the case:

United States v. Calandra, 414 U.S. at 343.

Calandra, 414 U.S. at 343.

414 U.S. at 343.

In law review text, the same forms may be used, but the citations should appear in footnotes. In any legal writing, a case that has been cited in full in the same general discussion may be referred to by one of the parties' names without further citation:

> The issue presented in *Bakke* has not been fully resolved.

Avoid using the name of a governmental litigant for any of these purposes. Thus, "*United States*, 414 U.S. at 343" is *not* a proper short form.

In footnotes any short form permitted in text may be used, provided it clearly identifies a case fully cited in the same footnote or named in the same general textual discussion to which the footnote is appended. Otherwise a full citation is required. Acceptable short forms include:

> United States v. Calandra, 414 U.S. at 343.
> *Calandra,* 414 U.S. at 343.

(b) Statutes. (i) In law review text and other places where full citation is not permitted, use forms like those in the "Law Review Text" column of the table below for citations to statutes. Add the remainder of the citation in a footnote the first time the statute is mentioned. Subsequent references in the same general discussion do not need full citations. (ii) In text of briefs and legal memoranda, the first mention of a statute within each general discussion should give a full citation or use one of the "Law Review Text" forms and add the remainder of the citation in a footnote. Subsequent references in the same general discussion may employ any short form that clearly identifies the statute (*see* "Suggested Short Forms" column below). (iii) In all forms of legal writing, footnotes may use any short form that clearly identifies a statute if the general discussion in text to which the footnote is appended has previously referred to the statute. Otherwise use the *full* citation form for the first citation to a statute in the footnote. Thereafter, any short form that clearly identifes the statute may be used in that footnote.

	Full citation	Law review text	Suggested short forms
named statutes	Administrative Procedure Act § 1, 5 U.S.C. § 551 (1976)	section 1 of the Administrative Procedure Act section 1	§ 1 5 U.S.C. § 551 Administrative Procedure Act § 1
United States Code provisions	42 U.S.C. § 1983 (1976)	42 U.S.C. § 1983	42 U.S.C. § 1983 § 1983
all other statutory material	DEL. CODE ANN. tit. 28, § 556 (Supp. 1978)	title 28, section 556 of the Delaware Code	title 28, § 556 § 556

(c) Constitutions. Do not use a short citation form for constitutions.

Quotations 5

Indentation, Quotation Marks, Citation, and Punctuation 5.1

(a) Quotations of fifty or more words should be indented left and right, without quotation marks, as follows:

> The need to develop all relevant facts in the adversary system is both fundamental and comprehensive. The ends of criminal justice would be defeated if judgments were to be founded on a partial or speculative presentation of the facts. The very integrity of the judicial system and public confidence in the system depend on full disclosure of all the facts, within the framework of the rules of evidence. To ensure that justice is done, it is imperative to the function of courts that compulsory process be available for the production of evidence needed either by the prosecution or by the defense.

United States v. Nixon, 418 U.S. 683, 709 (1974).

In briefs, law review footnotes, and other material in which citation is permitted, the citation should not be indented, but should appear at the margin, on the line immediately following the quotation, as shown above. In law review text and other material in which citations are not permitted, place the footnote number after the final punctuation of the quotation. See rule 5.4 for indentation to show paragraph structure.

(b) Quotations of forty-nine or fewer words should be enclosed in quotation marks, but do not otherwise set them off from the rest of the text. The citation or footnote number should follow immediately unless it is more convenient to place it elsewhere shortly before or after the quotation. Always place commas and periods inside the quotation marks; place other punctuation marks inside the quotation marks only if they are part of the matter quoted. When the material quoted is such that it would commonly be set off from the text, as would lines of poetry or dialogue from a play, the quotation may be printed according to rule 5.1(a), regardless of its length.

5.2 Alterations

When a letter must be changed from upper to lower case, or vice versa, enclose it in brackets. Substituted words or letters and other inserted material should also be bracketed. Thus:

> "[P]ublic confidence in the [adversary] system depend[s] on full disclosure of all the facts, within the framework of the rules of evidence."

Significant mistakes in the original should be followed by "[sic]," but otherwise left as they appear in the original:

> "The statue [sic] is offensive."

Indicate in a parenthetical clause after the citation any change of emphasis or omission of citations or footnote numbers. Thus:

> "The need to develop all relevant facts in the adversary system is *both* fundamental and comprehensive." United States v. Nixon, 418 U.S. 683, 709 (1974) (emphasis added).

Whenever possible, a quotation within a quotation should be attributed to its original source:

> The court in *Marks* noted "Congress' firm resolve to insure that the CIA's 'power that flows from money and stealth' could not be turned loose in domestic investigations of Americans." Marks v. CIA, 590 F.2d 997, 1008 (D.C. Cir. 1978) (footnote omitted) (quoting Weissman v. CIA, 565 F.2d 692, 695 (D.C. Cir. 1977)).

On related authority, see rule 2.6.

5.3 Omissions

Omission of a word or words is generally indicated by the insertion of three periods set off by a space before the first and after the last period (" . . . ") to take the place of the word or words omitted. This ellipsis signal should *never* be used to begin a quotation; nor should it be used when a word is merely altered. See rule 5.2 for how to alter words. The specific manner in which omission should be indicated depends on whether the quoted passage stands by itself as a full sentence.

If the quoted passage is used as a **phrase or clause**, do not indicate omission of matter before or after a quotation:

> Chief Justice Burger wrote that the availability of compulsory process is "imperative to the function of courts."

Indicate omission of matter within the phrase or clause thus:

> The Court warned that "judgments . . . founded on a partial or speculative presentation of the facts" would undermine the criminal justice system.

If the quoted language stands by itself as a **full sentence**: (i) Where language *beginning* the original sentence has been deleted, capitalize the first letter and place it in brackets if it is not already capitalized. If the sentence begins the quotation, do not otherwise indicate any omission. Thus:

> "[I]t is imperative to the function of courts that compulsory process be available for the production of evidence needed either by the prosecution or by the defense."

(ii) Use an ellipsis where language *from the middle* of a quoted sentence is omitted:

> "The very integrity of the judicial system . . . depend[s] on full disclosure of all the facts, within the framework of the rules of evidence."

(iii) Omission of language *at the end* of a quoted sentence should be indicated by an ellipsis between the last word quoted and the final punctuation:

> "To ensure that justice is done, it is imperative to the function of courts that compulsory process be available . . . ."

(iv) If language *after the end* of a quoted sentence is deleted and the sentence is followed by further quotation, retain the punctuation at the end of the sentence and insert three periods before the remainder of the quotation. Do not, however, indicate the deletion of matter after the period or other final punctuation that concludes the final quoted sentence. Thus:

> "The need to develop all relevant facts in the adversary system is both fundamental and comprehensive. . . . The very integrity of the judicial system and public confidence in the system depend on full disclosure of all the facts, within the framework of the rules of evidence."

Paragraph Structure 5.4

Do not indicate the original paragraph structure of quotations of **forty-nine or fewer words** enclosed in quotation marks according to rule 5.1(b). The paragraph structure of an indented quotation of **fifty or more words** should be indicated by further indenting the first line of each paragraph. However, indent the first sentence of the *first* quoted paragraph only if the first word of the quoted passage is also the first word of the original paragraph. If language at the beginning of the first paragraph is omitted, do not indent the first line or use an ellipsis. To indicate omission at the beginning of *subsequent paragraphs,* insert and indent an ellipsis. Indicate the omission of one or more entire paragraphs by inserting and indenting four periods (". . . .") on a new line. Thus, rules 5.1 and 5.2 might be quoted in part as follows:

> In briefs, law review footnotes, and other material in which citation is permitted, the citation should not be indented, but should appear at the margin, on the line immediately following the quotation . . . .
>
> . . . .
>
> . . . Indicate in a parenthetical clause after the citation any change of emphasis or omission of citations or footnote numbers.

6 Abbreviations, Numerals, and Symbols

Rules relating to abbreviations generally are given in rule 6.1; those relating particularly to abbreviations in languages other than English, in rule 6.2; and those relating to the use of numerals and symbols, in rule 6.3.

6.1 Abbreviations

The abbreviations of some specific types of words are found elsewhere in this book. (Note that the same word may be abbreviated differently for different uses.) Avoid use of abbreviations not listed in this book unless substantial space will be saved and the resulting abbreviation is unambiguous.

(a) Spacing. Close up adjacent single capitals except when an entity is abbreviated by widely recognized initials and combination of those initials with others would be confusing:

N.Y.L.J.

YALE L.J.

New York, N.H. & H.R.R.

But:

N.Y.U. L. REV.

Do not close up single capitals with longer abbreviations:

U. PA. L. REV.

NW. U.L. REV.

A

Individual numbers, including both numerals and ordinals, are treated as single capitals:

F.2d

Close up initials in personal names:

W.C. Fields

(b) Periods. Generally, every abbreviation, except those in which the last letter of the original word is included and set off from the rest of the abbreviation by an apostrophe, should be followed by a period. Thus:

Ave.
Bldg.
Gen.

But:

Ass'n
Dep't
Nat'l

Widely recognized initials that have come to be read out loud as initials rather than as the words they represent, e.g.:

NLRB, CBS, FDA, UN, USSR

may be used without periods in text, in case names, and as institutional authors, but not in reporter or code abbreviations, or as names of courts of decision. Thus:

NLRB v. Baptist Hosp., 442 U.S. 773 (1979).

But:

East Belden Corp., 239 N.L.R.B. 776 (1978).

Always retain periods after initials not commonly read aloud (e.g., N.Y., S.C.); do not omit periods in the abbreviation "U.S."

Abbreviations in Languages Other Than English 6.2

The abbreviations of foreign-language reporters, codes, statutory collections, and periodicals may be unfamiliar to the American reader. The full form should therefore be given the first time the source is cited, and the abbreviation should be given in brackets. Thereafter, the abbreviated form may be used without cross-reference. Thus:

[1] Astérix, Le Gaulois & Cie. v. Thomas, Dec. 10, 1934, Cour d'appel, Strasbourg, 1935 Recueil Périodique et Critique [D.P.] II 243.

[2] BÜRGERLICHES GESETZBUCH [BGB] art. 13 (W. Ger.).

[3] Swann v. DeCharlus, June 6, 1937, Cass. civ. 1re, Fr., 1937 D.P. I 167.

[4] BGB art. 12.

Abbreviations for some foreign reporters, codes, and statutory collections are given on pp. 179–200. Abbreviations for selected foreign periodicals are given on pp. 103–04. When abbreviating other foreign periodicals or services, follow the usage of the source.

6.3 Numerals and Symbols

(a) Numerals. In general, spell out the numbers zero to ninety-nine in text and zero to nine in footnotes; for larger numbers use numerals. This general rule is subject, however, to the following exceptions: (i) Any number that *begins a sentence* must be spelled out. (ii) "Hundred," "thousand," and similar *round numbers* may be spelled out, if done so consistently. (iii) When a *series* includes one or more numerals, numerals should be used for the entire series:

They burned, respectively, 117, 3, and 15 homes.

(iv) Numerals should be used if the number includes a *decimal point.* (v) Where material repeatedly refers to *percentages* or *dollar amounts,* numerals should be used for those percentages or amounts. (vi) Numerals should be used for *section or other subdivision* numbers.

In numbers containing five or more digits, use commas to separate groups of three digits:

1,234,567

H17,326

When referring to decades or centuries, insert an apostrophe:

1800's

1930's

(b) Section (§) and paragraph (¶) symbols. The first word of any sentence must be spelled out. Otherwise, in footnotes or citations the symbols should be used (except as noted in rule 3.4). In text the words should always be spelled out. There should be a *space* between "§" or "¶" and the numeral. *See also* rule 4.3(b) (textual citation of statutes).

(c) Dollar ($) and percent (%) symbols. These symbols should be used wherever numerals are used, and the words should be spelled out wherever numbers are spelled out, but a symbol should never begin a sentence. There should be *no space* between "$" or "%" and the numeral.

Italicization for Stylistic Purposes

7 A

Rules for the use of typefaces generally are discussed in rule 1. In addition, in all legal writing, italicize as a matter of style: (i) capital letters used to represent proper names of hypothetical parties or places:

A went to his bank *B* in state *X*.

(ii) the letter "l" when used as a subdivision:

§ 23(*l*)

(iii) words requiring italicization for emphasis, and (iv) words or phrases in languages other than English that have not been incorporated into common English usage. There is a strong presumption that Latin phrases commonly used in legal writing have been incorporated into common usage and thus should not be italicized.

Capitalization

8

In headings and titles, capitalize the initial word and all other words except articles, conjunctions, and prepositions of four or fewer letters. Follow the same rule in citing names or titles that are printed entirely in capitals; otherwise follow the capitalization of the cited source exactly. The following table indicates capitalization for commonly used words. For other words, use the table of capitalizations found in the *Government Printing Office Style Manual*.

Capitalize nouns referring to people or groups only when they identify specific persons, officials, groups, government offices, or government bodies:

the Federal Security Administrator

the Administrator

the NLRB

the Board

the FDA

the Agency

the Secretary of State

the Secretary

Congress

the President

But:

the congressional hearings
the presidential veto

Capitalize:

Act	Only when referring to a specific act: The Labor-Management Relations Act the Act
Circuit	Only when used with the circuit number: the Fifth Circuit
Code	Only when referring to a specific code: the 1939 and 1954 Codes
Court	Only when naming any court in full or when referring to the United States Supreme Court: the California Supreme Court the supreme court (referring to a state supreme court) the Court (referring to the United States Supreme Court) the court of appeals the Court of Appeals for the Fifth Circuit
Constitution	Only when naming any constitution in full or when referring to the United States Constitution. Parts are not capitalized: fifth amendment preamble article I, section 8, clause 17 But: Bill of Rights
Judge, Justice	Only when giving the name of a judge or justice or when referring to a Justice of the United States Supreme Court: Judge Newman Justice Holmes the Justice (referring to a Justice of the United States Supreme Court)

State	Only if the word it modifies is capitalized.
Term	Only when referring to a Term of the United States Supreme Court: 1978 Term this Term But: Michaelmas term

Titles of Judges, Officials, and Terms of Court 9

Justices are referred to as "Mr. Justice Blank," "Mme. Justice Blank," or "Justice Blank," and "Mr. Chief Justice Blank," "Mme. Chief Justice Blank," "Chief Justice Blank," or "the Chief Justice." Judges are referred to as "Judge Blank" and "Chief Judge Blank." Parenthetical references are to "Blank, J.," "Blank, C.J.," and "Blank & Space, JJ."

Titles of judges and officials may be abbreviated as follows:

Administrative Law Judge	A.L.J.	Judges, Justices	JJ.
Arbitrator	Arb.	Lord Justice	L.J.
Attorney General	Att'y Gen.	Magistrate	Mag.
Baron	B.	Master of the Rolls	M.R.
Chancellor	C.	Mediator	Med.
Chief Baron	C.B.	Referee	Ref.
Chief Judge, Chief Justice	C.J.	Representative	Rep.
Commissioner	Comm'r	Senator	Sen.
Judge, Justice	J.	Vice Chancellor	V.C.

As a matter of etiquette, lists of judges should be in the order indicated at the beginning of each volume of the official reporter for the court. Justices of the United States Supreme Court are always listed with the Chief Justice first, and then in order of seniority.

A term of court currently in progress may be referred to as "this term." The immediately preceding term, no longer in progress at time of publication, should be referred to as "last term." Any term may be indicated by year:

the 1979 term

Capitalize "term" only when referring to a Term of the United States Supreme Court. *See* rule 8.

B

Cases

Rule 10: Cases 35

Cases 10

Basic Citation Forms 10.1

(a) United States (federal and state), Commonwealth, and other common law jurisdictions.

	In law review footnotes	In briefs and legal memoranda
filed but not decided	Englert v. Tenenbaum, No. 85-345 (D. Mass. filed Sept. 18, 1985)	Englert v. Tenenbaum, No. 85-345 (D. Mass. filed Sept. 18, 1985)
unpublished interim order	Englert v. Tenenbaum, No. 85-345 (D. Mass. Oct. 25, 1985) (order granting preliminary injunction)	Englert v. Tenenbaum, No. 85-345 (D. Mass. Oct. 25, 1985) (order granting preliminary injunction)
published interim order	Englert v. Tenenbaum, 578 F. Supp. 1395 (D. Mass. 1985) (order granting preliminary injunction)	Englert v. Tenenbaum, 578 F. Supp. 1395 (D. Mass. 1985) (order granting preliminary injunction)
unpublished decision	Englert v. Tenenbaum, No. 85-345, slip op. at 6 (D. Mass. Dec. 4, 1985)	Englert v. Tenenbaum, No. 85-345, slip op. at 6 (D. Mass. Dec. 4, 1985)
decision published in service only	Englert v. Tenenbaum, 1985 FED. SEC. L. REP. (CCH) ¶ 102,342 (D. Mass. Dec. 4, 1985)	Englert v. Tenenbaum, 1985 Fed. Sec. L. Rep. (CCH) ¶ 102,342 (D. Mass. Dec. 4, 1985)
decision published in newspaper only	Englert v. Tenenbaum, N.Y.L.J., Dec. 5, 1985, at 1, col. 5 (D. Mass. Dec. 4, 1985)	Englert v. Tenenbaum, N.Y.L.J., Dec. 5, 1985, at 1, col. 5 (D. Mass. Dec. 4, 1985)
published decision	Englert v. Tenenbaum, 580 F. Supp. 1407, 1412 (D. Mass. 1985)	Englert v. Tenenbaum, 580 F. Supp. 1407, 1412 (D. Mass. 1985)
appeal docketed	Englert v. Tenenbaum, 580 F. Supp. 1407 (D. Mass. 1985), *appeal docketed,* No. 85-567 (1st Cir. Dec. 20, 1985)	Englert v. Tenenbaum, 580 F. Supp. 1407 (D. Mass. 1985), appeal docketed, No. 85-567 (1st Cir. Dec. 20, 1985)
brief, record, or appendix	Brief for Appellant at 7, Englert v. Tenenbaum, 776 F.2d 1427 (1st Cir. 1986)	Brief for Appellant at 7, Englert v. Tenenbaum, 776 F.2d 1427 (1st Cir. 1986)
disposition on appeal	Englert v. Tenenbaum, 776 F.2d 1427, 1430 (1st Cir. 1986)	Englert v. Tenenbaum, 776 F.2d 1427, 1430 (1st Cir. 1986)
disposition in lower court showing subsequent history	Englert v. Tenenbaum, 580 F. Supp. 1407, 1412 (D. Mass. 1985), *aff'd,* 776 F.2d 1427 (1st Cir. 1986)	Englert v. Tenenbaum, 580 F. Supp. 1407, 1412 (D. Mass. 1985), aff'd, 776 F.2d 1427 (1st Cir. 1986)

petition for certiorari filed	Englert v. Tenenbaum, 776 F.2d 1427 (1st Cir. 1986), *petition for cert. filed,* 55 U.S.L.W. 3422 (U.S. Jan. 14, 1987) (No. 86-212)	Englert v. Tenenbaum, 776 F.2d 1427 (1st Cir. 1986), petition for cert. filed, 55 U.S.L.W. 3422 (U.S. Jan. 14, 1987) (No. 86-212)
petition for certiorari granted	Englert v. Tenenbaum, 776 F.2d 1427 (1st Cir. 1986), *cert. granted,* 55 U.S.L.W. 3562 (U.S. Jan. 21, 1987) (No. 86-212)	Englert v. Tenenbaum, 776 F.2d 1427 (1st Cir. 1986), cert. granted, 55 U.S.L.W. 3562 (U.S. Jan. 21, 1987) (No. 86-212)
disposition in Supreme Court published only in service	Englert v. Tenenbaum, 55 U.S.L.W. 4420, 4421 (U.S. Feb. 4, 1987), *vacating as moot* 776 F.2d 1427 (1st Cir. 1986)	Englert v. Tenenbaum, 55 U.S.L.W. 4420, 4421 (U.S. Feb. 4, 1987), vacating as moot 776 F.2d 1427 (1st Cir. 1986)

(b) Civil law and other non-common-law jurisdictions.

published decision	Judgment of Jan. 10, 1935, Cour d'appel, Paris, 1935 Recueil Périodique et Critique [D.P.] II 758	Judgment of Jan. 10, 1935, Cour d'appel, Paris, 1935 Recueil Périodique et Critique [D.P.] II 758

A full Anglo-American case citation includes the name of the case (rule 10.2); the published sources in which it may be found, if any (rule 10.3); a parenthetical that indicates the court (rule 10.4) and the year or date of decision (rule 10.5); and the subsequent history of the case, if any (rule 10.7). It may also include additional parenthetical information (rule 10.6) and the prior history of the case (rule 10.7). Special citation forms for pending and unreported cases (rule 10.8.1); briefs, records, motions, and memoranda (rule 10.8.2); and civil law and other non-common-law cases (rule 10.8.3) are discussed in rule 10.8.

10.2 Case Names

Case names in briefs, legal memoranda, and law review text should conform to rule 10.2.1. Case names in law review footnotes should be further abbreviated according to rule 10.2.2. Special rules for the names of administrative cases and arbitrations appear in rule 10.2.3. Note that the examples throughout this rule (10.2) employ the typeface convention for law review footnotes. On typeface conventions, see rule 1.

10.2.1 Case Names in Text

In all places except law review footnotes, use the case name that appears at the beginning of the opinion in the official reporter, if any, as modified by the paragraphs below. If no name appears in the official reporter, use a popular name or cite as:

Judgment of [full date]

Always retain in full the first word in each party's name (including a relator) to facilitate index location, except as provided below. In long case names, omit words not necessary for identification; the running head (at the top of each page of the case) may serve as a guide. In all case names, make the following modifications:

(a) Actions and parties cited. If the case is a consolidation of two or more actions, cite only the first listed:

Shelley v. Kraemer

Not: Shelley v. Kraemer, McGhee v. Sipes

Omit all parties other than the first listed on each side, but do not omit the first-listed relator or any portion of a partnership name:

Barron v. Mayor of Baltimore

Not: Barron v. Mayor & City Council of Baltimore

But:

NAACP v. Alabama *ex rel.* Patterson

Eisen v. Carlisle & Jacquelin

Omit words indicating multiple parties, such as "et al." Also omit alternative names given for the first-listed party on either side:

Frankel v. Romano

Not: Frankel et al. v. Romano d/b/a Notes Department

Phrases or party names that would aid in identification of the case may be appended in parentheses after the formal case name:

ILGWU v. NLRB (Bernhard-Altmann Texas Corp.)

Thus, cite actions brought by or against a trustee in bankruptcy in bankruptcy court, or like actions, as adversary cases, with the name of the bankruptcy proceeding appended parenthetically:

Hart v. Roth (*In re* Campisano)

(b) Procedural phrases. Abbreviate "on the relation of," "for the use of," "on behalf of," and similar expressions to "*ex rel.*" Abbreviate "in the matter of," "petition of," and similar expressions to "*In re.*" Omit all procedural phrases except the first. When adversary parties are named, omit all procedural phrases except "*ex rel.*"

Feldman v. Snipes

Not: *In re* Feldman v. Snipes

But:

Massachusetts *ex rel.* Kennedy v. Carter

Ex parte Young

"Estate of" and "Will of" are not treated as procedural phrases and are not omitted:

In re Will of Smythe

Estate of Rusthoven v. Commissioner

Procedural phrases should always be italicized (or underscored), even in briefs, legal memoranda, law review text, and other contexts in which the case name is italicized (or underscored). Thus, in a brief:

Ex parte Young

(c) Abbreviations. Do not abbreviate the first word of a party's name, unless the full name of a party can be abbreviated to widely recognized initials:

NAACP v. Button

In briefs, memoranda, and law review text, do not otherwise abbreviate words making up the name of a case except for "Co.," "Corp.," "Inc.," "Ltd.," "&," and "No." In law review footnotes, abbreviate further according to rule 10.2.2.

(d) "The." Omit "The" as the first word of a party name, except as part of the name of the object of an in rem action, or in cases in which "The King" or "The Queen" is a party. Thus:

Network Project v. Corporation for Public Broadcasting

But:

Murray v. The Schooner Charming Betsy

The King v. Armstrong

Do not omit "The" in an established popular name, except when referring to the case textually. Thus:

The *Civil Rights Cases* stand for a proposition that neither *Civil Rights Cases* opinion intended to establish.

But:

See The Civil Rights Cases, 109 U.S. 3 (1883).

(e) Descriptive terms. Omit terms such as "administrator," "appellee," "executor," "licensee," and "trustee" that describe a party already named:

Stein v. Leffell

Not: Stein v. Leffell, Administrator

But:

Trustees of Dartmouth College v. Woodward

B

(f) Geographical terms. Omit "State of," "Commonwealth of," and "People of," except in citing decisions of the courts of that state, in which case only "State," "Commonwealth," or "People" should be retained:

State v. Mapp

Omit "City of" and like expressions unless the expression begins a party name:

Mayor of New York v. Miln

Not: Mayor of the City of New York v. Miln

But:

Lehman v. City of Shaker Heights

Omit all prepositional phrases of location not following "City," or like expressions, unless the omission would leave only one word in the name of a party or of a corporate or other entity:

Cooley v. Board of Wardens

Not: Cooley v. Board of Wardens of the Port of Philadelphia

But:

Bishop of Durham v. Trustees of the University of Cambridge

Include designations of national or larger geographical areas except in union names, but omit "of America" after "United States":

United States v. Aluminum Co. of America

Retain all geographical designations not introduced by a preposition:

Chicago Board of Trade v. Olsen

(g) Given names or initials. Generally, omit given names or initials of individuals, but not in names of business firms:

Kit Kinports, Inc. v. Neil P. Forrest & Co.

Thompson v. Madsen

Not: David K. Thompson v. Stephen Stewart Madsen

But:

Linda R.S. v. Richard D.

Given names that follow, rather than precede, a surname, however, should be retained; do not omit any part of a surname made up of more than one word:

Van der Velt v. Standing Horse

Abdul Ghani v. Subedar Shoedar Khan

Thus, retain the full name where the name is *entirely* in a language in which the surname is given first, such as Chinese or Korean:

Chang Meng Te v. Ng Fung Ho

But not: Wendy Yang v. Ng Fung Ho

Similarly, if a party's name is of Spanish or Portuguese derivation, cite by the surname and all names following:

Ortega y Gasset v. Feliciano Santiago

If in doubt, use the name under which the party appears in the index of the reporter cited.

(h) Business firm designations. Omit "Inc.," "Ltd.," and similar terms, if the name also contains words such as "Co.," "Bros.," and "Ass'n" clearly indicating that the party is a business firm:

Wisconsin Packing Co. v. Indiana Refrigerator Lines

Not: Wisconsin Packing Co., Inc. v. Indiana Refrigerator Lines, Inc.

Columbia Broadcasting System v. Loew's, Inc.

Not: Columbia Broadcasting System, Inc. v. Loew's, Inc.

But:

Wallace K. Lightsey, Ltd. v. Mark R. Merley, Inc.

In referring to a railroad company, omit "Co." as well, unless the full party name given in the official report is simply "Railroad Co."

(i) Union and local union names. Cite a union name exactly as given in the official report, except that (1) only the smallest unit should be cited:

NLRB v. Radio & Television Broadcast Engineers Local 1212

Not: NLRB v. Radio & Television Broadcast Engineers Local 1212, IBEW, AFL-CIO

(2) all craft or industry designations except the first *full* such designation should be omitted:

Douds v. Local 294, International Brotherhood of Teamsters

Not: Douds v. Local 294, International Brotherhood of Teamsters, Chauffeurs, Warehousemen & Helpers

But:

International Union of Doll & Toy Workers v. Local 379

(3) a widely recognized abbreviation of the union's name (e.g.,

UAW) may be used, (4) all prepositional phrases of location, including those of national or larger areas, should be omitted, and (5) modifications should be made as warranted by other paragraphs of this rule.

(j) Commissioner of Internal Revenue. Cite simply as "Commissioner."

Case Names in Footnotes 10.2.2

Cite case names in footnotes according to the rules given above, but with the following further modifications:

(a) Abbreviation. Always abbreviate any word listed below unless it is the first word of the name of a party (*including* a relator). Abbreviate states, countries, and other geographical units as indicated in the table on the inside back cover of this book. It is permissible to abbreviate other words of eight letters or more if *substantial* space is thereby saved and the result is unambiguous. Do not abbreviate "United States." Plurals are formed by adding the letter "s" inside the period, unless otherwise indicated.

Administrat[ive, ion]	Admin.	District	Dist.
Administrat[or, rix]	Adm'[r, x]	Division	Div.
America [n]	Am.	East [ern]	E.
Associate	Assoc.	Education [al]	Educ.
Association	Ass'n	Electric [al, ity]	Elec.
Atlantic	Atl.	Electronic	Elec.
Authority	Auth.	Engineer	Eng'r
Automobile	Auto.	Engineering	Eng'g
Avenue	Ave.	Enterprise	Enter.
Board	Bd.	Environment	Env't
Brotherhood	Bhd.	Environmental	Envtl.
Brothers	Bros.	Equipment	Equip.
Building	Bldg.	Exchange	Exch.
Central	Cent.	Execut[or, rix]	Ex'[r, x]
Chemical	Chem.	Federal	Fed.
Commission	Comm'n	Federation	Fed'n
Commissioner	Comm'r	Financ[e, ial, ing]	Fin.
Committee	Comm.	Foundation	Found.
Company	Co.	General	Gen.
Consolidated	Consol.	Government	Gov't
Construction	Constr.	Guaranty	Guar.
Cooperative	Coop.	Hospital	Hosp.
Corporation	Corp.	Housing	Hous.
Department	Dep't	Incorporated	Inc.
Development	Dev.	Indemnity	Indem.
Distribut[or, ing]	Distrib.	Independent	Indep.

Industr[y, ies, ial]	Indus.	Public	Pub.
Institut[e, ion]	Inst.	Railroad	R.R.
Insurance	Ins.	Railway	Ry.
International	Int'l	Refining	Ref.
Investment	Inv.	Road	Rd.
Liability	Liab.	Savings	Sav.
Limited	Ltd.	Securit[y, ies]	Sec.
Litigation	Litig.	Service	Serv.
Machine [ry]	Mach.	Society	Soc'y
Manufacturer	Mfr.	South [ern]	S.
Manufacturing	Mfg.	Steamship	S.S.
Market	Mkt.	Street	St.
Marketing	Mktg.	Surety	Sur.
Municipal	Mun.	System [s]	Sys.
Mutual	Mut.	Tele[phone, graph]	Tel.
National	Nat'l	Transport [ation]	Transp.
North [ern]	N.	University	Univ.
Organiz[ation, ing]	Org.	Utility	Util.
Pacific	Pac.	West [ern]	W.
Product [ion]	Prod.		

(b) Railroads. Abbreviate all geographical words other than the first word of a party's name to the initial letter or to recognized abbreviations, unless they complete the name of a state, city, or other entity begun by the first word:

Baltimore & O.R.R. v. Minneapolis, St. P. & S. Ste. M. Ry.

But:

Seaboard Air Line Ry. v. Lehigh Valley R.R.

Salt Lake City Elec. Ry. v. Chicago & E. Ill. R.R.

See also rule 10.2.1(h).

10.2.3 Names of Administrative Cases and Arbitrations

Cite administrative adjudications by the full reported name of the first-listed private party or by the official subject-matter title. Omit all procedural phrases.

Trojan Transp., Inc., 249 N.L.R.B. 642 (1980).

Great Lakes Area Case, 8 C.A.B. 360 (1947).

Cite the names of Tax Court and Board of Tax Appeals decisions as those of a court, not as those of an agency:

Jess v. Commissioner, 55 T.C. 3 (1970).

Treat arbitrations as court cases if adversary parties are named and as administrative adjudications if they are not. The arbitrator's name should be indicated parenthetically. Thus:

Kroger Co. v. Amalgamated Meat Cutters Local 539, 74 Lab. Arb. (BNA) 785, 787 (1980) (Doering, Arb.).

But:

Charles P. Ortmeyer, 23 Indus. Arb. 272 (1980) (Stern, Arb.).

Reporters and Other Sources 10.3

Which Source(s) to Cite 10.3.1

If possible, cite decisions of courts listed on pp. 133–200 to the reporter(s) indicated. Note that many decisions require parallel citations to two or more sources. Cite decisions of unlisted courts to the official reporter with a parallel citation to the preferred unofficial reporter (in the United States, the West reporter). Give the official reporter first. If a case has not yet appeared in the official reporter, cite instead to an official continuously paginated advance sheet service, if possible:

Reuben v. Jackson, 1985 Mass. Adv. Sh. 127, 476 N.E.2d 876.

Cite administrative adjudications to the official reporter if the case appears therein; if not, cite to an official release:

Tennessee Intrastate Rates & Charges, 286 I.C.C. 41 (1952).

Central & Southwest Corp., SEC Holding Co. Act Release No. 13,130 (Mar. 14, 1956).

Volumes of some official administrative reporters are initially distributed as slip opinions that are not consecutively paginated. Cite adjudications appearing in this form by case number, full date, and, if possible, parallel citation (to an unofficial reporter, service, or other source, in that order of preference). Thus, *before* the bound volume is issued:

LOF Glass, Inc., 249 N.L.R.B. No. 57, 1980 NLRB Dec. (CCH) ¶ 17,008 (1980).

But *after* the bound volume is issued:

LOF Glass, Inc., 249 N.L.R.B. 428 (1980).

For a list of official federal administrative reporters, see pp. 135–36; for a list of services, see rule 18.2.

If a case is available in any of the above forms, no further parallel citation should be given. If a case is not thus available, cite to another unofficial reporter, to a service (rule 18), or to a newspaper (rule 17), in that order of preference:

In re Saberman, 3 Bankr. L. Rep. (CCH) ¶ 67,416 (Bankr. N.D. Ill. Mar. 31, 1980).

United States v. Palermo, N.Y. Times, Aug. 27, 1957, at 24, col. 3 (S.D.N.Y. Aug. 26, 1957).

Cite unreported cases, including those that appear only in separately printed advance sheets, according to rule 10.8.1:

Englert v. Tenenbaum, No. 85-345 (D. Mass. Dec. 4, 1985).

10.3.2 Reporters

Bound publications that print only cases (or cases and annotations) are considered reporters and are cited in roman type. A citation to a reporter consists of a volume designation (rule 3.2), the abbreviated name of the reporter (as shown on pp. 133–200), and the page on which the case report begins (rule 3.3).

Environmental Defense Fund v. EPA, 465 F.2d 528 (D.C. Cir. 1972).

Early American reporters, even official reporters, were often named after their editors rather than after the courts whose cases they reported. Subsequently, official editor-named series have been combined into jurisdiction-named series with continuous volume numbering. Such reporters are now generally cited by the official series name and number only; the name of the reporter's editor is omitted:

Cobb v. Davenport, 32 N.J.L. 369 (Sup. Ct. 1867).

Not: 3 Vroom 369

But for United States Supreme Court reporters through 90 U.S. (23 Wall.), *see infra* p. 133, and a few early state reporters, *see infra* pp. 136–76, give the name of the reporter's editor and the volume of his series as well. If the pagination of the official jurisdiction-named reprints and the original reporters is the same, use the form:

Green v. Biddle, 21 U.S. (8 Wheat.) 1 (1823).

Hall v. Bell, 47 Mass. (6 Met.) 431 (1843).

If the pagination differs, however, give parallel citations to the reprints and the original reporters:

Wadsworth v. Ruggles, 23 Mass. 62, 6 Pick. 63 (1828).

10.4 Court and Jurisdiction

Every case citation must indicate which court decided the case. In American and other common law citations, give the full abbreviated name of the court (including its geographical jurisdiction) in the parenthetical phrase that immediately follows the citation and includes the date or year of decision:

Baker v. Fortney, 299 S.W.2d 563 (Mo. Ct. App. 1957).

Any information that is conveyed unambiguously by the reporter title may be eliminated from the parenthetical phrase:

Kidder v. Harding, 177 Mont. 499, 505, 582 P.2d 747, 750 (1978).

In civil law and other non-common-law citations, the court designation should appear immediately following the date (rule 10.8.3):

Judgment of Jan. 29, 1963, Finanzgericht Nürnberg, W. Ger., 11 FinG 358.

A more detailed court designation than that specified by the following paragraphs may be given if necessary.

(a) Federal courts. In citations to *United States Law Week,* the United States Supreme Court is indicated: "U.S." Cite a decision by a Supreme Court Justice sitting alone in his capacity as Circuit Justice:

Russo v. Byrne, 409 U.S. 1219 (Douglas, Circuit Justice 1972).

United States courts of appeals for numbered circuits, regardless of year, are indicated:

2d Cir.

Not: C.C.A.2d

And not: CA2

The United States Court of Appeals for the District of Columbia Circuit and all its predecessors are cited:

D.C. Cir.

For district court cases, give the district but not the division:

D.N.J.

D.D.C.

S.D. Cal.

Not: S.D. Cal. C.D.

Cite the old circuit courts (abolished 1912):

C.C.S.D.N.Y.

And cite the Judicial Panel on Multi-District Litigation:

J.P.M.D.L.

Cite decisions of bankruptcy courts and bankruptcy appellate panels:

Bankr. E.D. Va.

Bankr. 9th Cir.

(b) State courts. Include only the jurisdiction if the court of decision is the highest court thereof:

Reynolds v. Dougherty, 3 Serg. & Rawle 325 (Pa. 1817).

Omit the jurisdiction if it is unambiguously conveyed by the reporter title:

Roybal v. Martinez, 92 N.M. 630, 593 P.2d 71 (Ct. App. 1979).

When the name of the reporter is the same as the name of a jurisdiction, it is assumed that the decision is that of the highest court in the jurisdiction:

Putnam v. Wenbrand, 329 Mass. 453, 109 N.E.2d 123 (1952).

Do not indicate the department in citing decisions of intermediate state courts unless that information is of particular relevance:

Schiffman v. Corsi, 182 Misc. 498, 50 N.Y.S.2d 897 (Sup. Ct. 1944).

(c) English and other common law courts. If the report does not clearly indicate the court deciding the case, name the court parenthetically:

The King v. Lockwood, 99 Eng. Rep. 379 (K.B. 1782).

In citing to the K.B., Q.B., Ch., and P. reports (*Law Report* series), indicate the court of decision only if it is the Court of Appeal:

Hastings v. Perkins, 1930 P. 217 (C.A.).

For the App. Cas. and A.C. reports, indicate the court only if it is the Privy Council (P.C.).

In non-English cases, the jurisdiction as well as the court must be indicated parenthetically, if not unambiguously shown by the name of the report:

MacBayne v. Patience, 1940 Sess. Cas. 221 (Scot. 1st Div.).

But if the court involved is the highest court in the jurisdiction, only the jurisdiction need be identified:

Day v. Yates, 45 C.L.R. 32 (Austl. 1931).

Appleton v. Sweetapple, 1953 N.Z.L.R. 83 (1952).

In citing decisions of the Privy Council, House of Lords, or other court that hears appeals from more than one jurisdiction, indicate parenthetically the jurisdiction from which the appeal was taken if other than an English jurisdiction:

Water Works v. Electric Co., [1916] 1 A.C. 719 (P.C. 1915) (B.C.).

Barrett v. Murphy, 1932 A.C. 562 (Scot.).

Rex v. Akatia, 12 Sel. Judg. Ct. App. W. Afr. 98 (1946) (Gold Coast).

(d) Civil law and other non-common-law courts. *See* rule 10.8.3.

(e) Abbreviations. Abbreviate court designations in English as follows:

Admiralty [Court, Division]	Adm.
Appellate Department	App. Dep't
Appellate Division	App. Div.
Bankruptcy [Court, Judge]	Bankr.
Board of Tax Appeals	B.T.A.
Chancery [Court, Division]	Ch.
Children's Court	Child. Ct.
Circuit Court (old federal)	C.C.
Circuit Court (state)	Cir. Ct.
Circuit Court of Appeal [s] (state)	Cir. Ct. App.
Circuit Court of Appeals (federal)	Cir.
City Court	[name city] City Ct.
Civil Appeals	Civ. App.
Civil Court of Record	Civ. Ct. Rec.
Commerce Court	Comm. Ct.
Common Pleas	C.P. [when appropriate, name county or similar subdivision]
Commonwealth Court	Commw. Ct.
County Court	[name county] County Ct.
County Judge's Court	County J. Ct.
Court of Appeal (English)	C.A.
Court of Appeal [s] (state)	Ct. App.
Court of Appeals (federal)	Cir.
Court of Claims	Ct. Cl.
Court of Criminal Appeals	Crim. App.
Court of Customs and Patent Appeals	C.C.P.A.
Court of Customs Appeals	Ct. Cust. App.
Court of Errors and Appeals	Ct. Err. & App.
Court of International Trade	Ct. Int'l Trade
Court of Military Appeals	C.M.A.
Court of Military Review	C.M.R.
Court of [General, Special] Sessions	Ct. [Gen., Spec.] Sess.
Criminal Appeals	Crim. App.
Customs Court	Cust. Ct.
District Court (federal)	D.

District Court (state)	Dist. Ct.
District Court of Appeal [s]	Dist. Ct. App.
Domestic Relations Court	Dom. Rel. Ct.
Emergency Court of Appeals	Emer. Ct. App.
Equity Court or Division	Eq.
Family Court	Fam. Ct.
Judicial Panel on Multi-District Litigation	J.P.M.D.L.
Justice of the Peace's Court	J.P. Ct.
Juvenile Court	Juv. Ct.
Law Court	Law Ct.
Law Division	Law Div.
Magistrate's Court	Magis. Ct.
Municipal Court	[name city] Mun. Ct.
Orphans' Court	Orphans' Ct.
Probate Court	P. Ct.
Police Justice's Court	Police J. Ct.
Public Utilities Commission	P.U.C.
Real Estate Commission	Real Est. Comm'n
Special Court Regional Rail Reorganization Act	Regional Rail Reorg. Ct.
Superior Court	Super. Ct.
Supreme Court (federal)	U.S.
Supreme Court (other)	Sup. Ct.
Supreme Court, Appellate Division	App. Div.
Supreme Court, Appellate Term	App. Term
Supreme Judicial Court	Sup. Jud. Ct.
Surrogate's Court	Sur. Ct.
Tax Court	T.C.
Temporary Emergency Court of Appeals	Temp. Emer. Ct. App.
Workmen's Compensation Division	Workmen's Comp. Div.
Youth Court	Youth Ct.

10.5 Date or Year

Give the exact date for all unreported cases, for all cases cited to newspapers, periodicals, or looseleaf services, and for civil law and other non-common-law cases cited according to rule 10.8.3. Otherwise give only the year.

(a) Decisions. If possible, use the date or year of decision; use the year of the term of court only if the date or year of decision is unavailable. In case of ambiguity, follow the year given in the running head (at the top of each page) in the official report. Dates of United States Supreme Court cases, which usually are not given in the official reports before 108 U.S., may be found in *Lawyers' Edition* beginning with the December 1854 Term.

(b) Pending cases. Use the date or year of the most recent major disposition. If the significance of the date given is not indicated elsewhere, indicate that significance within the parenthetical phrase:

Englert v. Tenenbaum, No. 85-567 (1st Cir. argued Jan. 10, 1986).

Otherwise no such special notation is necessary:

Englert v. Tenenbaum, 580 F. Supp. 1407 (D. Mass 1985), *appeal docketed*, No. 85-567 (1st Cir. Dec. 20, 1985).

(c) Multiple decisions within a single year. In citing a case with several different decisions in the same year, include the year only with the last-cited decision in that year:

United States v. Eller, 114 F. Supp. 384 (M.D.N.C.), *rev'd,* 208 F.2d 716 (4th Cir. 1953), *cert. denied,* 347 U.S. 934 (1954).

However, if the exact date of decision is required in either case, include both dates:

United States v. Carlson, 617 F.2d 518 (9th Cir. 1980), *petition for cert. filed,* 49 U.S.L.W. 3053 (U.S. Aug. 6, 1980) (No. 80-191).

(d) Date included in designation of reporter or volume. When citing a report that uses a year as part of the volume designation, place the year in parentheses at the end of the citation only if it differs from the volume year:

Johnson v. Tigero, [1946] 1 K.B. 225 (1945).

Parenthetical Information Regarding Cases 10.6

When a case is cited for a proposition that is not the single, clear holding of a majority of the court (e.g., alternative holding; by implication; dictum; dissenting opinion; plurality opinion; holding unclear), indicate the fact parenthetically:

Parker v. Randolph, 442 U.S. 62, 84 (1979) (Stevens, J., dissenting).

Further information regarding the weight of the authority (e.g., 2-1 decision; Brandeis, J.; per curiam; mem.; en banc) and any other relevant information may be added in separate parenthetical phrases. Parenthetical phrases indicating the weight of the authority should precede those giving other information:

Green v. Georgia, 442 U.S. 95 (1979) (per curiam) (exclusion of relevant evidence at sentencing hearing constitutes a denial of due process).

National League of Cities v. Usery, 426 U.S. 833, 840 (1976) (5-4 decision) (quoting Fry v. United States, 421 U.S. 542, 547 (1975)).

Information about related authority (rule 2.6) or prior or subsequent history (rule 10.7) that can properly be included in an explanatory phrase should *not* be given parenthetically. Thus:

Wersba v. Seiler, 393 F.2d 937 (3d Cir. 1968) (per curiam).

But:

Wersba v. Seiler, 263 F. Supp. 838, 843 (E.D. Pa. 1967), *aff'd per curiam,* 393 F.2d 937 (3d Cir. 1968).

Parenthetical information about a case should always directly follow citation to that case, before any citation of prior or subsequent history:

Usery v. Allegheny County Inst. Dist., 544 F.2d 148, 154–56 (3d Cir. 1976) (rejecting *National League of Cities* attack on Equal Pay Act), *cert. denied,* 430 U.S. 946 (1977).

See rule 2.5 (parenthetical information generally).

10.7 Prior and Subsequent History

Whenever a decision is cited in full, give the entire *subsequent* history of the case, including disposition in the United States Supreme Court, but omit the history on remand or any denial of a rehearing unless relevant to the point for which the case is cited. Omit also any disposition withdrawn by the deciding authority, such as an affirmance followed by reversal on rehearing.

Give *prior* history only if significant to the point for which the case is cited or if the disposition cited does not intelligibly describe the issues in the case, as in a Supreme Court "mem." Give separate decisions of other issues in the case with their prior and subsequent history only if relevant.

10.7.1 Explanatory Phrases

The prior or subsequent history of a case is appended to the primary citation, and is introduced and explained by italicized words between the citations:

United States v. Kaiser Aetna, 584 F.2d 378 (9th Cir. 1978), *rev'd,* 444 U.S. 164 (1979).

If subsequent history itself has subsequent history, append the additional subsequent history with another explanatory phrase. For example, in the following case the Supreme Court reversed the Second Circuit:

Herbert v. Lando, 73 F.R.D. 387 (S.D.N.Y.), *rev'd,* 568 F.2d 974 (2d Cir. 1977), *rev'd,* 441 U.S. 153 (1979).

To show both prior and subsequent history, give the prior history first:

Kubrick v. United States, 581 F.2d 1092 (3d Cir. 1978), *aff'g* 435 F. Supp. 166 (E.D. Pa. 1977), *rev'd,* 444 U.S. 111 (1979).

Citations to prior or subsequent history should follow any parenthetical information given (rule 10.6). A partial list of explanatory phrases (as abbreviated) follows:

aff'd,
aff'd mem.,
aff'd [rev'd] on other grounds,
aff'd on rehearing,
aff'g [rev'g]
acq.
acq. in result
appeal denied,
appeal dismissed,
appeal filed,
argued,
cert. denied,
cert. dismissed,
cert. granted,
denying cert. to
dismissing appeal from
enforcing
modified,
modifying
nonacq.
petition for cert. filed,
prob. juris. noted,
reh'g granted [denied],
rev'd,
rev'd per curiam,
vacated,
withdrawn,

The word "mem." is used to designate dispositions without opinion. The phrase "per curiam" may be used to describe an opinion so denominated by the court in either English or Latin. Give the reason for a disposition if the disposition does not have the normal substantive significance:

vacated as moot,

appeal dismissed per stipulation,

Different Case Name on Appeal 10.7.2

When the name of the case differs in prior or subsequent history, the other name must be given, except: (1) when the parties' names are merely reversed, (2) when the citation in which the difference occurs is to a denial of certiorari or rehearing, or (3) when, in the appeal of an administrative action, the name of the private party remains the same:

United Dairy Farmers Coop. Ass'n, 194 N.L.R.B. 1094, *enforced,* 465 F.2d 1401 (3d Cir. 1972).

But:

Perma Vinyl Corp., 164 N.L.R.B. 968 (1967), *enforced sub nom.* United States Pipe & Foundry Co. v. NLRB, 398 F.2d 544 (1968).

A different name in *subsequent* history is indicated through the use of "*sub nom.*":

Great W. United Corp. v. Kidwell, 577 F.2d 1256 (5th Cir. 1978), *rev'd sub nom.* Leroy v. Great W. United Corp., 443 U.S. 173 (1979).

A different name in *prior* history is indicated:

Rederi v. Isbrandtsen Co., 342 U.S. 950 (1952) (per curiam), *aff'g by an equally divided Court* Isbrandtsen Co. v. United States, 96 F. Supp. 883 (S.D.N.Y. 1951).

10.8 Special Citation Forms

10.8.1 Pending and Unreported Cases

When a case is unreported or printed only in separately paginated advance sheets or separately printed slip opinions, give the docket number, the court, and the full date of the most recent major disposition of the case:

Groucho Marx Prods. v. Playboy Enters., No. 77 Civ. 1782 (S.D.N.Y. Dec. 30, 1977).

If the date is not that of decision and the significance of the date is not indicated elsewhere, indicate that significance within the parenthetical phrase containing the date:

Englert v. Tenenbaum, No. 85-345 (D. Mass. filed Sept. 18, 1985).

To cite to a particular page of an unpublished opinion, use the form:

Englert v. Tenenbaum, No. 85-345, slip op. at 6 (D. Mass. Dec. 4, 1985).

If dissenting or concurring opinions are separately paginated, be sure to indicate the author of the opinion cited:

Grehan v. Pincus, No. 84-2101, slip op. at 12 (D.C. Cir. Mar. 19, 1986) (Olenick, J., dissenting).

If an unreported case is available on a computerized legal research service, indicate that fact parenthetically:

Ostergaard v. DeMarco, No. 86-127 (D. Wyo. Aug. 7, 1987) (available Oct. 1, 1987, on LEXIS, Genfed library, Dist file).

When a pending case is reported, cite to the source in which it is reported, and append the docket number parenthetically. Note any renumbering of the docket thus:

United States v. Johnson, 425 F.2d 630 (9th Cir. 1970), *cert. granted,* 403 U.S. 956 (1971) (No. 577, 1970 Term; renumbered No. 70-8, 1971 Term).

Always give the full docket number:

No. 75-31

Not: No. 31

B

Briefs, Records, Motions, and Memoranda 10.8.2

Use the designation given on the document itself, followed by a full citation to the case to which it relates:

Appellant's Opening Brief at 5, Rosenthal v. Carr, 614 F.2d 1219 (9th Cir.), *cert. denied,* 447 U.S. 927 (1980).

Brief for the National Labor Relations Board at 7, NLRB v. J.C. Penney Co., 620 F.2d 718 (9th Cir. 1980).

A short form of the case name (rule 4.3) may be used, or the case name may be omitted, if the reference is unambiguous:

Record at 16, *Bakke*.

Record at 16.

Civil Law and Other Non-Common-Law Cases 10.8.3

Cite cases from countries listed on pp. 190–200 and from other non-common-law countries by full date of decision, court, jurisdiction, and source:

Judgment of Jan. 10, 1935, Cour d'appel, Paris, 1935 Recueil Périodique et Critique [D.P.] II 758.

(a) Name and date. Do not give the names of the parties; always use the form:

Judgment of [full date of decision]

(b) Court. Identify courts as indicated on pp. 190–200. Do not abbreviate the name of any court not listed on those pages unless the name is in English, in which case it may be abbreviated according to the list given in rule 10.4(e). Translate into English all court designations not in a Romance or Germanic language; do not add the name in the original language.

(c) Jurisdiction. Include the national jurisdiction abbreviated according to the table on the inside back cover of this book, unless the court designation (rule 10.8.3(b)) also includes a reference to some easily identifiable smaller geographic unit. Thus:

Corte cass., Italy

But:

Cour d'appel, Paris

(d) Reports and other sources. Cite to the sources listed, with their abbreviations, in the tables on pp. 190–200. Give the full form the first time a source is cited, indicating in brackets the abbreviation that will be used subsequently. Thereafter, the abbreviated form may be used. *See* rule 6.2.

(e) Annotations. Annotations to civil law cases are cited according to rule 3.5:

Judgment of Mar. 22, 1962, Cass. civ. soc., Fr., 1963 Recueil Sirey [S. Jur.] II 33 note R. Savatier.

C Constitutions, Statutes, and Legislative, Administrative, and Executive Materials

Rule 11: Constitutions 57

Rule 12: Statutes 57

Rule 13: Legislative Materials 71

Rule 14: Administrative and Executive Materials 75

Constitutions 11

Cite English-language constitutions by country or state and the word "CONST.":

U.S. CONST. art. I, § 9, cl. 2.

U.S. CONST. amend. XIV, § 2.

U.S. CONST. preamble.

N.M. CONST. art. IV, § 7.

Cite constitutions not in English by name, and append the English abbreviation of the jurisdiction in parentheses. Include a parenthetical translation of the names of constitutions not in a Germanic or Romance language:

GRUNDGESETZ [GG] art. 51 (W. Ger.).

KENPŌ (Constitution) art. VIII, para. 1 (Japan).

Cite constitutional provisions without date unless the cited provisions have been repealed or amended, in which case indicate parenthetically both the date of adoption and the date of repeal or amendment:

GRUNDGESETZ [GG] art. 92 (W. Ger. 1949, amended 1968).

Cite constitutions that have been totally superseded by year of adoption; if the specific provision cited was adopted in a different year, give that year parenthetically:

ARK. CONST. of 1868, art. III, § 2 (1873).

C

Statutes 12

Basic Citation Forms 12.1

(a) American jurisdictions.

cited to current official code	42 U.S.C. § 1983 (Supp. III 1979) National Environmental Policy Act of 1969, § 102, 42 U.S.C. § 4332 (1976) Probate, Estates and Fiduciaries Code, 20 PA. CONS. STAT. § 301 (1976)
cited to current unofficial code	12 U.S.C.A. § 635f (West Supp. 1981) Parking Authority Law, PA. STAT. ANN. tit. 53, § 342 (Purdon 1974)
cited to official session laws	National Environmental Policy Act of 1969, Pub. L. No. 91-190, § 102, 83 Stat. 852, 853 (1970) (prior to 1975 amendment)
cited to privately published session laws	Health Care Facilities Act, Act No. 1979-48, 1979 Pa. Legis. Serv. 114 (to be codified at 35 PA. CONS. STAT. §§ 448.101–.903)

cited to secondary source	International Air Transportation Competition Act of 1979, Pub. L. No. 96-192, § 17, 48 U.S.L.W. 80, 82 (1980) (to be codified at 49 U.S.C. § 1102)

(b) England and other Commonwealth jurisdictions.

pre-1962 uncodified	Supreme Court of Judicature Act, 1925, 15 & 16 Geo. 5, ch. 49, § 226, sched. 6
post-1962 uncodified	Sale of Goods Act, 1979, ch. 54
cited to compilation	Pacific Fur Seals Convention Act, CAN. REV. STAT. ch. F-33 (1970)
act subsequent to current compilation	Act of Dec. 23, 1971, ch. 63, 1970–1972 Can. Stat. 1311

(c) Civil law and other non-common-law jurisdictions.

code	CODE CIVIL [C. CIV.] art. 1097(2) (64e ed. Petits Codes Dalloz 1965)
session laws	Körperschaftsteuerreformgesetz [KStG] § 26(2), 1967 Bundesgesetzblatt [BGBl] I 2597 (W. Ger.)
	Aussensteuerreformgesetz [AStG], 1972 BGBl I 1713 (W. Ger.)

As the above table shows, American statutes may be cited to a current official or unofficial code (rule 12.3), official or privately published session laws (rule 12.4), or secondary sources (rule 12.5). Official and unofficial codes arrange statutes currently in force by subject matter. Official or privately published session laws report statutes in chronological order of enactment. Secondary sources—such as *United States Code Congressional and Administrative News,* looseleaf services, periodicals, or newspapers—print statutes that are unavailable elsewhere.

Rule 12.2 explains when to use each of these basic citation forms. The next three rules discuss in greater detail the citation forms for official and unofficial codes (rule 12.3), session laws (rule 12.4), and secondary sources (rule 12.5). Pages 133–200 of this book list citation forms for the codes and session laws of the federal government, each state, and many foreign countries. Rule 12.6 explains when the subsequent history of a statute must be cited, and rule 12.7 discusses the use of explanatory parenthetical phrases with statute citations. Finally, rule 12.8 outlines special citation forms for the Internal Revenue Code, ordinances, rules of evidence and procedure, uniform acts, model codes, restatements of the law, standards, the ABA Code of Professional Responsibility, and foreign statutes.

12.2 Choosing the Proper Citation Form

12.2.1 General Rule

If possible, cite statutes currently in force to the current official code or its supplement. Otherwise cite to a current unofficial code or its supplement, the official session laws, privately published session laws, *United States Code Congressional and Administrative News,* a looseleaf service, a periodical, or a newspaper—in that order of preference.

Cite statutes no longer in force to the current official or unofficial code if they still appear therein. Otherwise cite to the session laws or a secondary source. In any case, the fact of repeal or amendment *must* be noted parenthetically according to 12.6.1 or 12.6.2:

Clayton Act, ch. 323, § 7, 38 Stat. 730, 731–32 (1914) (current version at 15 U.S.C. § 18 (1976)).

Cite private laws to the session laws if therein; otherwise cite to a secondary source:

Priv. L. No. 94-75, 90 Stat. 2985 (1976).

C

Exceptions 12.2.2

(a) Historical fact. The historical fact of enactment, amendment, or repeal should be cited to the session laws. A parenthetical reference to the current version (*see* rules 12.6.2 and 12.7) may be added:

Two years later, Congress passed the Voting Rights Act of 1965, Pub. L. No. 89-110, 79 Stat. 437 (codified as amended at 42 U.S.C. §§ 1971, 1973 to 1973bb-1 (1976)).

(b) Materially different language. If the language in the current code (including its supplement) differs materially from the language in the session laws, and the relevant title has not been enacted into positive law, cite the session laws. A parenthetical reference to the code version, introduced by the phrase "codified with some differences in language at" may be given. If differences in the language merely reflect subsequent amendments, however, cite to the current code.

A current list of federal code titles that have been enacted into positive law appears in the preface to the latest edition or supplement of the United States Code. As of January 5, 1981, the titles so enacted were 1, 3–6, 9–11, 13, 14, 17, 18, 23, 28, 32, 35, 37–39, 44, and subtitle IV of 49. Similarly, state codes should indicate whether the titles contained therein have been enacted into positive law.

(c) Scattered statutes. Cite to the session laws if a statute appears in so many scattered sections or titles that no useful citation to the code is possible. Indicate parenthetically the general location of the codified sections. Thus:

Tax Reduction Act of 1975, Pub. L. No. 94-12, 89 Stat. 26 (codified as amended in scattered sections of 26 U.S.C.).

But:

Robinson-Patman Act, 15 U.S.C. §§ 13–13b, 21a (1976).

If the current version of a statute is split between the main body and the supplement of a code, it should be cited according to rule 3.2(c):

12 U.S.C. § 1451 (1976 & Supp. III 1979).

If the current version of a statute is split among different types of sources (not just a code and its supplement), it should be cited according to rule 12.6.2:

National Labor Relations Act § 19, 29 U.S.C. § 169 (1976), *as amended by* Act of Dec. 24, 1980, Pub. L. No. 96-593, 49 U.S.L.W. 227 (1981).

12.3 Current Official and Unofficial Codes

The official federal code is the *United States Code* (U.S.C.). Unofficial federal codes include the *United States Code Annotated* (U.S.C.A.) and the *United States Code Service* (U.S.C.S.). Official and unofficial codes for each state, as well as for many foreign countries, are listed on pp. 136–200 of this book.

All citations to codes contain the abbreviated name of the code (found on pp. 135–200) printed in large and small capitals; the section, paragraph, or article number(s) of the statute; and the year of the code (determined according to rule 12.3.1):

N.C. GEN. STAT. § 1-180 (1969).

Additional information may be required as follows:

(a) Name and original section number. Give the statute's name and original section number (found in the appropriate session laws) only if the statute is commonly cited that way or the information would otherwise aid in identification. An official name, a popular name, or both may be used:

Labor Management Relations (Taft-Hartley) Act § 301(a), 29 U.S.C. § 185(a) (1976).

(b) Title, chapter, or volume. If a code is divided into separately sectioned or paragraphed titles, chapters, or volumes, the title, chapter, or volume number must be indicated. When citing to the federal code, give the title number before the name of the code:

42 U.S.C. § 1983 (1976).

12 U.S.C.S. § 1710 (Law. Co-op. 1978).

The form for citation to state codes varies; the lists on pp. 136–76 indicate whether and in what manner to identify the title, chapter, or volume number of a state code. For example:

DEL. CODE ANN. tit. 13, § 1301 (1974).

Act of May 29, 1879, § 1, ILL. REV. STAT. ch. 21, § 13 (1979).

9 PA. CONS. STAT. § 301 (1977).

If each title, chapter, or volume of a code contains differently numbered sections or paragraphs, then the volume, chapter, or title number need not be given separately:

GA. CODE ANN. § 96-1005 (Supp. 1980).

(c) Subject-matter codes. If a separately sectioned or paragraphed portion of a code is identified by a subject-matter title rather than by a title, volume, or chapter number, give that subject-matter title as part of the code:

CAL. AGRIC. CODE § 408 (West 1968).

TEX. FAM. CODE ANN. § 5.01 (Vernon 1975).

The lists on pp. 136–76 of this book indicate which state codes require this treatment.

(d) Publisher, editor, or compiler. Unless a code is published, edited, or compiled by, or under the supervision of, the state or state officials, give the name of the publisher, editor, or compiler in the parenthetical phrase that also contains the year of the code:

42 U.S.C.A. § 300c-11 (West Supp. 1974–1979).

18 U.S.C.S. § 1761 (Law. Co-op. 1979 & Supp. 1980).

CAL. AGRIC. CODE § 306 (West 1968).

N.Y. JUD. LAW § 121 (McKinney 1968).

The lists on pp. 135–76 of this book indicate which federal and state codifications require this information.

(e) Supplements. Cite material appearing in supplements according to rule 3.2(c):

18 U.S.C. § 201(b) (Supp. III 1979).

12 U.S.C. § 1451 (1976 & Supp. III 1979).

(f) Compilations of uncodified laws. If a code contains uncodified laws printed in a separate compilation, cite in this manner:

N.Y. UNCONSOL. LAWS § 751 (McKinney 1979).

(g) Appendices. If a statute appears in an appendix to a code, and the statute is numbered and otherwise printed as if it were part of a code, cite according to rule 3.5:

50 U.S.C. app. § 5 (1976 & Supp. III 1979).

If the statute is not printed as if it were part of a code, cite the session laws and add an explanatory phrase (*see* rule 2.6(a)) showing that the statute is reprinted in the code's appendix:

Act of Aug. 31, 1970, ch. 842, 1970 Mass. Acts 732, *reprinted in* MASS. GEN. LAWS ANN. ch. 40 app. at 180 (West Supp. 1975).

(h) Differently numbered unofficial codes. If an unofficial code uses a numbering system that differs from the official code, cite the unofficial code only if the statute does not appear in the official code. Otherwise cite the official code. In the latter case, the unofficial code section may be given parenthetically:

MICH. COMP. LAWS § 551.151 (1967) (MICH. STAT. ANN. § 25.25 (Callaghan 1974)).

12.3.1 Year of Code

When citing a bound volume of the current official or unofficial code, give parenthetically the year that appears on the spine of the volume, the year that appears on the title page, or the latest copyright year—in that order of preference. If the date on the spine or title page spans more than one year, give all of the years covered. If the volume is a replacement of an earlier edition, use the year of the replacement volume, not of the original.

NEB. REV. STAT. § 33-116 (1978).

When citing a provision that appears in a supplement or pocket part, give the year that appears on the title page of the supplement or pocket part. If there is none, give the latest copyright year of the supplement or pocket part. In either case, if the date spans more than one year, give all years included:

IOWA CODE ANN. § 194.9 (West Supp. 1981–1982).

To cite material that appears in both the main volume and a supplement or pocket part, give both years:

VT. STAT. ANN. tit. 14, § 1492 (1974 & Supp. 1981).

If a code is published in looseleaf form, give the year on the page on which the provision is printed or the year on the first page of the subdivision in which the provision appears—in that order of preference—rather than the years indicated above:

ALASKA STAT. § 28.01.010 (1978).

In addition to the years discussed above, other dates (such as the date on which an act becomes effective) may be given parenthetically according to rule 12.7:

OKLA. STAT. tit. 10, § 1102.1 (Supp. 1980–1981) (effective Oct. 1, 1977).

Session Laws

12.4

When citing session laws, always give the name of the statute and the public law or chapter number; an official name, a popular name, or both may be used:

White-Slave Traffic (Mann) Act, ch. 395, 36 Stat. 825 (1910) (codified as amended at 18 U.S.C. §§ 2421–2424 (1976 & Supp. III 1979)).

If the statute has no official or popular name, use the form "Act of [full date of enactment or, if none, date of approval by executive or effective date]":

Act of Aug. 21, 1974, ch. 85, 1974 N.J. Laws 385.

Not: An Act concerning unemployment compensation for persons serving on jury duty, and amending R.S. 43:21-4, ch. 85, 1974 N.J. Laws 385.

Give the volume number (or, if none, year) of the session laws, followed by the abbreviated name of the session laws in ordinary roman type. The official federal session laws, *Statutes at Large,* are abbreviated "Stat." Abbreviations for official and privately published state session laws appear on pp. 136–76. When citing state session laws, the abbreviated title of the session laws should always begin with the abbreviated name of the state, even if the state name is not part of the official title; omit words in the official title not necessary for identification:

1978 Ark. Acts

1935–1936 Ill. Laws 4th Spec. Sess.

1878 Minn. Gen. Laws

Not: 1878 Gen. Laws of Minn.

When citing an entire act, give the page of the session laws on which the act begins:

National Environmental Policy Act of 1969, Pub. L. No. 91-190, 83 Stat. 852 (1970).

When citing only part of an act, give the page on which the act begins and the page(s) on which the relevant section(s) or subsection(s) appears. In the latter case, also give the section or subsection number. That number should appear after the public law or chapter number:

National Environmental Policy Act of 1969, Pub. L. No. 91-190, § 102, 83 Stat. 852, 853–54 (1970).

Give parenthetically the year the statute was passed by the legislature, unless the same year is part of the name of the statute or of the session laws:

McCarran-Ferguson Act, ch. 20, 59 Stat. 33 (1945) (codified as amended at 15 U.S.C. §§ 1011–1015 (1976)).

Act of Apr. 25, 1978, No. 515, § 3, 1978 Ala. Acts 569, 569 (codified at ALA. CODE § 9-3-12 (1980)).

If no date of enactment is identified, give the date the statute was approved by the executive or became effective. If the session laws were privately edited or compiled (i.e., not edited or compiled by the state), give the name of the editor or compiler in the same parenthetical phrase. The lists on pp. 135–76 indicate which session laws currently require this information.

If a statute has been or will ultimately be codified, and the code location is known, give that information parenthetically:

Act of Sept. 10, 1981, ch. 404, § 4, 1981 Cal. Legis. Serv. 1200, 1201 (West) (to be codified at CAL. PENAL CODE § 28).

Other parenthetical information, such as the date an act becomes effective, may be given according to rule 12.7.

12.5 Secondary Sources

When citing a statute to any source other than a code or session laws, give the name of the act and public law or chapter number as if citing to session laws (rule 12.4). When referring to a particular provision, give the section or subsection number after the public law or chapter number. If possible, cite to *United States Code Congressional and Administrative News*, indicating the volume and page number of *Statutes at Large* where the statute will appear:

Act of Feb. 7, 1981, Pub. L. No. 97-2, 1981 U.S. CODE CONG. & AD. NEWS (95 Stat.) 4.

When citing an entire act, give the page on which the act begins. When citing part of an act, give both the page on which the act begins and the pages on which the cited material appears. If the future code location of the statute is known, give that information parenthetically:

Act of Feb. 17, 1981, Pub. L. No. 97-4, 1981 U.S. CODE CONG. & AD. NEWS (95 Stat.) 6 (to be codified at 44 U.S.C. § 101).

Cite other secondary sources according to rule 18 (services), 16 (periodicals), or 17 (newspapers). Give the date or year appropriate for the cited source. If the name of a statute cited to a service includes the year, and the service was published in that year, the year of the service may be omitted. If the future location of the act in either a code or session laws is known, give that information parenthetically:

Soil and Water Resources Conservation Act of 1977, Pub. L. No. 95-192, [Federal Laws] ENV'T REP. (BNA) 71:8401 (to be codified at 16 U.S.C. §§ 2001–2009).

If a statute is too recent to appear in any published source, give only the name of the act; the public law or chapter number; the section or subsection number if referring only to part of the statute; the full date of enactment or, if none, date of approval by executive or effective date; and the future location in code or session laws if known:

Alabama Table Wine Act, No. 80-382 (May 7, 1980).

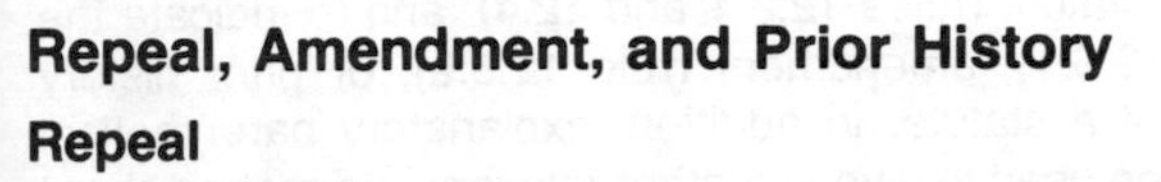

Repeal, Amendment, and Prior History 12.6

Repeal 12.6.1

When citing a statute no longer in force, either indicate the fact and date of repeal parenthetically or add a full citation to the repealing statute:

Law of June 1, 1895, ch. 4322, § 23, 1895 Fla. Laws 3, 20–21 (repealed 1969).

Act of Jan. 24, 1923, ch. 42, 42 Stat. 1174, 1208, *repealed by* Budget and Accounting Procedures Act of 1950, ch. 946, § 301(97), 64 Stat. 832, 844.

Amendment 12.6.2

When citing a version of a statute that is no longer in force, either indicate the fact and date of amendment parenthetically, cite the current amended version parenthetically, or cite the amending statute in full:

Supplemental Appropriation Act of 1955, Pub. L. No. 663, § 1311, 68 Stat. 800, 830 (1954) (amended 1959).

Clayton Act, ch. 323, § 7, 38 Stat. 730, 731–32 (1914) (current version at 15 U.S.C. § 18 (1976)).

33 U.S.C. § 1311 (1976), *amended by* 33 U.S.C. § 1311(g) (Supp. III 1979).

Prior History 12.6.3

When citing the current version of a statute, prior history may be given parenthetically if relevant:

33 U.S.C. § 1311(g) (Supp. III 1979) (amending 33 U.S.C. § 1311 (1976)).

28 U.S.C. § 1652 (1976) (originally enacted as Act of June 25, 1948, ch. 646, § 1652, 62 Stat. 869, 944).

28 U.S.C. § 1652 (1976) (corresponds to Judiciary Act of 1789, ch. 20, § 34, 1 Stat. 73, 92).

Clayton Act § 7, 15 U.S.C. § 18 (1976) (original version at ch. 323, § 7, 38 Stat. 730, 731–32 (1914)).

12.7 Explanatory Parenthetical Phrases

Explanatory parenthetical phrases are used to show the code location of statutes cited to session laws (rules 12.2.2 and 12.4) or secondary sources (rule 12.5); to give the unofficial code section when an unofficial code is numbered differently from an official code (rule 12.3(h)); to identify useful dates such as the effective date of a statute (rules 12.3.1 and 12.4); and to indicate the repeal (rule 12.6.1), amendment (rule 12.6.2), or prior history (rule 12.6.3) of a statute. In addition, explanatory parenthetical phrases may be used to give any other relevant information about a statute:

5 U.S.C. § 553(b) (1976) (requiring agencies to publish notice of proposed rulemaking in the *Federal Register*).

See generally rule 2.5 (parenthetical information).

12.8 Special Citation Forms

12.8.1 Internal Revenue Code

In citations to the Internal Revenue Code, "26 U.S.C." may be replaced with "I.R.C." Thus:

26 U.S.C. § 61 (1976)

becomes:

I.R.C. § 61 (1976).

In law review footnotes, the year of the current United States Code or its supplement (as appropriate) should always be given. Citations to the Internal Revenue Code as it appears in an unofficial code may also use this form. In that case, identify the unofficial code by placing the publisher's name in the parenthetical phrase containing the year of the version cited. Thus, citations to U.S.C.A. and U.S.C.S. could appear:

I.R.C. § 1371 (West Supp. 1980).

I.R.C. § 6323 (Law. Co-op. 1980).

In general, briefs and legal memoranda should cite the Internal Revenue Code in the same manner. However, citations to the current version of the Code in briefs and memoranda intended to be used for a very short time may omit the year and publisher:

I.R.C. § 61.

See also rule 4.3(b) (short form citation of statutes).

Ordinances 12.8.2

Cite ordinances analogously to statutes. Always give the name of the political subdivision (such as a city or county) and abbreviated state name at the beginning of the citation. If the ordinance is codified, give the name of the code, section or other subdivision, and the year of the code (determined according to rule 12.3.1). Print the political subdivision, state, and code name in large and small capitals:

MONTGOMERY, ALA., CODE § 3A-11 (1971).

PORTLAND, OR., POLICE CODE art. 30 (1933).

FORT WORTH, TEX., REV. ORDINANCES ch. 34, art. I, § 15 (1950).

If the ordinance is uncodified, give its number (or, if none, name) and exact date of adoption. Print the political subdivision, state, and ordinance name in ordinary roman type:

San Jose, Cal., Ordinance 16,043 (Jan. 17, 1972).

Halifax County, Va., Ordinance to Regulate the Solicitation of Membership in Organizations (Aug. 6, 1956).

Rules of Evidence and Procedure 12.8.3

Cite current rules of evidence or procedure in large and small capitals, without any date. Use abbreviations such as the following or abbreviations suggested by the rules themselves:

FED. R. CIV. P. 12.

FED. R. CRIM. P. 42(a).

FED. R. APP. P. 2.

1ST CIR. R. 6(a).

DEL. CT. C.P.R. 8(f).

FED. R. EVID. 410.

Cite rules no longer in force in ordinary roman type and give the most recent official source in which they appear:

Sup. Ct. R. 7, 266 U.S. 657 (1912).

Uniform Acts 12.8.4

When citing a uniform act as the law of a particular state, cite as a state statute:

12A PA. CONS. STAT. ANN. § 2-314 (Purdon 1970).

When not citing to the law of a particular state, cite as a separate code:

U.C.C. § 2-205 (1977).

A citation to *Uniform Laws Annotated* (U.L.A.) may be given:

UNIF. ADOPTION ACT § 10, 9 U.L.A. 35 (1971).

Give the year in which the uniform act was last amended, even if the section referred to was not amended at that time. If a uniform act or section has been withdrawn, superseded, or amended, indicate that fact parenthetically according to rule 12.6.1 or 12.6.2:

UNIF. R. EVID. 14(a) (section withdrawn 1911, act withdrawn 1921).

12.8.5 Model Codes, Restatements, and Standards

Cite model codes, restatements, standards, and similar materials in large and small capitals, by section, rule, or other relevant subdivision. Give the year in which the code, restatement, or set of standards was adopted, unless the version you are citing indicates that it incorporates subsequent amendments. In that case, give the year of the last amendment, even if you are citing a portion not amended at that time. Usually the cover or title page of the source will indicate the date of the most recent amendments incorporated. In naming the code, restatement, or set of standards, use abbreviations listed in rules 10.2.1 and 10.2.2 (abbreviation of case names) or suggested by the source itself:

MODEL BUSINESS CORP. ACT § 57 (1979).

MODEL CODE OF EVIDENCE Rule 502 (1942).

RESTATEMENT (SECOND) OF AGENCY § 20 (1957).

STANDARDS RELATING TO APPELLATE COURTS § 3.12 (1977).

If a code, restatement, or set of standards is a tentative or proposed draft, indicate that fact parenthetically and give the year of the draft:

MODEL LAND DEV. CODE § 2-402(2) (Proposed Official Draft 1975).

RESTATEMENT (SECOND) OF TORTS § 847A (Tent. Draft No. 17, 1974).

STANDARDS RELATING TO COURT ORG. § 1.40 (Tent. Draft 1973).

If the work was not authored by the American Law Institute or American Bar Association, indicate the author parenthetically:

MODEL CHILDREN'S CODE § 3.9B(2) (American Indian Law Center 1976).

STANDARDS FOR INMATES' LEGAL RIGHTS Right 18 (National Sheriffs' Ass'n 1974).

Comments, notes, and other addenda should be cited according to rule 3.5:

MODEL PENAL CODE § 223.6 note on status of section (Proposed Official Draft 1962).

RESTATEMENT (SECOND) OF CONFLICT OF LAWS § 305 comment b, illustration 1 (1969).

STANDARDS FOR TRAFFIC JUSTICE § 4.2 commentary at 9 (1975).

When citing a version of a code, restatement, or set of standards that has been withdrawn or amended, indicate that fact according to rule 12.6.1 or 12.6.2:

MODEL BUSINESS CORP. ACT § 2(f) (1969) (amended 1973).

C

ABA Code of Professional Responsibility and Opinions on Ethics — 12.8.6

Cite the old *Model Code of Professional Responsibility* and the new *Model Rules of Professional Conduct* according to rule 12.8.5:

MODEL CODE OF PROFESSIONAL RESPONSIBILITY Canon 2 (1979).

MODEL RULES OF PROFESSIONAL CONDUCT Rule 3.12 (Discussion Draft 1980).

Cite ethical considerations and disciplinary rules as follows:

MODEL CODE OF PROFESSIONAL RESPONSIBILITY EC 7-36 (1979).

MODEL CODE OF PROFESSIONAL RESPONSIBILITY DR 8-101 (1979).

Cite notes or other commentary according to rule 3.5:

MODEL RULES OF PROFESSIONAL CONDUCT Rule 1.15 comment (Discussion Draft 1980).

Cite formal and informal opinions of the Committee on Ethics and Professional Responsibility (or the older Committees on Professional Ethics (1958–1971) and on Professional Ethics and Grievances (1919–1958)) by issuing body, number, and year:

ABA Comm. on Professional Ethics and Grievances, Formal Op. 35 (1931).

ABA Comm. on Ethics and Professional Responsibility, Informal Op. 1414 (1978).

The subject of the opinion may be given parenthetically:

ABA Comm. on Ethics and Professional Responsibility, Formal Op. 338 (1974) (use of credit cards for the payment of legal services and expenses).

12.8.7 Commonwealth Statutes

(a) English. Cite English statutes enacted before 1962 by name (often including the year), if any, regnal year(s), chapter, section, and schedule, if any:

Supreme Court of Judicature Act, 1925, 15 & 16 Geo. 5, ch. 49, § 226, sched. 6.

Indicate regnal years by year(s) of reign, abbreviated name of the monarch, and numeric designation of the monarch in Arabic numerals; if the monarch was the first of that name, omit the numeric designation. Thus:

11 Hen. 7

But:

13 Eliz.

Abbreviate monarch's names as follows:

Charles	Car.	Philip & Mary	Phil. & M.
Edward	Edw.	Richard	Rich.
Elizabeth	Eliz.	Victoria	Vict.
George	Geo.	William	Will.
Henry	Hen.	William & Mary	W. & M.
James	Jac.		

If a short title has been established by the Short Titles Act or the Statute Law Revision Act, it may be indicated parenthetically:

Lord Campbell's Act (Fatal Accidents Act), 1846, 9 & 10 Vict., ch. 93.

If the name is omitted or does not include the date or year, give the year parenthetically at the end of the citation:

Hypnotism Act, 15 & 16 Geo. 6 & 1 Eliz. 2, ch. 44, § 117 (1952).

For statutes enacted since 1962, omit the regnal year:

Airports Authority Act, 1965, ch. 16.

(b) Canadian. Statutes appearing in the current national or provincial *Revision* (alphabetical consolidation of acts in force) are cited analogously to codified United States statutes:

Juvenile Delinquents Act, Can. Rev. Stat. ch. J-3, § 3(2) (1970).

Cite subsequent statutes to the *Annual* in a manner similar to that used for United States session laws:

Act of Dec. 23, 1971, ch. 63, 1970–1972 Can. Stat. 1311.

When citing an act appearing in the current *Revision* as well as the act's subsequent amendment, the name of the amendment need not be given:

Securities Act, Que. Rev. Stat. ch. V-1 (1977), *amended by* ch. 79, 1979 Que. Stat. 1227.

(c) Other. Cite like United States or Canadian statutes if the jurisdiction's statutes appear in a codification or other compilation. Otherwise cite like English statutes, noting the jurisdiction parenthetically at the end of the citation.

Civil Law and Other Non-Common-Law Statutes 12.8.8

Cite generally according to rules 12.1 to 12.7, but indicate the jurisdiction parenthetically if not apparent from the code's title. Give the publisher or editor of privately published sources only when citing to an annotation rather than to the code itself. Use the full publication name the first time the publication is cited, indicating in brackets the abbreviation that will be used subsequently. Thereafter, the abbreviated form may be used. *See* rule 6.2. Lists of codes and other statutory sources, with their abbreviations, are given on pp. 191–200.

Legislative Materials 13

Basic Citation Forms 13.1

federal bill (unenacted)	H.R. 3055, 94th Cong., 2d Sess., 122 Cong. Rec. 16,870–71 (1976)
federal resolution (unenacted)	H.R.J. Res. 1116, 95th Cong., 2d Sess., 124 Cong. Rec. H8790–91 (daily ed. Aug. 16, 1978)
state resolution	Okla. S. Res. 20, 37th Leg., 1979 Okla. Sess. Law Serv. A-159
committee hearing	*Panama Canal Treaty Implementation: Hearings on H.R. 1716 Before the Subcomm. on Immigration, Refugees, and International Law of the House Comm. on the Judiciary*, 96th Cong., 1st Sess. 68–70 (1979) (statement of Ambler H. Moss, Jr., U.S. Ambassador to the Republic of Panama)
federal report	H.R. Rep. No. 98, 92d Cong., 1st Sess. 4, *reprinted in* 1971 U.S. Code Cong. & Ad. News 1017, 1017

federal document	H.R. DOC. NO. 208, 94th Cong., 1st Sess. 2 (1975)
committee print	STAFF OF SENATE COMM. ON FINANCE, 93D CONG., 2D SESS., STAFF DATA AND MATERIALS ON UNITED STATES TRADE AND BALANCE OF PAYMENTS 52 (Comm. Print 1974)
congressional debate	126 CONG. REC. H6456 (daily ed. July 24, 1980) (statement of Rep. Levitas)
source reprinted in separately bound legislative history	SENATE COMM. ON LABOR AND PUBLIC WELFARE, LABOR-MANAGEMENT REPORTING AND DISCLOSURE ACT OF 1959, S. REP. NO. 187, 86th Cong., 1st Sess. 4, *reprinted in* 1959 U.S. CODE CONG. & AD. NEWS 2318, 2320, *and in* 1 NLRB, LEGISLATIVE HISTORY OF THE LABOR-MANAGEMENT REPORTING AND DISCLOSURE ACT OF 1959, at 397, 400 (1959)

Besides statutes (rule 12), the legislative process generates bills and resolutions (rule 13.2); committee hearings (rule 13.3); reports, documents, and committee prints (rule 13.4); floor debates (rule 13.5); and, sometimes, separately bound legislative histories (rule 13.6). When citing any United States legislative material except debates, identify the house, the number and session of the Congress, and the year of publication. State and foreign legislative materials are cited similarly except when this book indicates otherwise. For specific rules relating to English legislative materials, see p. 186.

13.2 Bills and Resolutions

(a) Unenacted federal bills and resolutions. Cite federal bills in the following manner:

S. 2830, 96th Cong., 2d Sess. § 8 (1980).

H.R. 3055, 94th Cong., 2d Sess. (1976).

Cite resolutions analogously, using the following abbreviations:

H.R. Res.

S. Res.

H.R. Con. Res.

S. Con. Res.

H.R.J. Res.

S.J. Res.

Thus:

H.R.J. Res. 1116, 95th Cong., 2d Sess. (1978).

If possible, cite to a printing of the bill or resolution in *Congressional Record*:

H.R. 3055, 94th Cong., 2d Sess., 122 CONG. REC. 16,870–71 (1976).

Otherwise cite to the reproduction of the bill in published hearings (rule 13.3). *See also* rule 3.4 (citation of section numbers in bills).

(b) Enacted federal bills and resolutions. Enacted bills and most joint resolutions are statutes (rule 12). They should be cited as statutes except when used to document legislative history, in which case they should be cited as unenacted bills. Cite simple resolutions to a printing of the resolution in *Congressional Record*:

S. Res. 218, 83d Cong., 2d Sess., 100 CONG. REC. 2972 (1954).

Cite concurrent resolutions (and joint resolutions that did not become statutes when enacted) to *Statutes at Large*:

S. Con. Res. 97, 90 Stat. 3024 (1976).

If they have not yet appeared in *Statutes at Large,* cite concurrent resolutions to *Congressional Record,* and cite joint resolutions as unpublished statutes (rule 12.5).

(c) State and foreign bills and resolutions. State and foreign bills and resolutions should be cited analogously to federal bills and resolutions:

H.R.J. Res. 1, 40th Leg., 2d Spec. Sess., 1974 Utah Laws 7.

C

Hearings 13.3

Cite as follows:

Discrimination on the Basis of Pregnancy, 1977: Hearings on S. 995 Before the Subcomm. on Labor of the Senate Comm. on Human Resources, 95th Cong., 1st Sess. 31 (1977) (statement of Ethel Walsh, Vice-Chairman, EEOC).

Always include the entire subject-matter title as it appears on the cover, the bill number (if any), the subcommittee name (if any), and the committee name.

Reports, Documents, and Committee Prints 13.4

Cite federal reports:

H.R. REP. NO. 353, 82d Cong., 1st Sess. 2 (1951).

S. REP. NO. 2, 84th Cong., 1st Sess. 7 (1955).

Cite federal documents analogously, using the following abbreviations:

H.R. DOC. NO.

S. DOC. NO.

H.R. EXEC. DOC. NO.

H.R. MISC. DOC. NO.

Drop any part of the report or document number that identifies the Congress:

S. REP. NO. 797

Not: S. REP. NO. 95-797

When possible, give a parallel citation to the permanent edition of *United States Code Congressional and Administrative News*:

S. REP. NO. 797, 95th Cong., 2d Sess. 4, *reprinted in* 1978 U.S. CODE CONG. & AD. NEWS 9260, 9262.

Titles of reports or documents may be indicated; if the title is given, the author should also be named (*see* rule 15.1(b) (institutional authors)):

HOUSE COMM. ON UN-AMERICAN ACTIVITIES, GUIDE TO SUBVERSIVE ORGANIZATIONS AND PUBLICATIONS, H.R. DOC. NO. 137, 82d Cong., 1st Sess. 12 (1951).

U.S. IMMIGRATION COMM'N, IMMIGRATION LEGISLATION, S. DOC. NO. 758, 61st Cong., 3d Sess. 613 (1911).

C. KOEPGE, THE ROAD TO INDUSTRIAL PEACE, H.R. DOC. NO. 563, 82d Cong., 2d Sess. 29–30 (1953).

Committee prints and unnumbered documents must be cited as works of institutional authors (rule 15.1(b)). Note that the Congress and session number are part of the author's name:

STAFF OF SENATE COMM. ON THE JUDICIARY, 81ST CONG., 2D SESS., REPORT ON ANTITRUST LAW 17 (Comm. Print 1950).

If the document is primarily the work of specific persons, that fact may be noted parenthetically.

Citations to state legislative reports, documents, and similar materials must include the date or session number of the legislature, the page number of the report or document (if citation is to a particular page or pages), and the date of publication:

LEGISLATIVE COUNCIL OF MARYLAND, REPORT TO THE GEN. ASSEMBLY OF 1968, at 437 (1967).

13.5 Debates

Cite congressional debates to *Congressional Record*; use the daily edition only for matter not yet in the bound edition:

123 CONG. REC. 17,147 (1977).

126 CONG. REC. S1986–87 (daily ed. Feb. 28, 1980) (statement of Sen. DeConcini).

Congressional debates prior to 1873 are cited according to the following models:

1789–1824	38 ANNALS OF CONG. 624 (1822) But for vol. 1, give editor(s) in parentheses: 1 ANNALS OF CONG. 486 (J. Gales ed. 1789)
1824–1837	10 CONG. DEB. 3472 (1834)
1833–1873	CONG. GLOBE, 36th Cong., 1st Sess. 1672 (1860)

Separately Bound Legislative Histories 13.6

C

The legislative histories of several important acts are published separately, e.g., the Administrative Procedure Act; titles VII & IX of the Civil Rights Act of 1964; the Clean Air Act Amendments of 1970; the Equal Employment Opportunity Act; the Internal Revenue Acts; the National Labor Relations Act; and the Occupational Safety and Health Act of 1970. A parallel citation may be given to such a separate publication:

H.R. REP. NO. 245, 80th Cong., 1st Sess. 6 (1947), *reprinted in* 1 NLRB, LEGISLATIVE HISTORY OF THE LABOR MANAGEMENT RELATIONS ACT, 1947, at 292, 297 (1948).

Internal Revenue Amendments, Pub. L. No. 87-834, § 15(a), 76 Stat. 960, 1041–42 (1962) (codified at I.R.C. § 1248(a) (1976)), *reprinted in* JOINT COMM. ON INT. REV. TAX., 90TH CONG., 1ST SESS., LEGISLATIVE HISTORY OF THE INTERNAL REVENUE CODE OF 1954, at 473–74 (1967).

Administrative and Executive Materials 14

Basic Citation Forms 14.1

federal rules and regulations (except Treasury)	
Code of Federal Regulations	EPA Effluent Limitations Guidelines, 40 C.F.R. § 405.53 (1980)
	47 C.F.R. § 73.609 (1980)
Federal Register	Amendments to Regulation A, 45 Fed. Reg. 41,629 (1980) (to be codified at 12 C.F.R. §§ 201.51–.53)
	45 Fed. Reg. 45,259 (1980) (to be codified at 14 C.F.R. § 39.13)
Treasury regulations	Treas. Reg. § 1.302(b) (1955)
agency adjudications (*see* rules 10.2.3 & 10.3.1)	Reichold Chems., Inc., 91 F.T.C. 246 (1978)
formal advisory opinions	39 Op. Att'y Gen. 484 (1940)

executive orders — Exec. Order No. 11,609, 3 C.F.R. 308 (1974), *reprinted in* 3 U.S.C. § 301 app. at 272–74 (1976)

Administrative and executive materials include administrative rules, regulations, and other publications (rule 14.2); advisory opinions (rule 14.3); federal taxation materials (rule 14.4); executive orders and other presidential papers (rule 14.5); and court administrative orders (rule 14.6). Administrative adjudications are cited according to rule 10. For additional information regarding citation of the administrative and executive materials of the various states, see the tables at pp. 136–76. Cite other state and foreign materials by analogy to the following federal examples.

14.2 Rules, Regulations, and Other Publications

Whenever possible, cite all federal rules and regulations, except Treasury materials (rule 14.4), to the *Code of Federal Regulations* (C.F.R.) by title, section (or, in certain circumstances, by page, *see, e.g.*, rule 14.5.1), and year:

47 C.F.R. § 73.609 (1980).

Each title of C.F.R. is revised at least once a year; cite to the most recent edition. If a rule or regulation is commonly known by name, its name should be given:

EPA Effluent Limitations Guidelines, 40 C.F.R. § 405.53 (1980).

The *Federal Register* (Fed. Reg.) publishes rules and regulations before they are entered in C.F.R. Citations of rules or regulations in *Federal Register* should give any commonly used name of the rule or regulation, the volume and page on which the rule or regulation begins, and the year. Give additional pages for more specific references. When the *Federal Register* indicates where the rule or regulation will appear in C.F.R., give that information parenthetically:

Amendments to Regulation A, 45 Fed. Reg. 41,629 (1980) (to be codified at 12 C.F.R. §§ 201.51–.53).

45 Fed. Reg. 45,259 (1980) (to be codified at 14 C.F.R. § 39.13).

Administrative notices (which are not transferred to C.F.R.) should be cited to *Federal Register.* In citing notices of proposed rules and regulations, follow the form for final rules, but parenthetically add the status and date:

45 Fed. Reg. 45,303 (1980) (to be codified at 10 C.F.R. pt. 20) (proposed June 23, 1980).

Cite other administrative notices by volume, page, and year. The citation may begin with a description or commonly used name:

Meeting Notice, 45 Fed. Reg. 41,711 (1980).

For rules and announcements not appearing in C.F.R. or Fed. Reg., cite to U.S.C., a service (rule 18), or the original form of issuance—in that order of preference. Regular reports by administrative agencies are cited like periodicals (rule 16). Always give the abbreviated agency name first and then use the abbreviations for periodical names given in rule 16.2:

4 NLRB ANN. REP. 93 (1939).

1942 ATT'Y GEN. ANN. REP. 22.

1955–1956 MICH. ATT'Y GEN. BIENNIAL REP. pt. 1, at 621.

Other publications are cited as works by institutional authors (rule 15.1(b)), unless issued as congressional documents (rule 13.4).

C

Adjudications and Advisory Opinions 14.3

Cite administrative adjudications as court cases. Be sure to follow rules 10.2.3 and 10.3.1:

Jess v. Commissioner, 55 T.C. 3 (1970).

Great Lakes Area Case, 8 C.A.B. 360 (1947).

Cite formal advisory opinions by volume, type of opinion (including issuing agency), page, and year:

42 Op. Att'y Gen. 111 (1962).

The name of the opinion may be included:

Legality of Revised Philadelphia Plan, 42 Op. Att'y Gen. 405 (1969).

To refer to a specific page or pages, use a pinpoint cite:

1 Op. Off. Legal Counsel 168, 173–74 (1977).

If an opinion appears only in unpaginated or separately paginated advance sheets, but will eventually be included in a volume, cite according to the examples given in rule 10.3.1:

Rights-of-Way Across National Forests, 43 Op. Att'y Gen. No. 26 (June 23, 1980).

Federal Taxation Materials 14.4

(a) Treasury regulations. If the section cited has never been amended, give the year of promulgation and cite without source:

Treas. Reg. § 1.761-1 (1956).

Treas. Reg. 118, § 39.23(p)-3 (1953).

If the regulation has been amended or for some other reason has appeared in substantially different versions, give a source in which the relevant language can be found:

Treas. Reg. 108, § 86.16a, T.D. 5902, 1952-1 C.B. 167, 168.

(b) Other Treasury determinations. Cite all other Treasury materials to *Cumulative Bulletin* (C.B.) or its advance sheet, the *Internal Revenue Bulletin* (I.R.B.); to *Customs Bulletin and Decisions* (Cust. B. & Dec.); or to *Treasury Decisions Under Customs and Other Laws* (Treas. Dec.) or *Treasury Decisions Under Internal Revenue Laws* (Treas. Dec. Int. Rev.)—in that order of preference:

T.D. 32,477, 22 Treas. Dec. 768 (1912).

Rev. Rul. 81-167, 1981-25 I.R.B. 5.

Cumulative Bulletin has been numbered in three series: 1919–1921, by volume number; 1921–1936, by volume number and part number; and 1937–date, by year and part number:

T.B.R. 29, 1 C.B. 230 (1919).

I.T. 2624, 11-1 C.B. 122 (1932).

Rev. Rul. 131, 1953-2 C.B. 112.

The abbreviations used in the above examples and other abbreviations are explained in the introductory pages of each volume of the *Cumulative Bulletin*.

14.5 Presidential Papers and Executive Orders

14.5.1 Executive Orders, Presidential Proclamations, and Reorganization Plans

Cite by page number to 3 C.F.R. (rule 14.2), with a parallel citation to U.S.C. (or, if that is unavailable, U.S.C.A. or U.S.C.S.) whenever possible:

Exec. Order No. 11,609, 3 C.F.R. 308 (1974), *reprinted in* 3 U.S.C. § 301 app. at 272–74 (1976).

Cite to *Federal Register* if the material is not in C.F.R.:

Exec. Order No. 12,217, 45 Fed. Reg. 41,623 (1980).

Proclamation No. 4771, 45 Fed. Reg. 45,247 (1980).

A parallel citation to *Statutes at Large* may also be given:

Reorg. Plan No. 1 of 1978, 3 C.F.R. 321 (1978), *reprinted in* 5 U.S.C.A. app. at 150 (West Supp. 1979), *and in* 92 Stat. 3781 (1978).

Other Presidential Papers 14.5.2

Presidential papers, speeches, and documents have been published in the *Public Papers of the Presidents* (PUB. PAPERS) since 1945. For material not recorded in *Public Papers,* the *Weekly Compilation of Presidential Documents* (WEEKLY COMP. PRES. DOC.), since 1965, or the *U.S. Code Congressional and Administrative News* (U.S. CODE CONG. & AD. NEWS) may be cited:

> President's Message to Congress Transmitting Rescissions and Deferrals, 11 WEEKLY COMP. PRES. DOC. 1334 (Dec. 1, 1975).

Court Administrative Orders 14.6

Cite to the official reporter if therein; give the title of the order, if any:

> Order Discharging the Advisory Committee, 352 U.S. 803 (1956).

D

Books, Pamphlets, Unpublished Materials, Periodicals, Newspapers

Rule 15: Books, Pamphlets, and Unpublished Materials 81

Rule 16: Periodicals 87

Rule 17: Newspapers 104

Books, Pamphlets, and Unpublished Materials 15

Cite books, pamphlets, and unpublished materials by volume, if more than one (rule 3.2); author (rule 15.1); title (rule 15.2); serial number, if any (rule 15.3); page, section, or paragraph (rules 3.3 and 3.4), if only part of a volume is cited; and edition, if more than one has appeared, and date (rule 15.4). Cite prefaces or forewords according to rule 15.2, supplements according to rule 3.2(c), and appendices according to rule 3.5.

Modify the above rules according to rule 15.5.2 when citing letters, interviews, speeches, unpublished works, or materials of limited circulation. Refer to rule 15.5.1 for special provisions governing the citation of essays in collection and rule 15.5.3 for other special citation forms.

Author 15.1

Always give at least the last name and first initial of the author, but give more if it would aid in identification; print the author's name in large and small capitals:

B. CARDOZO, THE GROWTH OF THE LAW (1924).

LOUIS M. BROWN, PREVENTIVE LAW (1950).

In citing a single volume of a multivolume work, give only the author(s) of the volume cited:

21 C. WRIGHT & K. GRAHAM, FEDERAL PRACTICE AND PROCEDURE § 5023 (1977).

If a book has multiple authors, a "hereinafter" form (described in rule 4.2(b)) may be used to shorten citations after the first full citation. Do not use "et al."

(a) Editor or translator. Generally, do not indicate an editor or translator. When a work is known by the name of the editor or translator, however, give his or her last name and first initial in a parenthetical phrase that also includes the year of publication and edition, if any:

L. BAR, THE THEORY AND PRACTICE OF PRIVATE INTERNATIONAL LAW 543–46 (G. Gillespie trans. 2d ed. 1892).

R. ROBERTSON & F. KIRKHAM, JURISDICTION OF THE SUPREME COURT OF THE UNITED STATES § 445 (R. Wolfson & P. Kurland 2d ed. 1951).

A work that has an editor rather than an author is cited:

1 HOLMES-LASKI LETTERS 86 (M. Howe ed. 1953).

5 WEST'S FEDERAL PRACTICE MANUAL § 5224 (M. Volz 2d ed. 1970).

If a work has no named editor, it may be necessary to designate an edition by the name of the publisher.

(b) Institutional authors. Citations to works by institutional authors must always begin with the author's complete name:

EASTERN AIR LINES, INC., 1978 ANNUAL REPORT 5 (1979).

NATIONAL MUNICIPAL LEAGUE, A MODEL ELECTION SYSTEM (1973).

Name first any subdivision preparing the work, then the body of which the subdivision is a part:

STATISTICAL ANALYSIS CENTER, STATE CRIME COMM'N, CRIME IN GEORGIA 41 (1980).

Abbreviate the name of an institutional author only if the result will be completely unambiguous. When abbreviating, use the abbreviations suggested for case names in footnotes (rules 10.2.1(c) and 10.2.2(a)) and the geographical abbreviations listed on the inside back cover. The words "United States" may be abbreviated:

CONSUMER DEPUTY PROGRAM, U.S. CONSUMER PROD. SAFETY COMM'N, CHILDREN'S SLEEPWEAR (1975).

15.2 Title

Cite the full main title as it appears on the title page; use large and small capitals. Do not abbreviate words in the title.

L. SULLIVAN, HANDBOOK OF THE LAW OF ANTITRUST (1977).

6 J. MOORE, W. TAGGART & J. WICKER, MOORE'S FEDERAL PRACTICE ¶ 56.07 (2d ed. 1981).

Give a subtitle only if it is particularly relevant. In citing a single volume of a multivolume work, give the main title of the volume cited. If the title ends with a date, the page number must be set off by a comma and the word "at" (rule 3.3(a)):

J. GRENVILLE, THE MAJOR INTERNATIONAL TREATIES, 1914–1973, at 114–15 (1974).

Cite a preface or foreword by someone other than the author:

Davis, *Foreword* to F. WIENER, EFFECTIVE APPELLATE ADVOCACY at v (1950).

Give the date of the book, not that of the foreword or preface.

Serial Number 15.3

(a) Series issued by the author. In citing a publication that is one of a series issued by the author, include the publication number as part of the title:

BUREAU OF INTELLIGENCE & RESEARCH, U.S. DEP'T OF STATE, PUB. NO. 8732, WORLD STRENGTH OF THE COMMUNIST PARTY ORGANIZATIONS 65 (1973).

WOMEN'S BUREAU, OFFICE OF THE SECRETARY, U.S. DEP'T OF LABOR, LEAFLET NO. 55, A WORKING WOMAN'S GUIDE TO HER JOB RIGHTS (1978).

(b) Series issued by one other than the author. To cite a publication that is one of a series issued by someone other than the author, indicate the series and number parenthetically:

W. HAMILTON & I. TILL, ANTITRUST IN ACTION 78–85 (TNEC Monograph No. 16, 1940).

G. SHEPHERD, JR., ANTI-APARTHEID 6 (Studies in Human Rights No. 3, 1977).

D

Edition and Date 15.4

Give the year of publication in parentheses following the author, title, and page(s), paragraph(s), or section(s) cited. Give the full date of publication only when it might be particularly helpful, as when citing a prospectus or citing works according to rule 15.5.2:

AIRBORNE FREIGHT CORP., PROSPECTUS (Sept. 8, 1965).

A work that has been published in only one edition is cited without any indication of edition, even if there have been multiple printings. In general, cite by the date of the edition, not by the date of a particular printing. If the printings differ in a respect relevant for the purposes of the citation, however, give the printing designation and use the date of the printing:

(12th ed. 6th printing 1980)

When citing a single volume of a multivolume work, give the date of the volume cited.

If there has been more than one edition, cite to the latest edition supporting the point under discussion, unless the original was published before 1870. In the latter case, see rule 15.4(b) and (c). Follow the publisher's terminology in designating an edition:

14 W. FLETCHER, CYCLOPEDIA OF THE LAW OF PRIVATE CORPORATIONS § 6687 (rev. perm. ed. 1980).

Some useful abbreviations follow:

abridge[d, ment]	abr.
annotated	ann.
anonymous	anon.
compil[ation, ed]	comp.
edit[ion, or]	ed.
manuscript	ms.
permanent	perm.
photoduplicated reprint	photo. reprint
replacement	repl.
revis[ed, ion]	rev.
special	spec.
temporary	temp.
translat[ion, or]	trans.

(a) Supplements. Cite pocket parts and bound supplements according to rule 3.2(c):

4 S. SCHWEITZER & J. RASCH, CYCLOPEDIA OF TRIAL PRACTICE § 895 (2d ed. Supp. 1979).

5 S. WILLISTON, A TREATISE ON THE LAW OF CONTRACTS § 661 (3d ed. 1961 & Supp. 1980).

(b) Star edition. In a very few well-known works, the page of the original edition (star page) is indicated by an asterisk (*) in either the margin or the text of all recent editions. In such cases the date and edition may be omitted and the citation made to the star page, unless the material cited was inserted by the editor of a special edition. There is no space between the asterisk and the page number:

2 W. BLACKSTONE, COMMENTARIES *152.

(c) Material published before 1870. Cite books and pamphlets published before 1870, and not appearing in star editions, to the first edition whenever possible. Indicate the place of publication unless a specific editor is given:

E. POWELL, THE PRACTICE OF THE LAW OF EVIDENCE 91 (Philadelphia 1858).

When citing to a later edition, indicate the date of the first edition parenthetically:

S. TOLLER, THE LAW OF EXECUTORS AND ADMINISTRATORS 227 (2d ed. London 1806) (1st ed. London 1800).

If the date or place of publication is not given, use the abbreviation "n.p." for no place or "n.d." for no date.

(d) Photoduplicated reprints. Cite photoduplicated reprints to the original, indicating in parentheses the publication date of the original, the existence of a reprint, and the date of the reprint:

P. GATES, HISTORY OF PUBLIC LAND LAW DEVELOPMENT 1 (1968 & photo. reprint 1979).

Special Citation Forms 15.5

Essays in Collection 15.5.1

If all essays are by the same author, print the author's name, including a first initial, in large and small capitals. The title of the essay is printed in italics; that of the volume, in large and small capitals:

O.W. HOLMES, *Law In Science and Science In Law*, in COLLECTED LEGAL PAPERS 210 (1920).

If the collected essays are by various authors, their names are printed in regular roman type, without any first initials. The titles of the essays are italicized and the volume title is printed in large and small capitals:

Maitland, *The Mystery of Seisin*, in 3 SELECT ESSAYS IN ANGLO-AMERICAN LEGAL HISTORY 591 (1909).

If the collection was edited by one person, give the editor's name in a parenthetical phrase that also contains the edition, if any, and the date of publication:

Wyzanski, *Constitutionalism: Limitation and Affirmation*, in GOVERNMENT UNDER LAW 473 (A. Sutherland ed. 1956).

Letters, Interviews, Speeches, Unpublished Works, and Other Materials of Limited Circulation 15.5.2

Cite letters, interviews, and speeches in ordinary roman type by exact date, if available. Use forms analogous to the following:

Letter from Louis Touton to Michael B. Reuben (June 13, 1981) (discussing Bluebook tab index).

Address by Senator Humphrey, *Harvard Law Review* Annual Banquet (Mar. 29, 1958).

Interview with Abner J. Whiteside, Director of the Education Department of New York, in New York City (Aug. 14, 1957).

Telephone interview with Alice A. Colburn, Editor-in-Chief of the *Yale Law Journal* (Nov. 6, 1979).

Cite unpublished works and materials of limited circulation like books, but print the title and author's name in ordinary roman type and give the exact date if available:

Comics Magazine Ass'n of America, Press Release No. 51 (Sept. 16, 1954).

S. Miller, The Care and Feeding of Summer Associates 11 (July 29, 1981) (unpublished manuscript).

If possible, include parenthetically information that would help locate the cited source, or cite a published work that reprints the material:

H. Wechsler, Remarks at the Meeting of the Bar of the Supreme Court of the United States in Memory of Chief Justice Stone 5 (Nov. 12, 1947) (available in Columbia Law School Library).

Letter from Samuel Bowles to David Dudley Field (Dec. 29, 1870), *reprinted in* A. KAUFMAN, PROBLEMS IN PROFESSIONAL RESPONSIBILITY 250 (1976).

15.5.3 Other Special Citation Forms

A few frequently cited works require special citation forms:

BALLENTINE'S LAW DICTIONARY 1190 (3d ed. 1969).

BLACK'S LAW DICTIONARY 712 (5th ed. 1979).

88 C.J.S. *Trial* § 192 (1955).

17 AM. JUR. 2D *Contracts* § 74 (1964).

In a brief:

17 Am. Jur. 2d Contracts § 74 (1964).

The Bible is cited as follows:

2 *Kings* 12:19.

If the version is important, it may be indicated parenthetically:

Mark 9:21 (King James).

Citations to the *Manual for Complex Litigation* prepared by the Federal Judicial Center are as follows:

MANUAL FOR COMPLEX LITIGATION § 2.1 (4th ed. 1977).

However, when citing an edition other than the edition prepared by the Federal Judicial Center, identify the source and publication date of the edition cited:

MANUAL FOR COMPLEX LITIGATION § 4.52 (1977) (supplement to C. WRIGHT & A. MILLER, FEDERAL PRACTICE AND PROCEDURE (1969–1980)).

Cite an entire *Federalist* paper without indicating a specific edition; include the author's name parenthetically:

THE FEDERALIST No. 23 (A. Hamilton).

But if citing to particular material, cite to the page of a specific edition:

THE FEDERALIST No. 47, at 329 (J. Madison) (J. Cooke ed. 1961).

Cite proceedings, regular publications by institutes, and reports by sections of the American Bar Association as periodicals (rule 16). Cite the ABA Code of Professional Responsibility and opinions of the ABA Committee on Ethics and Professional Responsibility according to rule 12.8.6. Cite model codes or statutes and restatements of the law according to rule 12.8.5.

Periodicals 16

(a) Basic citation forms. Cite authors and titles of works published in periodicals according to rule 16.1. Cite the name of the periodical in large and small capitals, abbreviated according to rule 16.2. If the periodical is paginated consecutively throughout each volume, cite works within the periodical by volume and page number, and enclose the year of publication in parentheses at the end of the citation:

COX, *Federalism and Individual Rights,* 73 NW. U.L. REV. 1 (1978).

If the periodical has no volume number, but is still consecutively paginated throughout each volume, use the year of publication as the volume number and omit the parenthetical reference to the year:

Burt, *The Constitution of the Family,* 1979 SUP. CT. REV. 329.

Note, *Substitution of Judges in Illinois Criminal Cases,* 1978 U. ILL. L.F. 519.

If the periodical is separately paginated within each issue, cite by the date or publication period of the issue, again omitting the parenthetical reference to the year:

Stuart, *Avoiding Costly Bond Problems,* PUB. UTIL. FORT., June 19, 1980, at 42.

Ward, *Progress for a Small Planet,* HARV. BUS. REV., Sept.–Oct. 1979, at 89, 90.

Always give the page on which the article begins. Cite additional pages to refer to material on those pages.

(b) Proceedings, regular publications by institutes, and ABA section reports. Cite as periodicals:

Goodrich, *Annual Report of Adviser on Professional Relations,* 16 A.L.I. PROC. 48 (1939).

Vranesh, *Water Planning for Municipalities,* 24 ROCKY MTN. MIN. L. INST. 865 (1978).

If the volumes are unnumbered, use either the number of the institute (or proceedings) or the year of publication as a volume number; in the latter case omit the parenthetical reference to the year:

Beck, *Crude Oil Issues,* 30 INST. ON OIL & GAS L. & TAX'N 1 (1979).

Sackman, *Landmark Cases on Landmark Law,* 1979 INST. ON PLAN. ZONING & EMINENT DOMAIN 241.

Curtin, *Reverse Discrimination and Affirmative Action: Practical Considerations for the Utilities Industry,* 1978 A.B.A. SEC. PUB. UTIL. L. REP. 26.

If the publication is organized by paragraph or section numbers, use those numbers in citations:

Gutierrez, *Estate Planning for the Unmarried Cohabitant,* 13 INST. ON EST. PLAN. ¶ 1600 (1979).

To cite part of an article, cite both the first paragraph or section number of the article and the paragraph or section number(s) where the relevant material appears. Add a page citation if necessary for further identification:

O'Connor, *Taxation of Foreign Investors,* 38 INST. ON FED. TAX'N § 22.01, § 22.04, at 22-10 (1980).

16.1 Authors and Titles

16.1.1 Articles

Except for student-written law review pieces, book reviews, and annotations, which are discussed below, cite the last name of the author in ordinary roman type and the article's title in italics; do not give the author's first initial:

Garvey, *The Attorney's Affidavit in Litigation Proceedings,* 31 STAN. L. REV. 191 (1979).

Black, *The Supreme Court, 1966 Term—Foreword: "State Action," Equal Protection, and California's Proposition 14,* 81 HARV. L. REV. 69 (1967).

If there is no author, give only the article's title:

The Development of the Law of Gambling: Arkansas, 13 ARK. LAW. 108 (1979).

Student-Written Law Review Materials 16.1.2

Cite student-written law review materials by the designation used in the periodical. Do not name the student author. Give the designation, such as "Note," "Comment," or "Special Project," in ordinary roman type and the title of the piece in italics:

Special Project, *The Remedial Process in Institutional Reform Litigation,* 78 COLUM. L. REV. 784 (1978).

Note, *A Framework for Preemption Analysis,* 88 YALE L.J. 363 (1978).

Comment, *The Lawyer's Moral Paradox,* 1979 DUKE L.J. 1335.

Case Comment, Bivens *Actions for Equal Protection Violations:* Davis v. Passman, 92 HARV. L. REV. 745 (1979).

When there is no separable designation, italicize the entire title:

Developments in the Law—Corporate Crime: Regulating Corporate Behavior Through Criminal Sanctions, 92 HARV. L. REV. 1227 (1979).

The Supreme Court, 1979 Term, 94 HARV. L. REV. 75, 241 n.73 (1980).

Fourth Annual Survey of Developments in Alabama Law: 1976–1977, 30 ALA. L. REV. 49 (1978).

Short commentary on recent developments, such as Recent Cases, Recent Statutes, Recent Decisions, Case Notes, Recent Developments, and Abstracts, may be cited without designation or title:

9 MEM. ST. U.L. REV. 339 (1979).

55 N.D.L. REV. 475 (1979).

Cite student-written book reviews according to rule 16.1.3.

Book Reviews 16.1.3

Give the last name of the reviewer, as well as the designation "Book Review," in ordinary roman type:

Westwood, Book Review, 45 U. CHI. L. REV. 255 (1977).

Cite student-written reviews by their designation alone:

Book Note, 126 U. PA. L. REV. 1447 (1978).

In either case, the author, title, and publication date of the book reviewed may be given parenthetically after the citation:

Moore, Book Review, 77 MICH. L. REV. 363 (1979) (reviewing D. ENGEL, CODE AND CUSTOM IN A THAI PROVINCIAL COURT (1978)).

If a book review has a title (other than the name of the book reviewed), this alternate citation form may be used:

Wisdom, *Rethinking Injunctions* (Book Review), 89 YALE L.J. 825 (1980).

16.1.4 Annotations

Cite discussions in selective case reporters (such as *American Law Reports* and *Lawyer's Reports Annotated*) by the designation "Annot." in ordinary roman; do not give the annotation's author or title:

Annot., 53 A.L.R. FED. 272 (1981).

Annot., 1918F L.R.A. 190, 192.

Note that the citation should give the page on which the annotation begins, rather than the initial page of the case as reprinted in the reporter. Use the date of the volume, not of the case.

16.1.5 Miscellaneous Matters

(a) Surveys and symposia. If an article is part of a survey of the law of one jurisdiction, the title of the article should incorporate the title of the survey:

Levasseur, *Sales, The Work of the Louisiana Appellate Courts for the 1977–1978 Term,* 39 LA. L. REV. 705 (1979).

Otherwise cite an individual article within a symposium or survey in the same manner as any other article:

Shaffer, *Advocacy as Moral Discourse,* 57 N.C.L. REV. 647 (1979).

Comment, *ABA Code of Professional Responsibility: Void for Vagueness?,* 57 N.C.L. REV. 671 (1979).

When citing the symposium as a unit, do not give any author:

Reflections on a Decade Under the Code of Professional Responsibility: The Need for Reform, 57 N.C.L. REV. 495 (1979).

(b) Multipart articles. To cite an entire article that appears in more than one part, identify the numbers of the parts in parentheses after the article's title and give the volume number, first page, and publication year for each part:

Stone, *The Equitable Rights and Liabilities of Strangers to a Contract* (pts. 1 & 2), 18 COLUM. L. REV. 291 (1918), 19 COLUM. L. REV. 177 (1919).

If all of the parts appear in one volume, use the shortened form:

Fuller, *Legal Fictions* (pts. 1–3), 25 ILL. L. REV. 363, 513, 877 (1930–1931).

To cite only some parts of a multipart article, indicate which part or parts are cited and give only the volume number, page number, and publication year of the part(s) cited:

Fuller, *Legal Fictions* (pt. 2), 25 ILL. L. REV. 513 (1931).

(c) Parallel citations. If an article has been reprinted, a parallel citation to the reprinting source may be given:

Loss, *The Conflict of Laws and the Blue Sky Laws,* 71 HARV. L. REV. 209 (1957), *reprinted in* L. LOSS & E. COWETT, BLUE SKY LAW 180 (1958).

Periodical Abbreviations 16.2

Periodicals with English-Language Titles 16.2.1

The following alphabetical list gives abbreviations for about 250 periodical titles that are commonly cited or difficult to abbreviate and for many words commonly found in periodical titles. In some cases, the list indicates that a word should not be abbreviated.

To use this list, first ascertain the correct name of the periodical you wish to cite. *Always use the title of the periodical that appears on the title page of the volume you are citing.* If the title of the periodical has changed over time, do not use an older or newer form of the title. Then check to see if the periodical title you wish to cite is listed in the left-hand column of this list. If it is, you will find the full abbreviation for that periodical in the right-hand column.

If the periodical you wish to cite is not given in full on this list, you may still determine the proper abbreviation by looking up each word in the periodical's title on this list and on the list of geographical abbreviations found on the inside back cover. Put together the abbreviations for each word to form the full abbreviated title. Omit the words "a," "at," "in," "of," and "the" from all abbreviated titles. If any other word is listed neither here nor on the inside back cover, use the full word in the abbreviated title unless an abbreviation would both save substantial space and be completely unambiguous. If a periodical title consists of only one word after the words "a," "at," "in," "of," and "the" have been omitted, do not abbreviate the word.

If a periodical title itself contains an abbreviation, use that abbreviation in the abbreviated title:

APLA Q.J.

IMF SURV.

Rule 6.1(a) explains the spacing of abbreviations.

Omit commas from periodical title abbreviations, but retain other punctuation:

> Pedowitz, *Title Problems in Bankruptcy,* 12 REAL PROP. PROB. & TR. J. 519 (1977).
>
> *Nineteen States Adopt Code of Judicial Conduct,* OYEZ! OYEZ!, Feb. 1974, at 11.

If a periodical has been renumbered in a new series, indicate that fact:

> Deutch, *Ten Answers to Substitute Brands,* 28 TRADE-MARK BULL. (n.s.) 6 (1933).

Periodical abbreviations

Academy	ACAD.
Account [ant, ants, ing, ancy]	ACCT.
Adelaide Law Review	ADEL. L. REV.
Administra[tive, tor, tion]	AD.
Administrative Law Review	AD. L. REV.
Advocate (first word)	ADVOCATE
Advoca[te, cy]	ADVOC.
Affairs	AFF.
Agricultural	AGRIC.
Air	AIR
Air Force	A.F.
Akron Law Review	AKRON L. REV.
Alabama Law Review	ALA. L. REV.
Albany Law Review	ALB. L. REV.
America [n, s]	AM.
American Bankruptcy Law Journal	AM. BANKR. L.J.
American Bar Association	A.B.A.
American Bar Association Journal	A.B.A. J.
American Journal of Jurisprudence	AM. J. JURIS.
American Law Institute	A.L.I.
American Law Reports	A.L.R.
American University Law Review	AM. U.L. REV.
and	&
Anglo-American	ANGLO-AM.
Annals	ANNALS
Annals of the American Academy of Political and Social Science	ANNALS
Annual	ANN.
Antitrust	ANTITRUST
Arbitrat[ion, ors]	ARB.
Arbitration Journal	ARB. J.

Refer to inside back cover for further abbreviations.

Arizona Law Review	ARIZ. L. REV.
Arizona State Law Journal	ARIZ. ST. L.J.
Arkansas Law Review	ARK. L. REV.
Articles	ARTICLES
Aspects	ASP.
Association	A.
Atlantic	ATL.
Atomic Energy Law Journal	ATOM. ENERGY L.J.
Attorney [s]	ATT'Y [S]
Auckland University Law Review	AUCKLAND U.L. REV.
Authorities [']	AUTH.
Banking Law Journal	BANKING L.J.
Bankruptcy	BANKR.
Bar	B.
Baylor Law Review	BAYLOR L. REV.
Behavior	BEHAV.
Beverly Hills	BEV. HILLS
Black Law Journal	BLACK L.J.
Boston	B.
Boston College Law Review	B.C.L. REV.
Boston University Law Review	B.U.L. REV.
Briefcase	BRIEFCASE
Brigham Young University Law Review	B.Y.U. L. REV.
British	BRIT.
Brooklyn Law Review	BROOKLYN L. REV.
Buffalo Law Review	BUFFALO L. REV.
Bulletin	BULL.
Business	BUS.
Business Lawyer	BUS. LAW.
Business Week	BUS. WK.
California Law Review	CALIF. L. REV.
California State Bar Journal	CAL. ST. B.J.
California Western Law Review	CAL. W.L. REV.
Cambridge Law Journal	CAMBRIDGE L.J.
Capital University Law Review	CAP. U.L. REV.
Cardozo Law Review	CARDOZO L. REV.
Case and Comment	CASE & COM.
Case Western Reserve	CASE W. RES.
Catholic Lawyer	CATH. LAW.
Catholic University Law Review	CATH. U.L. REV.
Central	CENT.
Chartered Life Underwriters	C.L.U.
Chicago	CHI.
Chicago[-]Kent Law Review	CHI.[-]KENT L. REV.
Chronicle	CHRON.

Refer to inside back cover for further abbreviations.

Cincinnati	CIN.
Civil	CIV.
Civil Liberties Review	CIV. LIB. REV.
Clearinghouse Review	CLEARINGHOUSE REV.
Cleveland State Law Review	CLEV. ST. L. REV.
Cleveland-Marshall Law Review	CLEV.-MAR. L. REV.
College	C.
Colorado Lawyer	COLO. LAW.
Columbia	COLUM.
Columbia Journal of Law & Social Problems	COLUM. J.L. & SOC. PROBS.
Columbia Law Review	COLUM. L. REV.
Commerc[e, ial]	COM.
Common Market Law Review	COMMON MKT. L. REV.
Communication [s]	COM.
Comparative	COMP.
Conference	CONF.
Congressional	CONG.
Congressional Digest	CONG. DIG.
Connecticut Bar Journal	CONN. B.J.
Connecticut Law Review	CONN. L. REV.
Constitution [al]	CONST.
Contemporary	CONTEMP.
Contract [s]	CONT.
Conveyancer and Property Lawyer (new series)	CONV. & PROP. LAW. (n.s.)
Copyright Law Symposium (American Society of Composers, Authors, and Publishers)	COPYRIGHT L. SYMP. (ASCAP)
Cornell	CORNELL
Cornell Law Review	CORNELL L. REV.
Corporat[e, ion]	CORP.
Counsel [or, ors, or's]	COUNS.
Court [s]	CT[S].
Creighton Law Review	CREIGHTON L. REV.
Crime	CRIME
Criminal	CRIM.
Criminology	CRIMINOLOGY
Cumberland Law Review	CUM. L. REV.
Cumberland-Samford Law Review	CUM.-SAM. L. REV.
Current Medicine for Attorneys	CURRENT MED. FOR ATT'YS
Dalhousie Law Journal	DALHOUSIE L.J.
De Paul Law Review	DE PAUL L. REV.
Defense	DEF.
Delinquency	DELINQ.
Denver	DEN.

Refer to inside back cover for further abbreviations.

Denver Law Journal	DEN. L.J.
Department of State Bulletin	DEP'T ST. BULL.
Detroit	DET.
Detroit College of Law Review	DET. C.L. REV.
Development	DEV.
Dickinson Law Review	DICK. L. REV.
Digest	DIG.
Diplomacy	DIPL.
Drake Law Review	DRAKE L. REV.
Duke Law Journal	DUKE L.J.
Duquesne Law Review	DUQ. L. REV.
East [ern]	E.
Ecology Law Quarterly	ECOLOGY L.Q.
Econom[ic, ics, y]	ECON.
Economist	ECONOMIST
Education [al]	EDUC.
Emory Law Journal	EMORY L.J.
English	ENG.
Environment	ENV'T
Environmental	ENVTL.
Environmental Law	ENVTL. L.
Estate [s]	EST.
Europe [an]	EUR.
Faculty of Law Review	FACULTY L. REV.
Family	FAM.
FDA Consumer	FDA CONS.
Federal	FED.
Federal Rules Decisions	F.R.D.
Federation	FED'N
Financ[e, ial]	FIN.
Florida State University Law Review	FLA. ST. U.L. REV.
Food Drug Cosmetic Law Journal	FOOD DRUG COSM. L.J.
for	FOR
Fordham Law Review	FORDHAM L. REV.
Foreign	FOREIGN
Forensic	FORENSIC
Fortnightly	FORT.
Fortune	FORTUNE
Forum	F.
The Forum	FORUM
Foundation [s]	FOUND.
General	GEN.
George Washington Law Review	GEO. WASH. L. REV.
Georgetown Law Journal	GEO. L.J.
Georgia Law Review	GA. L. REV.

Refer to inside back cover for further abbreviations.

Glendale Law Review	GLENDALE L. REV.
Golden Gate	GOLDEN GATE
Gonzaga Law Review	GONZ. L. REV.
Government	GOV'T
Guild Practitioner	GUILD PRAC.
Hamline Law Review	HAMLINE L. REV.
Harvard	HARV.
Harvard Civil Rights-Civil Liberties Law Review	HARV. C.R.-C.L. L. REV.
Harvard International Law Journal	HARV. INT'L L.J.
Harvard Journal on Legislation	HARV. J. ON LEGIS.
Harvard Law Review	HARV. L. REV.
Harvard Women's Law Journal	HARV. WOMEN'S L.J.
Hastings Constitutional Law Quarterly	HASTINGS CONST. L.Q.
Hastings International and Comparative Law Review	HASTINGS INT'L & COMP. L. REV.
Hastings Law Journal	HASTINGS L.J.
Histor[ical, y]	HIST.
Hofstra Law Review	HOFSTRA L. REV.
Hospital	HOSP.
Houston	HOUS.
Houston Law Review	HOUS. L. REV.
Howard Law Journal	HOW. L.J.
Human	HUM.
I.C.C. Practitioners' Journal	I.C.C. PRAC. J.
Idaho Law Review	IDAHO L. REV.
Idea	IDEA
Illinois Bar Journal	ILL. B.J.
Indiana Law Journal	IND. L.J.
Indiana Law Review	IND. L. REV.
Industrial	INDUS.
Industrial and Labor Relations Review	INDUS. & LAB. REL. REV.
Injury	INJ.
Institute	INST.
Institute on Estate Planning (University of Miami Law Center)	INST. ON EST. PLAN.
Institute on Federal Taxation (New York University)	INST. ON FED. TAX'N
Institute on Mineral Law (Louisiana State University)	INST. ON MIN. L.
Institute on Oil and Gas Law and Taxation (Southwestern Legal Foundation)	INST. ON OIL & GAS L. & TAX'N
Institute on Planning, Zoning, and Eminent Domain (Southwestern Legal Foundation)	INST. ON PLAN. ZONING & EMINENT DOMAIN

Refer to inside back cover for further abbreviations.

Institute on Private Investments and Investors Abroad	INST. ON PRIV. INV. & INV. ABROAD
Institute on Securities Regulation	INST. ON SEC. REG.
Insurance	INS.
Insurance Law Journal	INS. L.J.
Intellectual	INTELL.
International	INT'L
International and Comparative Law Quarterly	INT'L & COMP. L.Q.
The International Lawyer	INT'L LAW.
International Organization	INT'L ORG.
Intramural	INTRA.
Iowa Law Review	IOWA L. REV.
JAG	JAG
John Marshall	J. MAR.
John Marshall Journal of Practice and Procedure	J. MAR. J. PRAC. & PROC.
Journal	J.
Journal of Business Law	J. BUS. L.
Journal of Corporate Taxation	J. CORP. TAX'N
Journal of Family Law	J. FAM. L.
Journal of Products Liability	J. PROD. LIAB.
Journal of Taxation	J. TAX'N
Journal of the American Medical Association	J. A.M.A.
Journal of the Patent Office Society	J. PAT. OFF. SOC'Y
Judge [s]	JUDGE [S]
Judicature	JUDICATURE
Judicial	JUD.
Juridical	JURID.
Jurimetrics Journal	JURIMETRICS J.
Juris Doctor	JURIS DR.
Jurist	JURIST
Justice	JUST.
Justice of the Peace	JUST. P.
Justice System Journal	JUST. SYS. J.
Juvenile	JUV.
Kentucky Law Journal	KY. L.J.
Labo[r, ur]	LAB.
Labor Law Journal	LAB. L.J.
Land and Water Law Review	LAND & WATER L. REV.
Law (first word)	LAW
Law	L.
Law and Contemporary Problems	LAW & CONTEMP. PROBS.
Lawyer [s, s', 's]	LAW.

Refer to inside back cover for further abbreviations.

Lawyer's Reports Annotated	L.R.A.
Legal	LEGAL
Legislat[ion, ive]	LEGIS.
Librar[y, ian]	LIBR.
Lincoln Law Review	LINCOLN L. REV.
Los Angeles	L.A.
Louisiana Law Review	LA. L. REV.
Loyola	LOY.
Loyola Law Review (New Orleans)	LOY. L. REV.
Loyola of Los Angeles Law Review	LOY. L.A.L. REV.
Loyola University of Chicago Law Journal	LOY. U. CHI. L.J.
Magazine	MAG.
Maine Law Review	ME. L. REV.
Major Tax Planning (University of Southern California Tax Institute)	MAJOR TAX PLAN.
Management	MGMT.
Maritime	MAR.
Marquette Law Review	MARQ. L. REV.
Maryland Law Review	MD. L. REV.
Massachusetts Law Review	MASS. L. REV.
McGill Law Journal	MCGILL L.J.
Medic[al, ine]	MED.
Melbourne University Law Review	MELB. U.L. REV.
Memphis	MEM.
Memphis State University Law Review	MEM. ST. U.L. REV.
Mercer Law Review	MERCER L. REV.
Michigan Law Review	MICH. L. REV.
Military Law Review	MIL. L. REV.
Mineral	MIN.
Minnesota Law Review	MINN. L. REV.
Mississippi Law Journal	MISS. L.J.
Missouri Law Review	MO. L. REV.
Modern	MOD.
Monash University Law Review	MONASH U.L. REV.
Montana Law Review	MONT. L. REV.
Monthly	MONTHLY
Monthly Labor Review	MONTHLY LAB. REV.
Municipal	MUN.
The Nation	NATION
National	NAT'L
National Review	NAT'L REV.
Natural	NAT.
Natural Resources Journal	NAT. RESOURCES J.
Nebraska Law Review	NEB. L. REV.

Refer to inside back cover for further abbreviations.

Negligence	NEGL.
New England	NEW ENG.
New Law Journal	NEW L.J.
New Mexico Law Review	N.M.L. REV.
new series	(n.s.)
New York Law School Law Review	N.Y.L. SCH. L. REV.
New York State Bar Association Antitrust Law Symposium	N.Y. ST. B.A. ANTITRUST L. SYMP.
New York University Law Review	N.Y.U. L. REV.
New York University Review of Law and Social Change	N.Y.U. REV. L. & SOC. CHANGE
Newsletter	NEWSLETTER
NOLPE School Law Journal	NOLPE SCH. L.J.
North [ern]	N.
North Carolina Law Review	N.C.L. REV.
North Dakota Law Review	N.D.L. REV.
Northwest [ern]	NW.
Northwestern University Law Review	NW. U.L. REV.
Notre Dame Lawyer	NOTRE DAME LAW.
Office	OFF.
Ohio Northern University Law Review	OHIO N.U.L. REV.
Ohio State Law Journal	OHIO ST. L.J.
Oil and Gas Tax Quarterly	OIL & GAS TAX Q.
Oklahoma Law Review	OKLA. L. REV.
on	ON
Order	ORD.
Oregon Law Review	OR. L. REV.
Osgoode Hall Law Journal	OSGOODE HALL L.J.
Ottawa Law Review	OTTAWA L. REV.
Pacific	PAC.
Pacific Law Journal	PAC. L.J.
Patent	PAT.
Patent Law Annual (Southwestern Legal Foundation Institute on Patent Law)	PAT. L. ANN.
Pepperdine Law Review	PEPPERDINE L. REV.
Performing Arts Review	PERF. ARTS REV.
Personal	PERS.
Perspective	PERSP.
Philosoph[ical, y]	PHIL.
Planning	PLAN.
Police	POLICE
Policy	POL'Y
Politic[al, s]	POL.
Potomac	POTOMAC

Refer to inside back cover for further abbreviations.

Practi[cal, ce, tioners]	PRAC.
Practical Lawyer	PRAC. LAW.
Probate	PROB.
Probation	PROBATION
Problems	PROBS.
Proce[edings, dure]	PROC.
Profession [al]	PROF.
Property	PROP.
Psychiatry	PSYCHIATRY
Psychology	PSYCHOLOGY
Public	PUB.
Publishing, Entertainment, Advertising & Allied Fields Law Quarterly	PUB. ENT. ADVERT. & ALLIED FIELDS L.Q.
Quarterly	Q.
Record	REC.
Record of the Association of the Bar of the City of New York	REC. A.B. CITY N.Y.
Referees	REF.
Register	REG.
Regulation	REG.
Relations	REL.
Report [s, er]	REP.
Research	RESEARCH
Resources	RESOURCES
Responsibility	RESP.
Review	REV.
Rights	RTS.
Rocky Mountain Mineral Law Institute	ROCKY MTN. MIN. L. INST.
Rutgers	RUTGERS
Rutgers-Camden	RUT.-CAM.
Rutgers Law Journal	RUTGERS L.J.
Rutgers Law Review	RUTGERS L. REV.
St. John's Law Review	ST. JOHN'S L. REV.
Saint Louis University Law Journal	ST. LOUIS U.L.J.
St. Mary's Law Journal	ST. MARY'S L.J.
San Diego Law Review	SAN DIEGO L. REV.
San Fernando Valley Law Review	SAN FERN. V.L. REV.
Santa Clara Law Review	SANTA CLARA L. REV.
Saturday Review	SAT. REV.
School	SCH.
Scien[ce, ces, tific]	SCI.
Scientific American	SCI. AM.
Scottish	SCOT.
Section	SEC.
Securities	SEC.
Security	SECURITY

Refer to inside back cover for further abbreviations.

Seton Hall	SETON HALL
Social	SOC.
Social Service Review	SOC. SERV. REV.
Socialist	SOCIALIST
Society	SOC'Y
Sociolog[ical, y]	SOC.
Solicitor [s, s', 's]	SOLIC.
South [ern]	S.
South Carolina Law Review	S.C.L. REV.
South Dakota Law Review	S.D.L. REV.
South Texas Law Journal	S. TEX. L.J.
Southern California Law Review	S. CAL. L. REV.
Southwestern	SW.
Southwestern Law Journal	SW. L.J.
Stanford Law Review	STAN. L. REV.
State (first word)	STATE
State	ST.
Stetson Law Review	STETSON L. REV.
Street	ST.
Studies	STUD.
Suffolk University Law Review	SUFFOLK U.L. REV.
Supreme Court Review	SUP. CT. REV.
Survey	SURV.
Sydney Law Review	SYDNEY L. REV.
Symposium	SYMP.
Syracuse	SYRACUSE
Syracuse Law Review	SYRACUSE L. REV.
System	SYS.
Tax	TAX
Tax Adviser	TAX ADVISER
Tax Law Review	TAX L. REV.
Taxation	TAX'N
Taxes: The Tax Magazine	TAXES
Teacher [s]	TCHR[S].
Techn[ique, ology]	TECH.
Temple Law Quarterly	TEMP. L.Q.
Tennessee Law Review	TENN. L. REV.
Texas Law Review	TEX. L. REV.
Texas Tech Law Review	TEX. TECH L. REV.
Third Branch	THIRD BRANCH
Trademark	TRADEMARK
Trade-Mark	TRADE-MARK
Trade-Mark Reporter	TRADE-MARK REP.
Transnational	TRANSNAT'L

D

Refer to inside back cover for further abbreviations.

Transportation	TRANSP.
Trial Lawyer's Guide	TRIAL LAW. GUIDE
Trust [s]	TR.
Tulane Law Review	TUL. L. REV.
Tulane Tax Institute	TUL. TAX INST.
Tulsa Law Journal	TULSA L.J.
U.C. Davis Law Review	U.C.D. L. REV.
UCLA Law Review	UCLA L. REV.
U.C.L.A. [UCLA]-Alaska Law Review	U.C.L.A. [UCLA]-ALASKA L. REV.
UMKC Law Review	UMKC L. REV.
UN Monthly Chronicle	UN MONTHLY CHRON.
Unauthorized Practice News	UNAUTH. PRAC. NEWS
Uniform Commercial Code Law Journal	U.C.C. L.J.
United States	U.S.
Universit[ies, y]	U.
University of Arkansas at Little Rock Law Journal	U. ARK. LITTLE ROCK L.J.
University of Baltimore Law Review	U. BALT. L. REV.
University of Chicago Law Review	U. CHI. L. REV.
University of Cincinnati Law Review	U. CIN. L. REV.
University of Colorado Law Review	U. COLO. L. REV.
University of Dayton Law Review	U. DAYTON L. REV.
University of Detroit Journal of Urban Law	U. DET. J. URB. L.
University of Florida Law Review	U. FLA. L. REV.
University of Hawaii Law Review	U. HAWAII L. REV.
University of Illinois Law Forum	U. ILL. L.F.
University of Kansas Law Review	U. KAN. L. REV.
University of Miami Law Review	U. MIAMI L. REV.
University of Michigan Journal of Law Reform	U. MICH. J.L. REF.
University of Newark Law Review	U. NEWARK L. REV.
University of Pennsylvania Law Review	U. PA. L. REV.
University of Pittsburgh Law Review	U. PITT. L. REV.
University of Puget Sound Law Review	U. PUGET SOUND L. REV.
University of Richmond Law Review	U. RICH. L. REV.
University of San Francisco Law Review	U.S.F.L. REV.
University of Toledo Law Review	U. TOL. L. REV.
University of Toronto Faculty of Law Review	U. TORONTO FAC. L. REV.
University of Toronto Law Journal	U. TORONTO L.J.
University of West Los Angeles Law Review	U. WEST L.A. L. REV.

Refer to inside back cover for further abbreviations.

Urban	URB.
U.S. News and World Report	U.S. NEWS & WORLD REP.
Utah Law Review	UTAH L. REV.
Utilit[ies, y]	UTIL.
Valparaiso University Law Review	VAL. U.L. REV.
Vanderbilt	VAND.
Vanderbilt Law Review	VAND. L. REV.
Victoria	VICT.
Villanova Law Review	VILL. L. REV.
Virginia Law Review	VA. L. REV.
Vital Speeches of the Day	VIT. SPEECHES DAY
Wake Forest Law Review	WAKE FOREST L. REV.
Washburn Law Journal	WASHBURN L.J.
Washington & Lee Law Review	WASH. & LEE L. REV.
Washington Law Review	WASH. L. REV.
Washington Monthly	WASH. MONTHLY
Washington University Law Quarterly	WASH. U.L.Q.
Wayne Law Review	WAYNE L. REV.
Welfare	WELFARE
West [ern]	W.
West Virginia Law Review	W. VA. L. REV.
Whittier Law Review	WHITTIER L. REV.
Willamette Law Journal	WILLAMETTE L.J.
William and Mary Law Review	WM. & MARY L. REV.
William Mitchell Law Review	WM. MITCHELL L. REV.
Wisconsin Law Review	WIS. L. REV.
Yale	YALE
Yale Law Journal	YALE L.J.
Yearbook (or Year Book)	Y.B.

D

Periodicals with Foreign-Language Titles 16.2.2

Give the name of the periodical in full in the first citation; indicate in brackets the abbreviation, if any, to be used in subsequent citations:

[1] Groffier, *L'adoption en droit international privé comparé,* 65 REVUE CRITIQUE DE DROIT INTERNATIONAL PRIVÉ [R.C.D.I.P.] 603 (1976).

[2] Lyon-Caen, *La grève en droit international privé,* 66 R.C.D.I.P. 271 (1977).

The following list gives abbreviations for several periodicals with foreign-language titles:

Les Cahiers de Droit	C. DE D.
Lex et Scientia	LEX ET SCIENTIA

Revista del Colegio de Abogados de Puerto Rico	REV. COL. AB. P.R.
Revista de Derecho Puertorriqueño	REV. D.P.
Revista Juridica de la Universidad de Puerto Rico	REV. JUR. U.P.R.
Revue Critique de Droit International Privé	R.C.D.I.P.
Revue de Droit (Université de Sherbrooke)	R.D.U.S.
Revue de Droit International et de Droit Comparé	R. DR. INT. DR. COMP.
Revue Générale de Droit	REV. GÉN.
Revue Internationale de Droit Comparé	R.I.D.C.

For periodicals not on this list, use the abbreviations suggested in the periodical itself.

17 Newspapers

Cite newspapers in ordinary roman type, unless consecutively paged by volume. In the latter case, cite as a periodical in large and small capitals. Thus:

Boston Herald, Oct. 14, 1954, at 6, col. 1.

But:

34 THE TIMES (London) 950 (weekly ed. 1910).

54 N.Y.L.J. 2017 (1916).

Be certain that abbreviations of newspaper names are not confusing; use rule 16.2.1 as a general guide.

Give the page and first column of the material cited; do not give continuations on another page unless a specific reference is intended. Give the section of the paper if needed to identify unambiguously the material cited; the section name may also be given. Thus:

N.Y. Times, Jan. 19, 1958, § 6 (Magazine), at 8.

Id., Apr. 19, 1953, § 1, at 1, col. 4.

Note that, in some newspapers or editions, the section designation is included in the page number:

N.Y. Times, Aug. 11, 1980, at B3, col. 5.

Cite a signed article (not a news report) by author and title:

Friedman, *Five Examples of Fed Double-Talk,* Wall St. J., Aug. 21, 1975, at 6, col. 4.

News reports may be cited without title or byline:

Seattle Times, Feb. 25, 1981, at 2, col. 4.

If desired, the title alone or the title and byline together may be given:

> *Abscam Jury Sees Videotape of Deal,* San Francisco Chron., Aug. 14, 1980, at 14, col. 1.

If an edition other than the one that is bound or microfilmed is cited, indicate the edition parenthetically. For example, the *New York Times* is bound in the "late city" edition. Thus:

> N.Y. Times, Feb. 3, 1958, at 8, col. 2 (city ed.).

If a case is cited to a newspaper, both the date of decision and the date of the newspaper must be given:

> United States v. Palermo, N.Y. Times, Aug. 27, 1957, at 24, col. 3 (S.D.N.Y. Aug. 26, 1957).

Services

Rule 18: Services 107

Services 18

Cases, administrative materials, and brief commentaries are often published unofficially in topical compilations called "services," which appear in looseleaf form initially and sometimes are later published as bound volumes. Rule 18.1 provides rules for citing services. Rule 18.2 lists abbreviations for looseleaf services and their corresponding bound forms.

Citation Form for Services 18.1

Cite services by volume, abbreviated title, publisher, subdivision, and date. For looseleaf services, print the abbreviated title and publisher in large and small capitals:

In re Saberman, 3 BANKR. L. REP. (CCH) ¶ 67,416 (Bankr. N.D. Ill. Mar. 31, 1980).

Cite bound volumes of services in ordinary roman type:

SEC v. Texas Int'l Airlines, 29 Fed. R. Serv. 2d (Callaghan) 408 (D.D.C. 1979).

The publisher of bound services may be omitted:

29 Fed. R. Serv. 2d 408

In citing looseleaf material that will eventually be bound, add the name of the bound form in parentheses if it is different from the name of the looseleaf form; include the volume of the bound form if available:

Heaven Hill Distilleries, 3 LAB. REL. REP. (BNA) (74 Lab. Arb.) 42 (Jan. 9, 1980) (Beckman, Arb.).

(a) Volume. The volume designation of a looseleaf service may be a number, a year, a descriptive subtitle from the volume's spine, or a combination of these:

5 TRADE REG. REP.

1979-1 Trade Cas.

[Current Developments] HOUS. & DEV. REP.

[1979] 8 STAND. FED. TAX REP.

[2 Wages-Hours] LAB. L. REP.

[1 Estate & Gift] FED. TAXES

In citations to a transfer binder, the volume designation should indicate the years of material included in that binder:

[1979–1980 Transfer Binder] FED. SEC. L. REP.

See generally rule 3.2(a) (designation of volumes and use of brackets).

E

(b) Publisher. Every citation to a looseleaf service must indicate the publisher; citations to bound services may indicate the publisher. Enclose an abbreviation of the publisher's name in parentheses following the service's title:

4 LAB. L. REP. (CCH) ¶ 9046

1980-1 Trade Cas. (CCH) ¶ 63,053

Common abbreviations include:

Bureau of National Affairs	(BNA)
Callaghan & Co.	(Callaghan)
Commerce Clearing House	(CCH)
Matthew Bender	(MB)
Pike & Fischer	(P & F)
Prentice-Hall	(P-H)

(c) Subdivision. Cite services by paragraph or section number if possible, otherwise by page number. *See generally* rules 3.3 (pages and footnotes) & 3.4 (sections and paragraphs). A report number may be given if it would assist the reader in locating the cited material:

Rhode Island Insurance Agents Agree Not to Rig Bids, [Jan.–June] ANTITRUST & TRADE REG. REP. (BNA) No. 967, at D-11 (June 5, 1980).

(d) Date. When citing a case reported in a service, give the date (for looseleaf services) or year (for bound services) of the case (rule 10.5). When citing a statute or regulation, give the exact date of its enactment or promulgation unless either the full date or the year is indicated elsewhere in the citation:

Employment Standards Order 75-2, [2 Wages-Hours] LAB. L. REP. (CCH) ¶ 30,029 (NOV. 28, 1975).

Act of Aug. 24, 1974, ECON. STAND. (CCH) ¶ 6005.

Citations to other material (such as opinion letters or monographs) should give the exact date if available. When citing otherwise undated material in a looseleaf service, give the date of the page on which the material is printed or the date of the subsection in which it is printed:

Fed Proposes Streamlined Check-Clearing Procedures, [July–Dec.] WASH. FIN. REP. (BNA) No. 34, at A-23 (Aug. 25, 1980).

18.2 Service Abbreviations

Abbreviations for some commonly used services are listed below. Following each looseleaf service title, the list indicates the subdivision(s) by which the service is cited, the appropriate abbreviation of the service, the publisher, and corresponding bound services. Names of bound services that differ markedly from their looseleaf forms are printed in italics and cross-referenced to the looseleaf forms.

Service	Abbreviation
Abortion Law Reporter (topic and section number)	ABORTION L. REP. (NAT'L ABORTION RTS. ACT. LEAGUE)
Accountancy Law Reporter (¶)	ACCOUNTANCY L. REP. (CCH)
Administrative Law Reporter Second (page)	AD. L. REP. 2D (P & F)
bound in same name (page)	Ad. L. Rep. 2d (P & F)
All State Sales Tax Reporter (¶)	ALL ST. SALES TAX REP. (CCH)
American Federal Tax Reporter—see Federal Taxes	
American Labor Arbitration Service (¶)	AM. LAB. ARB. SERV. (P-H)
American Labor Arbitration Awards (¶)	Am. Lab. Arb. Awards (P-H)
American Stock Exchange Guide (¶)	AM. STOCK EX. GUIDE (CCH)
Antitrust & Trade Regulation Report (report number, section letter, and page)	ANTITRUST & TRADE REG. REP. (BNA)
Automobile Insurance Reporter (¶)	AUTO. INS. REP. (CCH)
Aviation Law Reporter (¶)	AV. L. REP. (CCH)
Aviation Cases (page)	Av. Cas. (CCH)
Balance of Payments Report (¶)	BALANCE OF PAYMENTS REP. (CCH)
Bankruptcy Court Decisions (page)	BANKR. CT. DEC. (CRR)
Bankruptcy Law Reporter (¶)	BANKR. L. REP. (CCH)
Benefits Review Board Service (page)	BEN. REV. BD. SERV. (MB)
Blue Sky Law Reporter (¶)	BLUE SKY L. REP. (CCH)
Board of Contract Appeals Decisions—see Contract Appeals Decisions	
British Columbia Tax Reporter (¶)	B.C. TAX REP. (CCH)
Canadian Commercial Law Guide (¶)	CAN. COM. L. GUIDE (CCH)
Canadian Sales Tax Reporter (¶)	CAN. SALES TAX REP. (CCH)
Canadian Tax Reporter (¶)	CAN. TAX REP. (CCH)
College & University Reporter (¶)	COLLEGE & UNIV. REP. (CCH)
College Law Digest (page)	COLLEGE L. DIG. (NAT'L ASS'N COLLEGE & UNIV. ATT'YS)
Collier Bankruptcy Cases, Second Series (page)	COLLIER BANKR. CAS. 2D (MB)

Commodity Futures Law Reporter (¶)	COMM. FUT. L. REP. (CCH)
Common Market Reporter (¶)	COMMON MKT. REP. (CCH)
Computer Law Service (page)	COMPUTER L. SERV. (CALLAGHAN)
Computer Law Service Reporter (page)	Computer L. Serv. Rep. (Callaghan)
Congressional Index (page)	CONG. INDEX (CCH)
Consumer Credit Guide (¶)	CONSUMER CRED. GUIDE (CCH)
Contract Appeals Decisions (¶)	CONT. APP. DEC. (CCH)
Board of Contract Appeals Decisions (¶)	B.C.A. (CCH)
Contracts Cases, Federal—see Government Contracts Reporter	
Copyright Law Reporter (¶)	COPYRIGHT L. REP. (CCH)
Corporation Guide (¶)	CORP. GUIDE (P-H)
Corporation Law Guide (¶)	CORP. L. GUIDE (CCH)
Cost Accounting Standards Guide (¶)	COST ACCOUNTING STAND. GUIDE (CCH)
Criminal Law Reporter (page)	CRIM. L. REP. (BNA)
Dominion Tax Cases (page)	DOMINION TAX CAS. (CCH)
Economic Standards (¶)	ECON. STAND. (CCH)
EEOC Compliance Manual (section and page) *See also* Equal Employment Opportunity Commission Compliance Manual	EEOC COMPL. MAN. (BNA)
Employment Practices Guide (¶)	EMPL. PRAC. GUIDE (CCH)
Employment Practices Decisions (¶) *See also* Labor Law Reporter	Empl. Prac. Dec. (CCH)
Energy Law Service (page)	ENERGY L. SERV. (CALLAGHAN)
Energy Management (¶)	ENERGY MGMT. (CCH)
Energy Users Report (section letter and page)	ENERGY USERS REP. (BNA)
Environment Regulation Handbook (section title and page)	ENV'T REG. HANDBOOK (ENV'T INFORMATION CENTER)
Environment Reporter (page)	ENV'T REP. (BNA)
Environment Reporter Cases (page)	Env't Rep. Cas. (BNA)
Environmental Law Reporter (page)	ENVTL. L. REP. (ENVTL. L. INST.)
Equal Employment Opportunity Commission Compliance Manual (¶) *See also* EEOC Compliance Manual	E.E.O.C. COMPL. MAN. (CCH)
Fair Employment Practices Cases—see Labor Relations Reporter	
Family Law Reporter (page)	FAM. L. REP. (BNA)
bound in same name (page)	Fam. L. Rep. (BNA)
Federal Banking Law Reporter (¶)	FED. BANKING L. REP. (CCH)

Service	Abbreviation
Federal Carriers Reporter (¶)	FED. CARR. REP. (CCH)
Federal Carriers Cases (¶)	Fed. Carr. Cas. (CCH)
Federal Controls (page)	FED. CONTROLS (BNA)
Federal Election Campaign Financing Guide (¶)	FED. ELECTION CAMP. FIN. GUIDE (CCH)
Federal Estate and Gift Tax Reporter (¶)	FED. EST. & GIFT TAX REP. (CCH)
U.S. Tax Cases (¶)	U.S. Tax Cas. (CCH)
Federal Excise Tax Reporter (¶)	FED. EX. TAX REP. (CCH)
Federal Power Service (page)	FED. POWER SERV. (MB)
Federal Rules of Evidence Service (page)	FED. R. EVID. SERV. (CALLAGHAN)
bound in same name (page)	Fed. R. Evid. Serv. (Callaghan)
Federal Rules Service, Second Series (page)	FED. R. SERV. 2D (CALLAGHAN)
bound in same name (page)	Fed. R. Serv. 2d (Callaghan)
Federal Securities Law Reporter (¶)	FED. SEC. L. REP. (CCH)
bound in same name (¶)	Fed. Sec. L. Rep. (CCH)
Federal Taxes (¶)	FED. TAXES (P-H)
American Federal Tax Reporter, Second Series (¶)	A.F.T.R.2d (P-H)
Fire & Casualty Cases—see Insurance Law Reporter	
Food Drug Cosmetic Law Reporter (¶)	FOOD DRUG COSM. L. REP. (CCH)
Government Contracts Reporter (¶)	GOV'T CONT. REP. (CCH)
Contracts Cases, Federal (¶)	Cont. Cas. Fed. (CCH)
Government Employee Relations Report (page)	GOV'T EMPL. REL. REP. (BNA)
Housing & Development Reporter (page)	HOUS. & DEV. REP. (BNA)
Income Taxes Worldwide (country and page)	INCOME TAXES WORLDWIDE (CCH)
Indian Law Reporter (section letter and page)	INDIAN L. REP. (AM. INDIAN LAW. TRAINING PROGRAM)
Industrial Relations Guide (¶)	INDUS. REL. GUIDE (P-H)
Inheritance, Estate & Gift Tax Reporter (jurisdiction and ¶)	INHER. EST. & GIFT TAX REP. (CCH)
Insurance Law Reporter (page)	INS. L. REP. (CCH)
Fire & Casualty Cases (¶)	Fire & Casualty Cas. (CCH)
Life Cases 2d (¶)	Life Cas. 2d (CCH)
Labor Arbitration Awards (¶)	LAB. ARB. AWARDS (CCH)
bound in same name (¶)	Lab. Arb. Awards (CCH)
Labor Law Reporter (¶)	LAB. L. REP. (CCH)
Labor Cases (¶)	Lab. Cas. (CCH)
NLRB Decisions (¶)	NLRB Dec. (CCH)
See also Employment Practices Guide	
Labor Relations Reporter (page)	LAB. REL. REP. (BNA)
Fair Employment Practices Cases (page)	Fair Empl. Prac. Cas. (BNA)

Service	Abbreviation
Labor Arbitration Reports (page)	Lab. Arb. (BNA)
Labor Relations Reference Manual (page)	L.R.R.M. (BNA)
Wage and Hour Cases (page)	Wage & Hour Cas. (BNA)
Life Cases—see Insurance Law Reporter	
Liquor Control Law Service (¶)	LIQUOR CONT. L. SERV. (CCH)
Manitoba & Saskatchewan Tax Reporter (province and ¶)	MAN. & SASK. TAX REP. (CCH)
Maritimes Law Reporter (province and ¶)	MARITIMES L. REP. (CCH)
Media Law Reporter (page)	MEDIA L. REP. (BNA)
bound in same name (page)	Media L. Rep. (BNA)
Medical Devices Reports (¶)	MED. DEVICES REP. (CCH)
Medicare and Medicaid Guide (¶)	MEDICARE & MEDICAID GUIDE (CCH)
Military Law Reporter (page)	MIL. L. REP. (PUB. L. EDUC. INST.)
Mutual Funds Guide (¶)	MUT. FUNDS GUIDE (CCH)
National Public Employment Reporter (page)	NAT'L PUB. EMPL. REP. (LAB. REL. PRESS)
New York Stock Exchange Guide (¶)	N.Y.S.E. GUIDE (CCH)
NLRB Decisions—see Labor Law Reporter	
Noise Regulation Reporter (current reports by report number, section letter, and page; reference file by page)	NOISE REG. REP. (BNA)
NOLPE School Law Reporter (page)	SCHOOL L. REP. (NAT'L ORG. ON LEGAL PROBS. IN EDUC.)
Nuclear Regulation Reporter (¶)	NUCLEAR REG. REP. (CCH)
Occupational Safety & Health Reporter (page)	O.S.H. REP. (BNA)
Occupational Safety & Health Cases (page)	O.S.H. Cas. (BNA)
Ontario Tax Reporter (¶)	ONT. TAX REP. (CCH)
Patents, Trademark & Copyright Journal (report number, section letter, and page)	PAT. TRADEMARK & COPYRIGHT J. (BNA)
Pension & Profit Sharing (¶)	PENS. & PROFIT SHARING (P-H)
Pension Plan Guide (¶)	PENS. PLAN GUIDE (CCH)
Pension Reporter (report number, section letter, and page)	PENS. REP. (BNA)
Pollution Control Guide (¶)	POLLUTION CONT. GUIDE (CCH)
Poverty Law Reporter (¶)	POV. L. REP. (CCH)
Private Foundations Reporter (¶)	PRIV. FOUND. REP. (CCH)
Product Safety & Liability Reporter (page)	PROD. SAFETY & LIAB. REP. (BNA)

Products Liability Reporter (¶)	PROD. LIAB. REP. (CCH)
Provincial Inheritance & Gift Tax Reporter (¶)	PROV. INHER. & GIFT TAX REP. (CCH)
Public Employee Bargaining Reports (¶)	PUB. EMPLOYEE BARGAINING REP. (CCH)
Public Bargaining Cases (¶)	Pub. Bargaining Cas. (CCH)
Public Utilities Reports (page)	PUB. UTIL. REP. (PUR)
bound in same name (page)	Pub. Util. Rep. (PUR)
Quebec Tax Reporter (¶)	QUE. TAX REP. (CCH)
Radio Regulation (¶)	RAD. REG. (P & F)
School Law Reporter (page)	SCHOOL L. REP. (NAT'L ORG. ON LEGAL PROBS. IN EDUC.)
Search & Seizure Bulletin (page)	SEARCH & SEIZURE BULL. (QUINLAN)
SEC Accounting Rules (¶)	SEC ACCOUNTING R. (CCH)
Secured Transactions Guide (¶)	SECURED TRANSACTIONS GUIDE (CCH)
Securities & Federal Corporate Law Report (page)	SEC. & FED. CORP. L. REP. (CLARK BOARDMAN)
Securities Regulation Guide (¶)	SEC. REG. GUIDE (P-H)
Securities Regulation & Law Report (report number, section letter, and page)	SEC. REG. & L. REP. (BNA)
Selective Service Law Reporter (page)	SEL. SERV. L. REP. (PUB. L. EDUC. INST.)
Standard Excess Profits Tax Reporter (¶)	STAND. EX. PROF. TAX REP. (CCH)
Standard Federal Tax Reporter (¶)	STAND. FED. TAX REP. (CCH)
U.S. Tax Cases (¶)	U.S. Tax Cas. (CCH)
State and Local Tax Service (¶)	ST. & LOC. TAX SERV. (P-H)
State and Local Taxes (¶ by section)	ST. & LOC. TAXES (BNA)
State Motor Carrier Guide (¶)	ST. MOT. CARR. GUIDE (CCH)
State Tax Cases Reporter (¶)	ST. TAX CAS. REP. (CCH)
State Tax Cases (¶)	St. Tax Cas. (CCH)
State Tax Reporter (¶) (designate volume by number and state in brackets preceding service abbreviation)	ST. TAX. REP. (CCH)
Tax Court Memorandum Decisions (CCH) (page) [or (P-H) (¶)]	TAX CT. MEM. DEC. (CCH) [or (P-H)]
bound in same name (same)	T.C.M. (CCH) [or (P-H)]
Tax Court Reported Decisions (¶)	TAX CT. REP. DEC. (P-H)
Tax Court Reporter (decision number)	TAX CT. REP. (CCH)
Tax Management (series, section, and page)	TAX MGMT. (BNA)
Tax Treaties (¶)	TAX TREATIES (CCH)
Trade Regulation Reporter (¶)	TRADE REG. REP. (CCH)
Trade Cases (¶)	Trade Cas. (CCH)

E

Unemployment Insurance Reporter (jurisdiction and ¶)	UNEMPL. INS. REP. (CCH)
Uniform Commercial Code Reporting Service (page)	U.C.C. REP. SERV. (CALLAGHAN)
bound in same name (page)	U.C.C. Rep. Serv. (Callaghan)
United States Law Week (page)	U.S.L.W. (BNA—publisher need not be indicated)
United States Patents Quarterly (page)	U.S.P.Q. (BNA)
bound in same name (page)	U.S.P.Q. (BNA)
Urban Affairs Reporter (¶)	URB. AFF. REP. (CCH)
U.S. Supreme Court Bulletin (page)	S. CT. BULL. (CCH)
U.S. Tax Cases—see Federal Estate and Gift Tax Reporter; Standard Federal Tax Reporter	
Utilities Law Reporter (¶)	UTIL. L. REP. (CCH)
Wage and Hour Cases—see Labor Relations Reporter	
Washington Financial Reports (report number, section letter, and page)	WASH. FIN. REP. (BNA)
Wills, Estates and Trust Service (¶)	WILLS EST. & TR. (P-H)
Workmen's Compensation Law Reporter (¶)	WORKMEN'S COMP. L. REP. (CCH)

E

International Materials

Rule 19: International Materials 117

International Materials 19

Basic Citation Forms 19.1

(a) Treaties and other international agreements (rule 19.2).

bilateral or trilateral, U.S. a party	Treaty of Friendship, Commerce and Navigation, Apr. 2, 1953, United States-Japan, art. X, 4 U.S.T. 2063, 2071, T.I.A.S. No. 2863, at 10
bilateral or trilateral, U.S. not a party	Treaty of Neutrality, Jan. 5, 1929, Hungary-Turkey, 3 Recueil de Traités (Turk.) 457, 100 L.N.T.S. 137
multilateral, U.S. a party	Agreement on International Classification of Trademarked Goods and Services, June 15, 1957, 23 U.S.T. 1336, T.I.A.S. No. 7418, 550 U.N.T.S. 45
	Treaty on the Non-Proliferation of Nuclear Weapons, *opened for signature* July 1, 1968, 21 U.S.T. 483, T.I.A.S. No. 6839, 729 U.N.T.S. 161

(b) International law cases and arbitrations (rule 19.3).

World Court cases	Fisheries Jurisdiction (U.K. v. Ice.), 1972 I.C.J. 12 (Interim Protection Order of Aug. 17)
Common Market cases	Imperial Chem. Indus. v. Commission des Communautés européennes, 1972 C.J. Comm. E. Rec. 619, [1971–1973 Transfer Binder] Common Mkt. Rep. (CCH) ¶ 8161
international arbitrations	Savarkar Case (Fr. v. Gr. Brit.), Hague Ct. Rep. (Scott) 275 (Perm. Ct. Arb. 1911)

F

(c) United Nations materials (rule 19.4).

included in an official record	UNICEF Financial Report, 10 U.N. GAOR Supp. (No. 6A) at 5, U.N. Doc. A/2905 (1955)
UN charter	U.N. Charter art. 2, para. 4
documents without UN number	U.N. Economic Committee for Europe, 29 Economic Bulletin for Europe 9, U.N. Sales No. E.78.II.E.4 (1977)

(d) Materials of other international organizations (rule 19.5).

European Community	1961–1962 Eur. Parl. Deb. (No. 38) 5 (Mar. 7, 1961)
	O.J. Eur. Comm. (No. 261) 7 (1980) (Debates of European Parliament)
	1972–1973 Eur. Parl. Doc. (No. 258) 5 (1973)
Council of Europe	Eur. Consult. Ass. Deb. 10th Sess. 639 (Oct. 16, 1958)
	Reply of the Comm. of Ministers, Eur. Consult. Ass., 12th Sess., Doc. No. 1126 (1960)

(e) Yearbooks (rule 19.6).

United Nations	Summary Records of the 187th Meeting, [1953] 1 Y.B. Int'l L. Comm'n 17, U.N. Doc. A/CN.4/SER.A/1953
other	*Certain Expenses of the United Nations* (summary), 1961–1962 I.C.J.Y.B. 78 (1962)

19.2 Treaties and Other International Agreements

A citation to a treaty or other international agreement should include the agreement's name (rule 19.2.1), date of signing (rule 19.2.2), parties (rule 19.2.3), and the sources in which it can be found (rule 19.2.4):

Agreement on Weather Stations, Apr. 27–May 13, 1964, United States-Colombia, 15 U.S.T. 1355, T.I.A.S. No. 5604.

In citing only part of an agreement (or an appended document), give the subdivision (or appendix) after the parties:

Treaty on Commerce and Navigation, Dec. 3, 1938, United States-Iraq, art. III, para. 2, 54 Stat. 1790, 1792, T.S. No. 960, at 3.

For a discussion of citations to subdivisions and appendices, see rule 3.

19.2.1 Name of the Agreement

Give the name in English. If the agreement is widely known by a popular name, use that name. Thus:

Treaty of Brest-Litovsk
Geneva Convention of 1927

If an agreement has no popular name, give its form (e.g., Convention, Treaty, Understanding) and subject matter (e.g., for the Repression of Brigandage):

Agreement on Aerospace Disturbances, Jan. 31–Feb. 26, 1975, United States-Australia, 26 U.S.T. 446, T.I.A.S. No. 8043.

The subject matter and form may appear in either order:

Consular Convention, Mar. 22, 1963, United States-Japan, 15 U.S.T. 768, T.I.A.S. No. 5602.

(a) Form of agreement. Use the first form designation that appears on the title page; omit all others. Thus:

Convention

Not: Convention & Supplementary Protocol

Cite lesser included documents as subdivisions:

Partial Revision of Radio Regulations, Nov. 8, 1963, Additional Protocol, 15 U.S.T. 887, T.I.A.S. No. 5603.

(b) Subject matter. If necessary, shorten the subject-matter description that appears on the title page. Thus:

Protocol Respecting Sugar Regulation

Not: Protocol Governing the International Agreement of May 6, 1937, Respecting Regulation of Production and Marketing of Sugar

Date of Signing 19.2.2

Give the exact date of signing unless the popular name includes the date or year of the agreement. Thus:

Treaty of Brest-Litovsk, Mar. 3, 1918

But:

Geneva Convention of 1927

Where dates of signing are given for an agreement or exchange of notes with three or fewer parties, give the first and last dates of signing:

Agreement on Weather Stations, Apr. 27–May 13, 1964, United States-Colombia, 15 U.S.T. 1355, T.I.A.S. No. 5604.

If a treaty with four or more parties is not signed on a single date, use the date on which the treaty is opened for signature, done, approved, or adopted, and indicate the significance of the date:

Constitution of the World Health Organization, *opened for signature* July 22, 1946, 62 Stat. 2679, T.I.A.S. No. 1808, 14 U.N.T.S. 185.

The date of entry into force or another date may be added parenthetically at the end of the citation if of particular relevance.

Parties to the Agreement 19.2.3

When citing an agreement with three or fewer parties, indicate all parties:

United States-Japan
Belgium-Netherlands-Luxembourg

Names of countries may be shortened by omitting words. Thus:

Jordan

Not: Government of the Hashemite Kingdom of Jordan

Ordinarily, words in a party name should not be abbreviated. Thus:

France-West Germany

Not: Fr.-W. Ger.

But:

U.S.S.R.

Parties need not be given if there are four or more.

19.2.4 Treaty Series and Other Sources

(a) Bilateral or trilateral agreements to which United States is party. Cite to one official source and to one State Department source.

official sources		
U.S. Treaties and Other International Agreements	Jan. 1, 1950–date	x U.S.T. xxx
Statutes at Large	to Dec. 31, 1949 (indexed at 64 Stat. B1107)	x Stat. xxx
State Department sources		
Treaties and Other International Acts Series	1945–date	T.I.A.S. No. x
Treaty Series	to 1945	T.S. No. x
Executive Agreement Series	to 1945	E.A.S. No. x

(b) Bilateral or trilateral agreements to which United States is not party. Cite to the official source of one signatory (preferably to sources in English or a Germanic or Romance language) and give a parallel citation to U.N.T.S. or L.N.T.S. or, if not therein, to another international treaty series (*see* table below):

> Treaty of Neutrality, Jan. 5, 1929, Hungary-Turkey, 3 Recueil de Traités (Turk.) 457, 100 L.N.T.S. 137.
>
> Agreement for the Avoidance of Double Taxation, Apr. 25, 1952, Netherlands-Sweden, art. 4, 1952 Tractatenblad van het Koninkrijk der Nederlanden No. 88, 163 U.N.T.S. 131, 136.

primary international treaty sources	
United Nations Treaty Series	U.N.T.S.
League of Nations Treaty Series	L.N.T.S.
other international treaty sources	
Pan-American Treaty Series	Pan-Am. T.S.
European Treaty Series	Europ. T.S.
Nouveau recueil général des traités	Martens Nouveau Recueil
Parry's Consolidated Treaty Series	Parry's T.S.
International Legal Materials	I.L.M.

If the official English source is Great Britain Treaty Series, include the Command number parenthetically:

> 1949 Gr. Brit. T.S. No. 76 (Cmd. 7854)

Other official sources include:

> 1950 Can. T.S. No. 21
>
> 1956 N.Z.T.S. No. 11

(c) Multilateral agreements. If the United States is a party, cite to one official source (U.S.T. or Stat.), to one State Department source (T.I.A.S., T.S., or E.A.S.), and to one international treaty series (e.g., U.N.T.S., L.N.T.S.). If the United States is not a party, cite only to U.N.T.S. or L.N.T.S. or, if not therein, to another international treaty collection.

International Law Cases and Arbitrations 19.3

Generally, cite international law cases and arbitrations according to rule 10 as modified by the following instructions:

(a) World Court. Citations to a case in the International Court of Justice and the Permanent Court of International Justice should include the case name, the names of the parties, the designation of the volume in which the material may be found, the abbreviated name of the issuing tribunal, the designation of the publication, the page on which it begins or the number of the material, and a parenthetical description of the material cited and the exact date of issuance. All of this information may be found on the first pages of each report.

Give the case name as found on the first pages of the report, but omit introductory articles such as "The." Also omit the word "case," unless the case name is a person's name. In general, do not otherwise abbreviate case names.

The names of the parties involved should be given in a parenthetical phrase immediately following the case name:

(Italy v. Ice.)

Abbreviate the names of countries according to the inside back cover of this book. "United States" should be abbreviated to "U.S." in this parenthetical phrase (but not in case names). Names of other parties should be abbreviated according to rule 10.2.2, even in law review text.

Identify the volume according to rule 3.2(a). Abbreviate the issuing tribunal:

I.C.J.

P.C.I.J.

The International Court of Justice publishes two reporter series, *Report of Judgments, Advisory Opinions and Orders* and *Pleadings, Oral Arguments and Documents*. Cite them:

1972 I.C.J. 12

1948 I.C.J. Pleadings 17

For materials of the Permanent International Court of Justice, designate the publication by series (A through F).

P.C.I.J. materials are cited by number; I.C.J. materials are cited to the page on which they begin:

1937 P.C.I.J., ser. A/B, No 70.

1972 I.C.J. 12

In referring to specific pages, give them in a pinpoint cite:

1933 P.C.I.J., ser. C, No. 62, at 12.

1948 I.C.J. Pleadings 17, 19.

Generally, use the following forms as a guide:

International Court of Justice

cases	Fisheries Jurisdiction (U.K. v. Ice.), 1972 I.C.J. 12 (Interim Protection Order of Aug. 17)
separately published pleadings	Memorial of the United Kingdom (U.K. v. Alb.), 1948 I.C.J. Pleadings (1 Corfu Channel) 17 (Memorial dated Sept. 30, 1947)
yearbooks	1948–1949 I.C.J.Y.B. 85 (1949)

Permanent Court of International Justice

cases	Diversion of Water from the Meuse (Neth. v. Belg.), 1937 P.C.I.J., ser. A/B, No. 70, at 7 (Judgment of June 28)
	Pajzs, Csáky and Esterházy Case (Hung. v. Yugo.), 1936 P.C.I.J., ser. A/B, No. 68 (Judgment of Dec. 16)
collateral materials	Memorial of Denmark, Legal Status of Eastern Greenland (Den. v. Nor.), 1933 P.C.I.J., ser. C, No. 62, at 12 (Memorial presented Oct. 31, 1931)
annual reports	13 P.C.I.J. ANN. R., ser. E, No. 13, at 61

(b) Court of Justice of the European Communities (Common Market cases). Citations to Common Market cases should include the case name; the volume designation (which is the same as the year); the reporter cited (E. Comm. Ct. J. Rep. or C.J. Comm. E. Rec.); the page on which the case begins, and, if only a portion of the case is cited, a pinpoint cite. Shorten case names according to rule 10.2.1 (case names in text). In law review footnotes (but not in briefs, memoranda, or law review text), abbreviate case names according to rule 10.2.2 (case names in footnotes). In shortening case names, foreign words may be treated like their English counterparts.

Cite to the English, instead of the French, version wherever possible (all decisions after 1972 are published in English; translations of past opinions are currently in progress):

Office Nat'l des Pensions pour Ouvriers v. Couture, 1967 E. Comm. Ct. J. Rep. 379 (Preliminary Ruling).

Rabe v. Commission des Communautés européennes, 1971 C.J. Comm. E. Rec. 297.

If possible, give a parallel citation to *Common Market Law Reports* (Comm. Mkt. L.R.) or *Common Market Reporter* (COMMON MKT. REP. (CCH)):

Imperial Chem. Indus. v. Commission des Communautés européennes, 1972 C.J. Comm. E. Rec. 619, [1971–1973 Transfer Binder] COMMON MKT. REP. (CCH) ¶ 8161.

(c) Other multinational courts. Cite to *International Law Reports* (1950–date) or to *Annual Digest and Reports of Public International Law Cases* (1919–1950). Volume numbers, rather than years, should be used; early issues of *Annual Digest* have been renumbered according to tables appearing in all volumes after volume 25:

Loomba v. Food & Agriculture Org. of the United Nations, 47 I.L.R. 382 (Int'l Lab. Org. Admin. Trib. 1970).

Mayras v. Secretary-General of the League of Nations, 13 Ann. Dig. 199 (Admin. Trib. of the League of Nations 1946).

(d) International cases in national courts. If an international case is decided by a national court whose reporter is not indicated on pp. 179–200, cite to I.L.R., Ann. Dig., Common Mkt. L.R., or COMMON MKT. REP. (CCH), described in the two preceding paragraphs, or to a yearbook (rule 19.6):

Ko Maung Tin v. U Gon Man, 14 Ann. Dig. 233 (Burma High Ct. 1947).

Abdul Ghani v. Subedar Shoedar Khan, 38 I.L.R. 3 (W. Pak. High Ct. 1964).

Even if the reporter of the deciding court appears on pp. 179–200, a parallel citation to one of the above international reporters should be added in law review citations, although such a parallel citation is unnecessary in other contexts:

Blackburn v. Attorney Gen., [1971] 1 W.L.R. 1037, 10 Common Mkt. L.R. 784 (C.A.).

F

(e) International arbitrations. If adversary parties are named, give the name as if it were a court case:

Massaut v. Stupp

Otherwise cite by the name of the first party plaintiff, or by the subject matter if no name is given. Indicate parenthetically the nations involved, except in cases before the Mixed Arbitral Tribunals of the 1920's:

Dillon Case (U.S. v. Mex.)

The Montijo (U.S. v. Colom.)

Cite arbitration awards to the official source (unless it is a pamphlet containing only a single judgment) and to one unofficial source, if possible. Frequently cited arbitration reporters include the *Tribunaux Arbitraux Mixtes* (Trib. Arb. Mixtes); the *United Nations Reports of International Arbitral Awards* (R. Int'l Arb. Awards); and the *Hague Court Reports, First Series* (Hague Ct. Rep. (Scott)) and *Second Series* (Hague Ct. Rep. 2d (Scott)). The latter two are single volumes and do not require volume numbers. Do not name the court unless it is the Permanent Court of Arbitration.

Massaut v. Stupp, 9 Trib. Arb. Mixtes 316 (1929).

Richeson Case (U.S. v. Pan.), United States and Panamanian General Claims Arbitration 216, 6 R. Int'l Arb. Awards 325 (1933).

Savarkar Case (Fr. v. Gr. Brit.), Hague Ct. Rep. (Scott) 275 (Perm. Ct. Arb. 1911).

19.4 United Nations Materials

19.4.1 Basic Citation Forms

Every United Nations citation, except as specified in rule 19.4.2, must include the volume designation, the subdivision, the page or paragraph, the UN document number, and the year:

20 U.N. TCOR Annex (Agenda Item 5) at 1, U.N. Doc. T/L.764 (1957).

Any citation may also include the author or title in ordinary roman type:

UNICEF Financial Report, 10 U.N. GAOR Supp. (No. 6A) at 5, U.N. Doc. A/2905 (1955).

Certain documents available for sale to the public are assigned a sales number, which should be included if the UN has not assigned a document number:

U.N. Economic Committee for Europe, 29 Economic Bulletin for Europe 9, U.N. Sales No. E.78.II.E.4 (1977).

The sales number may also be included following the document number of other United Nations materials (e.g., Yearbooks (rule 19.4.2(h))).

Official records are published by four of the five principal UN organs—the General Assembly (GAOR), the Security Council (SCOR), the Economic and Social Council (ESCOR), and the Trusteeship Council (TCOR)—and by a variety of subsidiary organs responsible to the five principal organs. (Most Secretariat materials are published as part of the records of other bodies.) The records of each of these publishing organizations ordinarily appear in four parts each session: plenary materials, committee materials, annexes, and supplements. Each part may occupy several volumes. The plenary volumes include verbatim or summary reports of the body's plenary meetings; the committee volumes, summary reports of committee meetings. Committee reports and other materials gathered for consideration as part of the principal organ's agenda are published in the annexes. Resolutions and other documents appear in the supplements.

(a) Volume designation. On each volume, three types of information should appear: the session number; the publishing organization; and whether the volume contains plenary materials, committee materials, annexes, or supplements. (If only the session number and the organization are given, the volume contains plenary materials.) Unless an author or title is given, this information—the volume designation—forms the first part of a UN citation:

8 U.N. GAOR

5 U.N. GAOR C.4

45 U.N. ESCOR Annex 1

22 U.N. TCOR Supp.

If a given session has been divided into two or more parts, that fact must be indicated:

3(1) U.N. GAOR

(b) Subdivisions. Since UN volumes are not continuously paginated, the separately paginated subdivision must be indicated parenthetically after the volume designation; plenary and committee materials are ordinarily divided by meeting:

8 U.N. GAOR (462d plen. mtg.)

27 U.N. GAOR Special Political Comm. (806th mtg.)

22 U.N. SCOR (1360th mtg.)

Annexes are ordinarily divided by agenda item:

22 U.N. GAOR Annex 1 (Agenda Item 23, addendum part 1)

24 U.N. GAOR Annex 2 (Agenda Item 72)

Supplement volumes are divided by supplement number or other designation:

8 U.N. GAOR Supp. (No. 19)

17 U.N. SCOR Supp. (Jan.–Mar. 1962)

(c) Page(s) or paragraph(s). The volume and subdivision designations should be followed by the page(s) or paragraph(s) to which reference is intended; when citing to page(s), introduce the page number(s) with the word "at":

8 U.N. GAOR (462d plen. mtg.) at 345

27 U.N. GAOR Special Political Comm. (806th mtg.) at 5

20 U.N. TCOR Annex (Agenda Item 5) at 1

17 U.N. SCOR Supp. (Jan.–Mar. 1962) at 63

Because United Nations materials may be published in several languages, and because pagination may vary from version to version, if a non-English version is used, that fact should be indicated parenthetically.

Many United Nations materials are numbered by paragraph as well as by page. Paragraph numbers may be used in lieu of page numbers in citations to United Nations materials. If paragraph numbers are used, it is unnecessary to specify which lingual version has been used:

29 U.N. GAOR C.3 (2058th mtg.) para. 9, U.N. Doc. A/C.3/SR.2058 (1974).

(d) United Nations document number system. Every UN citation, except as specified in rule 19.4.2, must also include the document number or, if none, the sales number given on the publication itself. The UN document numbering system parallels its volume system. Each of the main and specialized bodies has its own series symbol, as does each committee or other subdivision. Thus "A/SPC" refers to the Special Political Committee of the General Assembly. After these letters might come a subseries designation—for example, "SR." (summary records). Thus the document number for the summary report of the 806th meeting of the Special Political Committee would be:

U.N. Doc. A/SPC/SR.806

A full UN citation might therefore look like this:

27 U.N. GAOR Special Political Comm. (806th mtg.) at 5, U.N. Doc. A/SPC/SR.806 (1972).

A fuller explanation of document numbering system symbols can be found in United Nations Library, List of United Nations Document Series Symbols, U.N. Doc. ST/LIB/SER.B/5/Rev.2 (1970).

19.4.2 Specific Types of Materials

(a) General Assembly official records. Cite according to rule 19.4.1. Resolutions of the fifth and subsequent sessions have been published in the supplements:

G.A. Res. 832, 9 U.N. GAOR Supp. (No. 21) at 19, U.N. Doc. A/2890 (1954).

Resolutions before 1950 (the first four sessions) are cited without the ordinary volume designation:

G.A. Res. 133, U.N. Doc. A/519, at 43 (1947).

Verbatim transcripts are rarely kept for committee meetings; citations thus refer to summary records:

5 U.N. GAOR C.4 (187th mtg.) at 285, U.N. Doc. A/C.4/SR.187 (1950).

Specify annexes by volume or committee number when appropriate:

21 U.N. GAOR Annex 2 (Agenda Item 27) at 1, U.N. Doc. A/6529 (1966).

Permanent Missions to the U.N.: Report of the Secretary-General, 4 U.N. GAOR C.6 Annex (Agenda Item 50) at 16, U.N. Doc. A/939/Rev.1 (1949).

(b) Security Council official records. Cite according to rule 19.4.1. Records of meetings after 1950 are cited:

22 U.N. SCOR (1360th mtg.) at 1, U.N. Doc. S/P.V.1360 (1967).

Records of debates before 1951 do not have document numbers:

1 U.N. SCOR (3d mtg.) at 22 (1946).

The Security Council publishes no annexes; its supplements are denominated by the time periods they cover:

17 U.N. SCOR Supp. (Jan.–Mar. 1962) at 63, U.N. Doc. S/5073 (1962).

(c) Economic and Social Council and Trusteeship Council official records. Cite according to rule 19.4.1. The session numbers for these bodies do not correspond to those of the General Assembly or Security Council. Verbatim transcripts are not kept.

32 U.N. ESCOR (1156th mtg.) at 29, U.N. Doc. E/SR.1156 (1961).

Resolutions appear in the supplements:

T.C. Res. 1909, 22 U.N. TCOR Supp. (No. 1) at 3, U.N. Doc. T/1403 (1958).

E.S.C. Res. 337, 11 U.N. ESCOR Supp. (No. 1A) at 91, U.N. Doc. E/1849/Add.1 (1950).

Specify annexes by volume number when appropriate:

45 U.S. ESCOR Annex 1 (Agenda Item 6) at 1, U.N. Doc. E/4597 (1968).

(d) Official records of subsidiary organs. Cite materials published by the Development Programme, the UN Special Fund, and other subsidiary organs according to rule 19.4.1:

United Nations Regular Programme of Technical Cooperation, Report by the Secretary-General, 9 U.N. De-

F

velopment Programme (Agenda Item 11) 1, 3, U.N. Doc. DP/RP/8 (1969).

Decisions of the Administrative Tribunal should be cited to *Judgements of the U.N. Administrative Tribunal* (Judgements U.N. Admin. Trib.) by judgement (retaining the "e") number:

Eldridge v. Secretary-General of the United Nations, Judgements U.N. Admin. Trib. No. 32, at 144, U.N. Doc. AT/DEC/32 (1953).

(e) Provisional editions of official records. Indicate the provisional nature of the material parenthetically:

Sub-Committee II of the Committee on the Peaceful Uses of the Sea-Bed, 28 U.N. GAOR (75th mtg. of the subcomm.) at 1, U.N. Doc. A/A.C.138/S.C.II/SR.75 (prov. ed. 1973).

(f) United Nations Charter. Cite as a constitution (rule 11), giving only the appropriate article and paragraph:

U.N. CHARTER art. 2, para. 4.

(g) Founding documents. Cite documents of the initial conferences at San Francisco to *United Nations Conference on International Organization Documents* (U.N.C.I.O. Docs.), including the document number and committee print specification:

Doc. 463, II/3/19, 10 U.N.C.I.O. Docs. 51 (1945).

(h) Yearbooks. United Nations yearbooks collect summaries of subsidiary organizations and related documents. Original material is cited:

Summary Records of the 187th Meeting, [1953] 1 Y.B. INT'L L. COMM'N 17, U.N. Doc. A/CN.4/SER.A/1953.

Material reprinted in yearbooks from other UN documents should be cited to the original source or to the official records of a UN organ:

Report of the International Law Commission to the General Assembly, 19 U.N. GAOR Supp. (No. 9) at 1, U.N. Doc. A/5509 (1963), *reprinted in* [1963] 2 Y.B. INT'L L. COMM'N 187, U.N. Doc. A/CN.4/SER.A/1963/Add.1.

19.5 Materials of Other International Organizations

Generally, cite by analogy to UN materials and to the forms given below. Cite to English-language publications whenever possible.

League of Nations Materials 19.5.1

Cite the League of Nations Covenant as a constitution (rule 11):

LEAGUE OF NATIONS COVENANT art. 15, para. 6.

Cite the official journal:

12 LEAGUE OF NATIONS O.J. 56 (1931).

LEAGUE OF NATIONS O.J. Spec. Supp. 154, at 11 (1936).

Cite to other League of Nations materials by document number followed by the year of issuance in parentheses; the title may be included:

Report Presented by the Comm. of Technical Experts on Double Taxation and Tax Evasion, League of Nations Doc. C.216 M.85 1927 II (1927).

European Community Materials 19.5.2

Publications of the Council and of the Commission are cited to *Official Journal of the European Community* (O.J. EUR. COMM.) after 1972 and whenever available; otherwise cite to *Journal Officiel des Communautés européennes* (J.O. COMM. EUR.). Citations to the *Journal* after 1967 must include the subdivision number:

14 J.O. COMM. EUR. (No. L 20) 1 (1971).

16 O.J. EUR. COMM. (No. L 337) 7 (1973).

But:

7 J.O. COMM. EUR. 1710 (1964).

Debates of the European Parliamentary Assembly are cited:

1961–1962 EUR. PARL. DEB. (No. 38) 5 (Mar. 7, 1961).

Before debates are bound, cite them by *Journal* annex number:

Remarks of President Ortoli, O.J. EUR. COMM. (No. 193) 123 (July 9, 1975) (Debates of European Parliament).

Cite documents to *European Parliament Working Documents* (EUR. PARL. DOC.) if therein; otherwise cite to *Parlement Européen Documents de Séance* (PARL. EUR. DOC.). Include the document number:

1972–1973 EUR. PARL. DOC. (No. 258) 5 (1973).

1963–1964 PARL. EUR. DOC. (No. 64) 6 (1963).

A parallel citation may be given to either *Common Market Law Reports* (Common Mkt. L.R.) or *Common Market Reporter* (COMMON MKT. REP. (CCH)).

F

19.5.3 Council of Europe Materials

Debates of the Consultative Assembly should be cited to the official reports:

EUR. CONSULT. ASS. DEB. 10TH SESS. 639 (Oct. 16, 1958).

Documents should be cited:

Reply of the Comm. of Ministers, Eur. Consult. Ass., 12th Sess., Doc. No. 1126 (1960).

Cite cases before the European Court or Commission of Human Rights to the Yearbook:

Lawless Case, 1960 Y.B. EUR. CONV. ON HUMAN RIGHTS 492 (Eur. Comm'n on Human Rights) (preliminary objections).

19.6 Yearbooks

Cite United Nations yearbooks according to rule 19.4.2(h). Cite other international yearbooks or annual reports as periodicals (rule 16). Italicize article titles, but do not italicize the names of materials not ordinarily italicized—such as case names in footnotes. Give the yearbook title in the original language (*see* rule 16.2.2) and, if not obvious, the name of the issuing organization:

Certain Expenses of the United Nations (summary), 1961–1962 I.C.J.Y.B. 78 (1962).

Revised Staff Regulations, 1922–1925 P.C.I.J. ANN. REP., ser. E, No. 1, at 81 (1925).

Human Rights in the Union of Burma in 1953, 1953 Y.B. ON HUMAN RIGHTS 31 (United Nations).

X v. Belgium, 1961 Y.B. EUR. CONV. ON HUMAN RIGHTS 224 (Eur. Comm'n on Human Rights).

Boulouis, *Cour de Justice des Communautés Européennes,* 1965 ANNUAIRE FRANÇAIS DE DROIT INTERNATIONAL 333 (Centre National de la Recherche Scientifique).

Recommendations of the Customs Co-Operation Council on the Customs Treatment of Products Imported for Testing, 1972 EUR. Y.B. 429 (Council of Europe).

Other frequently cited yearbooks include those of the Union of International Associations (Y.B. INT'L ORG.), the United Nations (U.N.Y.B., U.N. JURIDICAL Y.B., Y.B. INT'L L. COMM'N), and the British Yearbook of international Law (BRIT. Y.B. INT'L L.).

G Tables: United States

Federal 133

State 136

Federal

United States

Supreme Court (U.S.): Cite to U.S., S. Ct., or U.S.L.W., in that order of preference. Do not give a parallel citation.

United States Reports		
91 U.S. to date	1875–date	U.S.
Wallace	1863–1874	e.g., 68 U.S. (1 Wall.)
Black	1861–1862	e.g., 66 U.S. (1 Black)
Howard	1843–1860	e.g., 42 U.S. (1 How.)
Peters	1828–1842	e.g., 26 U.S. (1 Pet.)
Wheaton	1816–1827	e.g., 14 U.S. (1 Wheat.)
Cranch	1801–1815	e.g., 5 U.S. (1 Cranch)
Dallas	1790–1800	e.g., 1 U.S. (1 Dall.)
Supreme Court Reporter	1882–date	S. Ct.
United States Law Week	1933–date	U.S.L.W.

Circuit Justices (e.g., Rehnquist, Circuit Justice): Cite to U.S., S. Ct., or U.S.L.W. if therein, in that order of preference.

United States Reports	1969–date	U.S.
Supreme Court Reporter	1926–date	S. Ct.
United States Law Week	1933–date	U.S.L.W.

(A few other opinions are reported in other reporters. E.g., United States v. Motlow, 10 F.2d 657 (Butler, Circuit Justice 1926).)

Courts of Appeals (e.g., 1st Cir., D.C. Cir.), previously **Circuit Courts of Appeals** (e.g., 1st Cir.), and **Court of Appeals of/for the District of Columbia** (D.C. Cir.): Cite to F. or F.2d.

Federal Reporter	1891–date	F., F.2d

Circuit Courts (e.g., C.C.S.D.N.Y., C.C.D. Cal.) (abolished 1912): Cite to F. Cas. or F.

Federal Cases	1789–1880	F. Cas.

(Citations to F. Cas. should give the case number parenthetically. E.g., Hochman v. Sobeloff, 18 F. Cas. 598 (C.C.W.D. Pa. 1859) (No. 10,444).)

Federal Reporter	1880–1912	F.

Emergency Court of Appeals (Emer. Ct. App.), **Temporary Emergency Court of Appeals** (Temp. Emer. Ct. App.), and **Commerce Court** (Comm. Ct.): Cite to F. or F.2d.

Federal Reporter	1926–date	F., F.2d

Court of Claims (Ct. Cl.), **Claims Court** (Cl. Ct.), **Court of Customs and Pat-**

ent Appeals (C.C.P.A.), **Court of Appeals for the Federal Circuit** (Fed. Cir.), **Customs Court** (Cust. Ct.), and **Court of International Trade** (Ct. Int'l Trade): Cite to F.2d or F.Supp. if therein; otherwise cite to the respective official reporter.

Federal Reporter	1929–date	F.2d
Federal Supplement	1932–date	F. Supp.
Court of Claims Reports	1956–date	Ct. Cl.
Court of Customs and Patent Appeals Reports	1929–date	C.C.P.A.
Customs Court Reports	1938–1980	Cust. Ct.
Court of International Trade Reports	1980–date	Ct. Int'l Trade

District Courts (e.g., D. Mass., S.D.N.Y.): For cases after 1932, cite to F. Supp., F.R.D., or Bankr. if therein; otherwise cite to Fed. R. Serv. or Fed. R. Serv. 2d. For prior cases, cite to F., F.2d, or F. Cas. if therein.

Federal Supplement	1932–date	F. Supp.
Federal Rules Decisions	1938–date	F.R.D.
Bankruptcy Reporter	1979–date	Bankr.
Federal Rules Service	1938–date	Fed. R. Serv. (Callaghan), Fed. R. Serv. 2d (Callaghan)
Federal Reporter	1880–1932	F., F.2d
Federal Cases	1789–1880	F. Cas.

(Citations to F. Cas. should give the case number parenthetically. E.g., *Ex parte* McKean, 16 F. Cas. 186 (E.D. Va. 1878) (No. 8848).)

Bankruptcy Courts (e.g., Bankr. N.D. Cal.) and **Bankruptcy Appellate Panels** (e.g., Bankr. 1st Cir.): Cite to Bankr. if therein; otherwise cite to a service (rule 18).

Bankruptcy Reporter	1979–date	Bankr.

Judicial Panel on Multi-District Litigation (J.P.M.D.L.) and **Special Court Regional Rail Reorganization Act** (Regional Rail Reorg. Ct.): Cite to F. Supp.

Federal Supplement	1968–date	F. Supp.

Tax Court (T.C.) and **Board of Tax Appeals** (B.T.A.): Cite to T.C. or B.T.A. if therein; otherwise cite to T.C.M. (CCH), T.C.M. (P-H), or B.T.A.M. (P-H).

Tax Court of the United States Reports	1942–date	T.C.
Board of Tax Appeals Reports	1924–1942	B.T.A
Tax Court Memorandum Decisions	1942–date	T.C.M. (CCH) [or (P-H)]
Board of Tax Appeals Memorandum Decisions	1924–1942	B.T.A.M. (P-H)

Court of Military Appeals (C.M.A.): Cite to C.M.A. if therein and to M.J. or C.M.R.

Court of Military Appeals Reports	1951–1975	C.M.A.
Military Justice Reporter	1975–date	M.J.
Court Martial Reports	1951–1977	C.M.R.

Courts of Military Review (e.g., A.C.M.R., A.F.C.M.R.), previously **Boards of Review** (e.g., A.B.R.): For cases after 1950, cite to M.J. or C.M.R. For earlier cases, cite to the official reporter.

Military Justice Reporter	1975–date	M.J.
Court Martial Reports	1951–1977	C.M.R.

Statutory compilations: Cite to U.S.C. if therein.

United States Code (26 U.S.C. may be abbreviated as I.R.C.)	x U.S.C. § x (19xx)
United States Code Annotated	x U.S.C.A. § x (West 19xx)
United States Code Service	x U.S.C.S. § x (Law. Co-op. 19xx)

Session laws

United States Statutes at Large (Cite public laws before 1957 by chapter number; cite subsequent acts by public law number.)	x Stat. xxx (1xxx)

United States official administrative publications

Administrative Decisions under Immigration and Nationality Laws	1940–date	I. & N. Dec.
Agricultural Decisions	1942–date	Agric. Dec.
Atomic Energy Commission Reports	1956–1975	A.E.C.
Civil Aeronautics Board Reports (vol. 1 by C.A.A.)	1940–date	C.A.B.
Copyright Decisions	1909–date	Copy. Dec.
Court of Customs Appeals Reports	1910–1929	Ct. Cust. App.
Cumulative Bulletin	1919–date	C.B.
Customs Bulletin and Decisions	1967–date	Cust. B. & Dec.
Decisions of the Comptroller General	1921–date	Comp. Gen.
Decisions of the Employees' Compensation Appeals Board	1947–date	Empl. Comp. App. Bd.
Decisions of the Department of the Interior (from vol. 53)	1930–date	Interior Dec.
Decisions of the Federal Maritime Commission	1947–date	F.M.C.
Decisions of the United States Maritime Commission	1919–1947	Dec. U.S. Mar. Comm'n
Decisions of the United States Merit Systems Protection Board	1979–date	M.S.P.B.
Department of the Interior, Decisions Relating to Public Lands (vols. 1–52)	1881–1929	Pub. Lands Dec.
Federal Communications Commission Reports	1934–date	F.C.C., F.C.C.2d
Federal Energy Regulatory Commission Reports	1977–date	F.E.R.C.
Federal Power Commission Reports	1931–1977	F.P.C.
Federal Reserve Bulletin	1915-date	Fed. Res. Bull.
Federal Trade Commission Decisions	1915-date	F.T.C.

G

Interstate Commerce Commission Reports	1887-date	I.C.C.
Interstate Commerce Commission, Valuation Reports	1929–date	I.C.C. Valuation Rep.
Motor Carrier Cases	1936–date	M.C.C.
National Labor Relations Board Decisions and Orders	1935–date	N.L.R.B.
National Railroad Adjustment Board, 1st–4th Div.	1934–date	e.g., N.R.A.B. (1st Div.)
National Transportation Safety Board Decisions	1967–date	N.T.S.B.
Nuclear Regulatory Commission Issuances	1975–date	N.R.C.
Official Gazette of the United States Patent Office	1872–date	Off. Gaz. Pat. Office
Official Opinions of the Solicitor for the Post Office Department	1873–1951	Op. Solic. P.O. Dep't
Opinions of the Attorney General	1789–date	Op. Att'y Gen.
Opinions of Office of Legal Counsel	1977–date	Op. Off. Legal Counsel
Patents, Decisions of the Commissioner and of U.S. Courts	1869–date	Dec. Comm'r Pat.
Securities and Exchange Commission Decisions and Reports	1934–date	S.E.C.
Treasury Decisions Under Customs and Other Laws	1898–1966	Treas. Dec.
Treasury Decisions Under Internal Revenue Laws	1898–1942	Treas. Dec. Int. Rev.

State

Alabama

Supreme Court (Ala.): Cite to a reporter below if therein and to So. or So. 2d.

Alabama Reports	1840–1976	Ala.
Porter	1834–1839	Port.
Stewart and Porter	1831–1834	Stew. & P.
Stewart	1827–1831	Stew.
Minor	1820–1826	Minor
Southern Reporter	1886–date	So., So. 2d

Court of Civil Appeals (Ala. Civ. App.) and **Court of Criminal Appeals** (Ala. Crim. App.), before 1969 **Court of Appeals** (Ala. Ct. App.): Cite to Ala. App. if therein and to So. or So. 2d.

Alabama Appellate Court Reports	1910–1976	Ala. App.
Southern Reporter	1911–date	So., So. 2d

Statutory compilation

Code of Alabama		ALA. CODE § x (19xx)

Session laws

Acts of Alabama		19xx Ala. Acts xxx

Alaska

Supreme Court (Alaska): Cite to P.2d.

Pacific Reporter	1960–date	P.2d

Court of Appeals (Alaska Ct. App.): Cite to P.2d.

Pacific Reporter	1980–date	P.2d

District Court of Alaska (D. Alaska): This court had local jurisdiction from 1884 to 1959. Cite to F., F.2d, or F. Supp. if therein; otherwise cite to Alaska.

Alaska Reports	1900–1959	Alaska
Federal Reporter	1884–1932	F., F.2d
Federal Supplement	1932–1959	F. Supp.

United States District Courts for California and **Oregon**, and **District Court of Washington** (D. Cal., D. Or., D. Wash.): These courts had local jurisdiction in Alaska until 1883. Cite to F. Cas. or F.

Federal Reporter	1880–1884	F.
Federal Cases	1867–1880	F. Cas.

(Citations to F. Cas. should give the case number parenthetically. *See supra* pp. 133, 134.)

Statutory compilation

Alaska Statutes		ALASKA STAT. § x (19xx)

Session laws

Alaska Session Laws		19xx Alaska Sess. Laws xxx

Administrative compilation

Alaska Administrative Code (with quarterly registers)		ALASKA ADMIN. CODE tit. x, § x (month 19xx)

American Samoa

High Court of American Samoa (Am. Samoa): Cite to Am. Samoa if therein.

American Samoa Reports	1900–1975	Am. Samoa

Statutory compilation

American Samoa Code Annotated		AM. SAMOA CODE ANN. § x (19xx)

Arizona

Supreme Court (Ariz.): Cite to Ariz. and to P. or P.2d.

Arizona Reports	1866–date	Ariz.
Pacific Reporter	1866–date	P., P.2d

Court of Appeals (Ariz. Ct. App.): Cite to Ariz. App. or Ariz. and to P.2d.

Arizona Appeals Reports	1965–1976	Ariz. App.
Arizona Reports	1976–date	Ariz.
Pacific Reporter	1965–date	P.2d

Statutory compilation

Arizona Revised Statutes Annotated	ARIZ. REV. STAT. ANN. § x (19xx)

Session laws: Cite to Ariz. Sess. Laws if therein.

Session Laws, Arizona	19xx Ariz. Sess. Laws xxx
Arizona Legislative Service (West)	19xx Ariz. Legis. Serv. xxx (West)

Administrative compilation

Official Compilation of Administrative Rules and Regulations	ARIZ. ADMIN. COMP. R. x (19xx)

Administrative register

Administrative Digest	Ariz. Admin. Dig.

Arkansas

Supreme Court (Ark.): Cite to Ark. and to S.W. or S.W.2d.

Arkansas Reports	1837–date	Ark.
Southwestern Reporter	1885–date	S.W., S.W.2d

Court of Appeals (Ark. Ct. App.): Cite to S.W.2d if therein.

Southwestern Reporter	1979–date	S.W.2d

Statutory compilation

Arkansas Statutes Annotated	ARK. STAT. ANN. § x (19xx)

Session laws

General Acts of Arkansas	19xx Ark. Acts xxx

Administrative register

Arkansas Register	Ark. Admin. Reg.

California

Supreme Court (Cal.): Cite to Cal., Cal. 2d, or Cal. 3d, to P. or P.2d, and to Cal. Rptr., if therein.

California Reports	1850–date	Cal., Cal. 2d, Cal. 3d
Pacific Reporter	1883–date	P., P.2d
West's California Reporter	1959–date	Cal. Rptr.
California Unreported Cases	1855–1910	Cal. Unrep.

Court of Appeal (Cal. Ct. App.), previously **District Court of Appeal** (Cal. Dist. Ct. App.): Cite to Cal. App., Cal. App. 2d, or Cal. App. 3d, and to Cal. Rptr. (after 1959) or P. or P.2d (before 1960).

California Appellate Reports	1905–date	Cal. App., Cal. App. 2d, Cal. App. 3d
Pacific Reporter	1905–1959	P., P.2d
West's California Reporter	1959–date	Cal. Rptr.

Appellate Departments of the Superior Court (Cal. App. Dep't Super. Ct.): Cite to Cal. App. Supp., Cal. App. 2d Supp., or Cal. App. 3d Supp., and to Cal. Rptr. (after 1959) or P. or P.2d (before 1960).

California Appellate Reports Supplement (bound with Cal. App.)	1929–date	Cal. App. Supp., Cal. App. 2d Supp., Cal. App. 3d Supp.
West's California Reporter	1959–date	Cal. Rptr.
Pacific Reporter	1929–1959	P., P.2d

Statutory compliations: Cite to either the West or the Deering subject matter code if therein; otherwise cite to *Deering's California General Laws Annotated.*

West's Annotated California Code	CAL. [subject] CODE § x (West 19xx)
Deering's Annotated California Code	CAL. [subject] CODE § x (Deering 19xx)
Agricultural (renamed "Food and Agricultural" in 1972)	AGRIC.
Business and Professions	BUS. & PROF.
Civil	CIV.
Civil Procedure	CIV. PROC.
Commercial	COM.
Corporations	CORP.
Education	EDUC.
Elections	ELEC.
Evidence	EVID.
Financial	FIN.
Fish and Game	FISH & GAME
Food and Agricultural (formerly "Agricultural")	FOOD & AGRIC.
Government	GOV'T
Harbors and Navigation	HARB. & NAV.
Health and Safety	HEALTH & SAFETY
Insurance	INS.
Labor	LAB.
Military and Veterans	MIL. & VET.
Penal	PENAL
Probate	PROB.
Public Resources	PUB. RES.
Public Utilities	PUB. UTIL.
Revenue and Taxation	REV. & TAX.

Streets and Highways	STS. & HY.
Unemployment Insurance	UNEMP. INS.
Uniform Commercial	COM.
Vehicle	VEH.
Water	WATER
Welfare and Institutions	WELF. & INST.
Deering's California General Laws Annotated (compiling uncodified acts)	CAL. GEN. LAWS ANN. act x, § x (Deering 19xx)

Session laws: Cite to Cal. Stat. if therein.

Statutes of California	19xx Cal. Stat. xxx
California Legislative Service (West)	19xx Cal. Legis. Serv. xxx (West)
California Advance Legislative Service (Deering)	19xx Cal. Adv. Legis. Serv. xxx (Deering)

Administrative compilation

California Administrative Code	CAL. ADMIN. CODE tit. x, R. x (19xx)

Administrative register

California Administrative Register	Cal. Admin. Reg.

Canal Zone

United States District Court for the District of the Canal Zone (D.C.Z.): Cite to F. Supp.

Federal Supplement	1946–date	F. Supp.

Statutory compilation

Panama Canal Code (enacted as Canal Zone Code, Pub. L. No. 87-845, 76A Stat. 1 (1962), and redesignated and continued partially in force by the Panama Canal Act of 1979, Pub. L. No. 96-70, § 3303(b), 93 Stat. 452, 499)	C.Z. CODE tit. x, § x (19xx)

Administrative compilation

Panama Canal Regulations	35 C.F.R. § x (19xx)

Colorado

Supreme Court (Colo.): Cite to Colo. if therein and to P. or P.2d.

Colorado Reports	1864–1980	Colo.
Pacific Reporter	1883–date	P., P.2d

Court of Appeals (Colo. Ct. App.): Cite to Colo. App. if therein and to P. or P.2d.

Colorado Court of Appeals Reports	1891–1905, 1912–1915, 1970–1980	Colo. App.
Pacific Reporter	1891–1905	P.
	1912–1915	P.
	1970–date	P.2d

Statutory compilation

Colorado Revised Statutes		COLO. REV. STAT. § x (19xx)

Session laws

Session Laws of Colorado		19xx Colo. Sess. Laws xxx

Administrative compilation

Code of Colorado Regulations		COLO. ADMIN. CODE

Administrative register

Colorado Register		Colo. Admin. Reg.

Connecticut

Supreme Court (Conn.), previously **Supreme Court of Errors** (Conn.): Cite to Conn., Day, or Root and to A. or A.2d.

Connecticut Reports	1814–date	Conn.
Day	1802–1813	Day
Root	1789–1798	Root
Atlantic Reporter	1885–date	A., A.2d

Superior Court (Conn. Super. Ct.) and **Court of Common Pleas** (Conn. C.P.): Cite to Conn. Supp. and to A.2d.

Connecticut Supplement	1935–date	Conn. Supp.
Atlantic Reporter	1954–date	A.2d

Circuit Court (Conn. Cir. Ct.): Cite to Conn. Cir. Ct. if therein and to A.2d.

Connecticut Circuit Court Reports	1961–1974	Conn. Cir. Ct.
Atlantic Reporter	1961–date	A.2d

Statutory compilations: Cite to CONN. GEN. STAT. if therein.

General Statutes of Connecticut (1977)		CONN. GEN. STAT. § x (19xx)
Connecticut General Statutes Annotated		CONN. GEN. STAT. ANN. § x (West 19xx)

Session laws: Cite to Conn. Acts, Conn. Pub. Acts, or Conn. Spec. Acts, if therein.

Connecticut Public & Special Acts	1971–date	19xx Conn. Acts xxx (Reg. [Spec.] Sess.)

G

Connecticut Public Acts	1650–1971	1xxx Conn. Pub. Acts xxx
Connecticut Special Acts (published under various titles—i.e., Resolves & Private Laws, Private & Special Laws, Special Laws, Resolves & Private Acts, Resolutions & Private Acts, Private Acts & Resolutions, and Special Acts & Resolutions—and with various volume designations—i.e., by year or volume number)	1789–1971	1xxx Conn. Spec. Acts xxx
Connecticut Legislative Service (West)		19xx Conn. Legis. Serv. xxx (West)

Administrative compilation

Regulations of Connecticut State Agencies	CONN. AGENCIES REGS.

Delaware

Supreme Court (Del.), previously **Court of Errors and Appeals** (Del.): Cite to Del. or Del. Cas. if therein and to A. or A.2d.

Delaware Reports		
31 Del. to 59 Del.	1920–1966	Del.
Boyce	1909–1919	e.g., 24 Del. (1 Boyce)
Pennewill	1897–1909	e.g., 17 Del. (1 Penne.)
Marvel	1893–1897	e.g., 15 Del. (1 Marv.)
Houston	1855–1893	e.g., 6 Del. (1 Houst.)
Harrington	1832–1855	e.g., 1 Del. (1 Harr.)
Delaware Cases	1792–1830	Del. Cas.
Atlantic Reporter	1884–date	A., A.2d

Court of Chancery (Del. Ch.): Cite to Del. Ch. or Del. Cas. if therein and to A. or A.2d.

Delaware Chancery Reports	1814–1968	Del. Ch.
Atlantic Reporter	1886–date	A., A.2d

Superior Court (Del. Super. Ct.), previously **Superior Court and Orphans' Court** (Del. Super. Ct. & Orphans' Ct.): Cite to official reporters listed under **Supreme Court**, if therein, and to A.2d.

Atlantic Reporter	1951–date	A.2d

Family Court (Del. Fam. Ct.): Cite to A.2d.

Atlantic Reporter	1977–date	A.2d

Statutory compilation

Delaware Code Annotated	DEL. CODE ANN. tit. x, § x (19xx)

Session laws

Laws of Delaware (by volume number)	x Del. Laws xxx (19xx)

District of Columbia

Court of Appeals (D.C.), previously **Municipal Court of Appeals** (D.C.): Cite to A.2d.

Atlantic Reporter	1943–date	A.2d

United States Court of Appeals for the District of Columbia Circuit (D.C. Cir.), previously **Court of Appeals of/for the District of Columbia** (D.C. Cir.), previously **Supreme Court of the District of Columbia** (D.C.): Cite to F. or F.2d if therein; otherwise cite to U.S. App. D.C., App. D.C., D.C., or Hay. & Haz.

Federal Reporter	1918–date	F., F.2d
United States Court of Appeals Reports	1941–date	U.S. App. D.C.
Appeal Cases, District of Columbia	1893–1941	App. D.C.
District of Columbia Reports		
Tucker and Clephane	1892–1893	21 D.C. (Tuck. & Cl.)
Mackey	1880–1892	e.g., 12 D.C. (1 Mackey)
MacArthur and Mackey	1879–1880	11 D.C. (MacArth. & M.)
MacArthur	1873–1879	e.g., 8 D.C. (1 MacArth.)
Mackey	1863–1872	e.g., 6 D.C. (1 Mackey)
Cranch	1801–1841	e.g., 1 D.C. (1 Cranch)
Hayward & Hazelton	1841–1862	Hay. & Haz.

Statutory compilations: Cite to D.C. CODE ANN. if therein.

District of Columbia Code Annotated (1973 & Supp. VII 1980)	D.C. CODE ANN. § x (19xx)
District of Columbia Code Encyclopedia (West) (current through 1978)	D.C. CODE ENCYCL. § x (West 19xx)

Session laws: Cite to Stat. or to D.C. Stat. if therein; otherwise cite to D.C. Reg.

United States Statutes at Large	x Stat. xxx (1xxx)
District of Columbia Statutes at Large	19xx D.C. Stat. xxx
District of Columbia Register	x D.C. Reg. xxx (19xx)
D.C. Code Legislative and Administrative Service (West) (current through 1978)	19xx D.C. Code Legis. & Ad. Serv. xxx (West)

Municipal regulations: The District was granted limited home rule in 1975. Cite to D.C. Mun. Regs. for acts of the new Council of the District of Columbia. For older acts, cite to D.C. R. & Regs.

D.C. Municipal Regulations	D.C. Mun. Regs. tit. x, § x (19xx)
D.C. Rules and Regulations	e.g., D.C. R. & Regs. tit. 5N, § 2.2 (1970)

Florida

Supreme Court (Fla.): Cite to Fla. if therein and to So. or So. 2d.

Florida Reports	1846–1948	Fla.
Southern Reporter	1886–date	So., So. 2d

District Court of Appeal (Fla. Dist. Ct. App.): Cite to So. 2d.

Southern Reporter	1957–date	So. 2d

Circuit Court (Fla. Cir. Ct.), **County Court** (e.g., Orange County Ct.), **Public Service Commission** (Fla. P.S.C.), and other lower courts of record: Cite to Fla. Supp.

Florida Supplement	1948–date	Fla. Supp.

Statutory compilations: Cite to FLA. STAT. if therein.

Florida Statutes	FLA. STAT. § x (19xx)
Florida Statutes Annotated (West)	FLA. STAT. ANN. § x (West 19xx)

Session laws: Cite to Fla. Laws if therein.

Laws of Florida	19xx Fla. Laws xxx
Florida Session Law Service (West)	19xx Fla. Sess. Law Serv. xxx (West)

Administrative compilation

Florida Administrative Code	FLA. ADMIN. CODE

Administrative register

Florida Administrative Weekly	Fla. Admin. Weekly

Georgia

Supreme Court (Ga.): Cite to Ga. and to S.E. or S.E.2d.

Georgia Reports	1846–date	Ga.
Southeastern Reporter	1887–date	S.E., S.E.2d

Court of Appeals (Ga. Ct. App.): Cite to Ga. App. and to S.E. or S.E.2d.

Georgia Appeals Reports	1907–date	Ga. App.
Southeastern Reporter	1907–date	S.E., S.E.2d

Statutory compilations: Cite to the official version of GA. CODE ANN. if therein.

Code of Georgia Annotated	GA. CODE ANN. § x (19xx)
Code of Georgia Annotated (Harrison)	GA. CODE ANN. § x (Harrison 19xx)

Session laws

Georgia Laws	19xx Ga. Laws xxx

Administrative compilation

Official Compilation Rules & Regulations of the State of Georgia	GA. ADMIN. COMP. ch. x (19xx)

Guam

District Court of Guam, Appellate Division (D. Guam App. Div.): Cite to F. Supp. if therein; otherwise cite to Guam.

Federal Supplement	1951–date	F. Supp.
Guam Reports	1955–date	Guam

Statutory compilations

Guam Civil Code	GUAM CIV. CODE § x (19xx)
Guam Code of Civil Procedure	GUAM CIV. PROC. CODE § x (19xx)
Guam Probate Code	GUAM PROB. CODE § x (19xx)
Guam Government Code	GUAM GOV'T CODE § x (19xx)
Guam Penal Code	GUAM PENAL CODE § x (19xx)
Guam Code Annotated (will eventually replace all other statutory compilations)	x GUAM CODE ANN. § x (19xx)

Administrative compilation

Administrative Rules & Regulations of the Government of Guam	GUAM ADMIN. R.

Hawaii

Supreme Court (Hawaii): Cite to Hawaii and to P.2d if therein.

Hawaii Reports	1847–date	Hawaii
Pacific Reporter	1959–date	P.2d

Intermediate Court of Appeals (Hawaii Ct. App.): Cite to P.2d.

Pacific Reporter	1980–date	P.2d

Statutory compilation

Hawaii Revised Statutes	HAWAII REV. STAT. § x (19xx)

Session laws

Session Laws of Hawaii	19xx Hawaii Sess. Laws xxx

Idaho

Supreme Court (Idaho): Cite to Idaho and to P. or P.2d.

Idaho Reports	1866–date	Idaho
Pacific Reporter	1881–date	P., P.2d

Statutory compilation

Idaho Code	IDAHO CODE § x (19xx)

Session laws

Session Laws, Idaho	19xx Idaho Sess. Laws xxx

G

Illinois

Supreme Court (Ill.): Cite to Ill. or Ill. 2d and to N.E. or N.E.2d.

Illinois Reports		
11 Ill. to date	1849–date	Ill., Ill. 2d
Gilman	1844–1849	e.g., 6 Ill. (1 Gilm.)
Scammon	1832–1844	e.g., 2 Ill. (1 Scam.)
Breese	1819–1831	1 Ill. (Breese)
Northeastern Reporter	1885–date	N.E., N.E.2d

Appellate Court (Ill. App. Ct.): Cite to Ill. App., Ill. App. 2d, or Ill. App. 3d and to N.E.2d.

Illinois Appellate Court Reports	1877–date	Ill. App., Ill. App. 2d, Ill. App. 3d
Northeastern Reporter	1936–date	N.E.2d

Court of Claims (Ill. Ct. Cl.)

Illinois Court of Claims Reports	1889–date	Ill. Ct. Cl.

Statutory compilations: Cite to ILL. REV. STAT. if therein. Because the numbering system is not official, however, always give the name of the act and the original section number (rule 12.3(a)).

Illinois Revised Statutes	ILL. REV. STAT. ch. x, § x (19xx)
Smith-Hurd Illinois Annotated Statutes	ILL. ANN. STAT. ch. x, § x (Smith-Hurd 19xx)

Session laws: Cite to Ill. Laws if therein.

Laws of Illinois	19xx Ill. Laws xxx
Illinois Legislative Service (West)	19xx Ill. Legis. Serv. xxx (West)

Administrative register

Illinois Register	Ill. Admin. Reg.

Indiana

Supreme Court (Ind.): Cite to Ind. or Blackf. and to N.E. or N.E.2d if therein.

Indiana Reports	1848–date	Ind.
Blackford	1817–1847	Blackf.
Northeastern Reporter	1885–date	N.E., N.E.2d

Court of Appeals (Ind. Ct. App.), previously **Appellate Court** (Ind. App.): Cite to Ind. App. and to N.E. or N.E.2d.

Indiana Court of Appeals Reports (prior to 1972, Indiana Appellate Court Reports)	1891–date	Ind. App.
Northeastern Reporter	1891–date	N.E., N.E.2d

Statutory compilations: Cite to IND. CODE if therein.

Indiana Code	IND. CODE § x (19xx)
Burns Indiana Statutes Annotated Code Edition	IND. CODE ANN. § x (Burns 19xx)
West's Annotated Indiana Code	IND. CODE ANN. § x (West 19xx)

Session laws

Acts, Indiana	19xx Ind. Acts xxx

Administrative compilation

Burns Indiana Administrative Rules & Regulations	IND. ADMIN. R. x (Burns 19xx)

Iowa

Supreme Court (Iowa): Cite to Iowa, Greene, Morris, or Bradf., if therein, and to N.W. or N.W.2d.

Iowa Reports	1855–1968	Iowa
Greene	1847–1854	Greene
Morris	1839–1846	Morris
Bradford	1839–1841	Bradf.
Northwestern Reporter	1878–date	N.W., N.W.2d

Court of Appeals (Iowa Ct. App.): Cite to N.W.2d.

Northwestern Reporter	1977–date	N.W.2d

Statutory compilations: Cite to IOWA CODE if therein.

Code of Iowa	IOWA CODE § x (19xx)
Iowa Code Annotated (West)	IOWA CODE ANN. § x (West 19xx)

Session laws: Cite to Iowa Acts if therein.

Acts and Joint Resolutions of the State of Iowa	19xx Iowa Acts xxx
Iowa Legislative Service (West)	19xx Iowa Legis. Serv. xxx (West)

Administrative compilation

Iowa Administrative Code	IOWA ADMIN. CODE

Administrative register

Iowa Administrative Bulletin	Iowa Admin. Bull.

Kansas

Supreme Court (Kan.): Cite to Kan. and to P. or P.2d.

Kansas Reports	1862–date	Kan.
McCahon	1858–1868	McCahon
Pacific Reporter	1883–date	P., P.2d

Court of Appeals (Kan. Ct. App.): Cite to Kan. App. or Kan. App. 2d and to P. or P.2d.

Kansas Court of Appeals Reports	1895–1901	Kan. App.
	1977–date	Kan. App. 2d
Pacific Reporter	1895–1901	P.
	1977–date	P.2d

Statutory compilations

Kansas Statutes Annotated	KAN. STAT. ANN. § x (19xx)
Vernon's Kansas Statutes Annotated	
Uniform Commercial Code	KAN. U.C.C. ANN. § x (Vernon 19xx)
Code of Civil Procedure	KAN. CIV. PROC. CODE ANN. § x (Vernon 19xx)
Criminal Code	KAN. CRIM. CODE ANN. § x (Vernon 19xx)
Code of Criminal Procedure	KAN. CRIM. PROC. CODE ANN. § x (Vernon 19xx)
Corporation Code	KAN. CORP. CODE ANN. § x (Vernon 19xx)

Session laws

Session Laws of Kansas	19xx Kan. Sess. Laws xxx

Administrative compilation

Kansas Administrative Regulations (1978)	KAN. ADMIN. REGS. x (19xx)

Kentucky

Supreme Court (Ky.), before 1976 **Court of Appeals** (Ky.): Cite to Ky. or Ky. Op. and to S.W. or S.W.2d.

Kentucky Reports		
78 Ky. to 314 Ky.	1879–1951	Ky.
Bush	1866–1879	e.g., 64 Ky. (1 Bush)
Duvall	1863–1866	e.g., 62 Ky. (1 Duv.)
Metcalf	1858–1863	e.g., 58 Ky. (1 Met.)
Monroe, Ben	1840–1857	e.g., 40 Ky. (1 B. Mon.)
Dana	1833–1840	e.g., 31 Ky. (1 Dana)
Marshall, J. J.	1829–1832	e.g., 24 Ky. (1 J. J. Marsh.)
Monroe, T. B.	1824–1828	e.g., 17 Ky. (1 T. B. Mon.)
Littell	1822–1824	e.g., 11 Ky. (1 Litt.)
Marshall, A. K.	1817–1821	e.g., 8 Ky. (1 A. K. Marsh.)
Bibb	1808–1817	e.g., 4 Ky. (1 Bibb)

Hardin	1805–1808	3 Ky. (Hard.)
Sneed	1801–1805	2 Ky. (Sneed)
Hughes	1785–1801	1 Ky. (Hughes)
Kentucky Opinions	1864–1886	Ky. Op.
Southwestern Reporter	1886–date	S.W., S.W.2d

Court of Appeals (Ky. Ct. App.) (for decisions before 1977, see **Kentucky Supreme Court**): Cite to S.W.2d.

Southwestern Reporter	1977–date	S.W.2d

Statutory compilations: Cite to KY. REV. STAT. if therein.

Kentucky Revised Statutes	KY. REV. STAT. § x (19xx)
Baldwin's Kentucky Revised Statutes Annotated	KY. REV. STAT. ANN. § x (Baldwin 19xx)
Kentucky Revised Statutes Annotated (Bobbs-Merrill)	KY. REV. STAT. ANN. § x (Bobbs-Merrill 19xx)

Session laws: Cite to Ky. Acts if therein.

Kentucky Acts	19xx Ky. Acts xxx
Kentucky Revised Statutes and Rules Service (Baldwin)	19xx Ky. Rev. Stat. & R. Serv. xxx (Baldwin)

Administrative compilation

Kentucky Administrative Regulations Service	x KY. ADMIN. REGS. x:x (19xx)

Administrative register

Administrative Register	Ky. Admin. Reg.

Louisiana

Supreme Court (La.), before 1813 the **Superior Court of Louisiana** (La.) and the **Superior Court of the Territory of Orleans** (Orleans): Cite to La., La. Ann., Rob., or Mart., if therein, and to So. or So. 2d.

Louisiana Reports	1900–1972	La.
Louisiana Annual Reports	1846–1900	La. Ann.
Robinson	1841–1846	Rob.
Louisiana Reports	1830–1841	La.
Martin (Louisiana Term Reports)	1809–1830	Mart., Mart. (n.s.)
Southern Reporter	1887–date	So., So. 2d

Court of Appeal (La. Ct. App.): Cite to La. App., Pelt., Teiss., or McGl., if therein, and to So. or So. 2d.

Louisiana Courts of Appeal Reports	1924–1932	La. App.
Peltier's Decisions, Court of Appeal, Parish of Orleans	1917–1923	Pelt.
Teisser's Court of Appeal, Parish of Orleans Reports	1903–1917	Teiss.

G

McGloin's Louisiana Courts of Appeal Reports	1881–1884	McGl.
Southern Reporter	1928–date	So., So. 2d

Statutory compilations

West's Louisiana Revised Statutes Annotated	LA. REV. STAT. ANN. § x (West 19xx)
West's Louisiana Civil Code Annotated	LA. CIV. CODE ANN. art. x (West 19xx)
West's Louisiana Code of Civil Procedure Annotated	LA. CODE CIV. PROC. ANN. art. x (West 19xx)
West's Louisiana Code of Criminal Procedure	LA. CODE CRIM. PROC. ANN. art. x (West 19xx)

Session laws: Cite to La. Acts if therein.

State of Louisiana: Acts of the Legislature	19xx La. Acts xxx
Louisiana Session Law Service (West)	19xx La. Sess. Law Serv. xxx (West)

Administrative compilation

Louisiana Administrative Code	LA. ADMIN. CODE

Administrative register

Louisiana Register	La. Admin. Reg.

Maine

Supreme Judicial Court (Me.): Cite to Me. and to A. or A.2d.

Maine Reports	1820–1965	Me.
Atlantic Reporter	1885–date	A., A.2d

Statutory compilation

Maine Revised Statutes Annotated	ME. REV. STAT. ANN. tit. x, § x (19xx)

Session laws: Cite to Me. Laws if therein.

Laws of the State of Maine	19xx Me. Laws xxx
Acts, Resolves and Constitutional Resolutions of the State of Maine	19xx Me. Acts xxx
Maine Legislative Service	19xx Me. Legis. Serv. xxx

Maryland

Court of Appeals (Md.): Cite to Md., Gill, G. & J., H. & G., H. & J., or H. & McH. and to A. or A.2d.

Maryland Reports	1851–date	Md.
Gill	1843–1851	Gill
Gill and Johnson	1829–1842	G. & J.

Harris and Gill	1826–1829	H. & G.
Harris and Johnson	1800–1826	H. & J.
Harris and McHenry	1785–1799	H. & McH.
Atlantic Reporter	1885–date	A., A.2d

Court of Special Appeals (Md. Ct. Spec. App.): Cite to Md. App. and to A.2d.

Maryland Appellate Reports	1967–date	Md. App.
Atlantic Reporter	1967–date	A.2d

Statutory compilations: Cite to the Maryland subject-matter code if therein; otherwise cite to MD. ANN. CODE of 1957. Titles of the subject-matter code available as of March 1982 are followed by the year of their publication.

Annotated Code of Maryland	MD. [subject] CODE ANN. § x (19xx)
Agriculture (1974)	AGRIC.
Business Regulation	BUS. REG.
Commercial Law (1975)	COM. LAW
Corporations and Associations (1975)	CORPS. & ASS'NS
Courts and Judicial Proceedings (1974)	CTS. & JUD. PROC.
Criminal Law	CRIM. LAW
Education (1978)	EDUC.
Elections	ELEC.
Estates and Trusts (1974)	EST. & TRUSTS
Family Law	FAM. LAW
Financial Institutions (1980)	FIN. INST.
General Provisions	GEN. PROV.
Health Occupations (1981)	HEALTH OCC.
Local Government	LOCAL GOV'T
Natural Resources (1974)	NAT. RES.
Occupations and Professions	OCC. & PROF.
Public Health	PUB. HEALTH
Public Safety	PUB. SAFETY
Real Property (1974)	REAL PROP.
Social Services	SOC. SERV.
State Government	STATE GOV'T
Taxation and Revenue	TAX. & REV.
Transportation (1977)	TRANSP.
Annotated Code of Maryland (1957)	MD. ANN. CODE art. x, § x (19xx)

Session laws

Laws of Maryland	19xx Md. Laws xxx

Administrative compilation

Code of Maryland Regulations	MD. ADMIN. CODE tit. x, § x (19xx)

Administrative register

Maryland Register		Md. Admin. Reg.

Massachusetts

Supreme Judicial Court (Mass.): Cite to Mass. or Mass. Adv. Sh. and to N.E. or N.E.2d if therein.

Massachusetts Reports		
97 Mass. to date	1868–date	Mass.
Allen	1861–1867	e.g., 83 Mass. (1 Allen)
Gray	1854–1860	e.g., 67 Mass. (1 Gray)
Cushing	1848–1853	e.g., 55 Mass. (1 Cush.)
Metcalf	1840–1847	e.g., 42 Mass. (1 Met.)
Pickering	1822–1839	e.g., 18 Mass. (1 Pick.)
1 Mass. to 17 Mass.	1804–1821	Mass.
Massachusetts S.J.C. Advance Sheets		19xx Mass. Adv. Sh. xxx
Northeastern Reporter	1884–date	N.E., N.E.2d

Appeals Court (Mass. App. Ct.): Cite to Mass. App. Ct. or Mass App. Ct. Adv. Sh. and to N.E.2d if therein.

Massachusetts Appeals Court Reports	1976–date	Mass. App. Ct.
Massachusetts Appeals Court Advance Sheets		19xx Mass. App. Ct. Adv. Sh. xxx
Northeastern Reporter	1972–date	N.E.2d

District Court (Mass. Dist. Ct.): Cite to Mass. App. Div. and Mass. App. Dec. if therein.

Appellate Decisions	1941–date	Mass. App. Dec.
Appellate Division Reports	1936–1950	Mass. App. Div.

Statutory compilations: Cite to either the West or Michie/Law. Co-op. edition.

Massachusetts General Laws Annotated (West)	MASS. GEN. LAWS ANN. ch. x, § x (West 19xx)
Annotated Laws of Massachusetts (Michie/Law. Co-op.)	MASS. ANN. LAWS ch. x, § x (Michie/Law. Co-op. 19xx)

Session laws

Acts and Resolves of Massachusetts	19xx Mass. Acts xxx
Massachusetts Advance Legislative Service (Law. Co-op.)	19xx Mass. Adv. Legis. Serv. xxx (Law. Co-op.)

Administrative compilation

Code of Massachusetts Regulations	MASS. ADMIN. CODE tit. x, § x (19xx)

Administrative register

Massachusetts Register	Mass. Admin. Reg.

Michigan

Supreme Court (Mich.): Cite to Mich. or Doug. and to N.W. or N.W.2d.

Michigan Reports	1847–date	Mich.
Douglass	1843–1847	Doug.
Northwestern Reporter	1879–date	N.W., N.W.2d

Court of Appeals (Mich. Ct. App.): Cite to Mich. App. and to N.W.2d.

Michigan Appeals Reports	1965–date	Mich. App.
Northwestern Reporter	1965–date	N.W.2d

Court of Claims (Mich. Ct. Cl.): Cite to Mich. Ct. Cl.

Michigan Court of Claims Reports	1938–1942	Mich. Ct. Cl.

Statutory compilations: Cite to MICH. COMP. LAWS if therein; otherwise cite to MICH. COMP. LAWS ANN. Cite to MICH. STAT. ANN. only under rule 12.3(h).

Michigan Compiled Laws (1970)	MICH. COMP. LAWS § x (19xx)
Michigan Compiled Laws Annotated (West)	MICH. COMP. LAWS ANN. § x (West 19xx)
Michigan Statutes Annotated (Callaghan)	MICH. STAT. ANN. § x (Callaghan 19xx)

Session laws: Cite to Mich. Pub. Acts if therein.

Public and Local Acts of the Legislature of the State of Michigan	19xx Mich. Pub. Acts xxx
Michigan Legislative Service (West)	19xx Mich. Legis. Serv. xxx (West)

Administrative compilation

Michigan Administrative Code (1954) (updated by supplements)	MICH. ADMIN. CODE R. x (19xx)

Minnesota

Supreme Court (Minn.): Cite to Minn. if therein and to N.W. or N.W.2d if therein.

Minnesota Reports	1851–1977	Minn.
Northwestern Reporter	1879–date	N.W., N.W.2d

Statutory compilations: Cite to MINN. STAT. if therein.

Minnesota Statutes (even-numbered years & Supp. odd-numbered years)	MINN. STAT. § x (19xx)
Minnesota Statutes Annotated (West)	MINN. STAT. ANN. § x (West 19xx)

Session laws: Cite to Minn. Laws if therein.

Laws of Minnesota	19xx Minn. Laws xxx
Minnesota Session Law Service (West)	19xx Minn. Sess. Law Serv. xxx (West)

Administrative compilation

Minnesota Code of Agency Rules		x MINN. CODE AGENCY R. § x (19xx)

Administrative register

Minnesota State Register		Minn. Admin. Reg.

Mississippi

Supreme Court (Miss.): Cite to Miss. if therein and to So. or So. 2d.

Mississippi Reports		
23 Miss. to 254 Miss.	1850–1966	Miss.
Smedes and Marshall	1843–1850	e.g., 9 Miss. (1 S. & M.)
Howard	1834–1843	e.g., 2 Miss. (1 Howard)
Walker	1818–1832	1 Miss. (1 Walker)
Southern Reporter	1886–date	So., So. 2d

Statutory compilation

Mississippi Code Annotated		MISS. CODE ANN. § x (19xx)

Session laws

General Laws of Mississippi		19xx Miss. Laws xxx

Missouri

Supreme Court (Mo.): Cite to Mo. if therein and to S.W. or S.W.2d.

Missouri Reports	1821–1956	Mo.
Southwestern Reporter	1886–date	S.W., S.W.2d

Court of Appeals (Mo. Ct. App.): Cite to Mo. App. if therein and to S.W. or S.W.2d.

Missouri Appeal Reports	1876–1951	Mo. App.
Southwestern Reporter	1902–date	S.W., S.W.2d

Statutory compilations: Cite to MO. REV. STAT. if therein.

Missouri Revised Statutes		MO. REV. STAT. § x (19xx)
Vernon's Annotated Missouri Statutes		MO. ANN. STAT. § x (Vernon 19xx)

Session laws: Cite to Mo. Laws if therein.

Laws of Missouri		19xx Mo. Laws xxx
Missouri Legislative Service		19xx Mo. Legis. Serv. xxx (Vernon)

Administrative compilation

Missouri Code of State Regulations		MO. ADMIN. CODE

Administrative register

Missouri Register		Mo. Admin. Reg.

Montana

Supreme Court (Mont.): Cite to Mont. and to P. or P.2d.

Montana Reports	1868–date	Mont.
Pacific Reporter	1882–date	P., P.2d

Statutory compilation

Montana Code Annotated		MONT. CODE ANN. § x (19xx)

Session laws

Laws of Montana		19xx Mont. Laws xxx

Administrative compilation

Administrative Rules of Montana		MONT. ADMIN. R. x (19xx)

Administrative register

Montana Administrative Register		Mont. Admin. Reg.

Nebraska

Supreme Court (Neb.): Cite to Neb. and to N.W. or N.W.2d.

Nebraska Reports	1860–date	Neb.
Northwestern Reporter	1879–date	N.W., N.W.2d

Statutory compilation

Revised Statutes of Nebraska		NEB. REV. STAT. § x (19xx)

Session laws

Laws of Nebraska		19xx Neb. Laws xxx

Administrative compilation

Nebraska Administrative Rules & Regulations		NEB. ADMIN. R. x (19xx)

Nevada

Supreme Court (Nev.): Cite to Nev. and to P. or P.2d.

Nevada Reports	1865–date	Nev.
Pacific Reporter	1882–date	P., P.2d

Statutory compilation

Nevada Revised Statutes		NEV. REV. STAT. § x (19xx)

Session laws

Statutes of Nevada		19xx Nev. Stat. xxx

Administrative compilation

Nevada Administrative Code		NEV. ADMIN. CODE

New Hampshire

Supreme Court (N.H.): Cite to N.H. and to A. or A.2d.

New Hampshire Reports	1816–date	N.H.
Atlantic Reporter	1886–date	A., A.2d

Statutory compilation

New Hampshire Revised Statutes Annotated		N.H. REV. STAT. ANN. § x (19xx)

Session laws

Laws of the State of New Hamsphire		19xx N.H. Laws xxx

Administrative compilation

New Hampshire Code of Administrative Rules		N.H. ADMIN. CODE

New Jersey

Supreme Court (N.J.), previously **Court of Errors and Appeals** (N.J.): Cite to N.J., N.J.L., N.J. Eq., or N.J. Misc. and to A. or A.2d.

New Jersey Reports	1948–date	N.J.
New Jersey Law Reports	1790–1948	N.J.L.
New Jersey Equity Reports	1830–1948	N.J. Eq.
New Jersey Miscellaneous Reports	1923–1949	N.J. Misc.
Atlantic Reporter	1885–date	A., A.2d

Superior Court (N.J. Super. Ct. App. Div., N.J. Super. Ct. Ch. Div., N.J. Super. Ct. Law Div.), previously **Court of Chancery** (N.J. Ch.), **Supreme Court** (N.J. Sup. Ct.), and **Prerogative Court** (N.J. Prerog. Ct.): Cite to N.J. Super., N.J.L., N.J. Eq., or N.J. Misc. and to A. or A.2d.

New Jersey Superior Court Reports	1948–date	N.J. Super.
New Jersey Law Reports	1790–1948	N.J.L.
New Jersey Equity Reports	1830–date	N.J. Eq.
New Jersey Miscellaneous Reports	1923–1949	N.J. Misc.
Atlantic Reporter	1885–date	A., A.2d

County Court (e.g., Essex County Ct.) and other lower courts: Cite to N.J. Super. or N.J. Misc. and to A.2d.

Statutory compilations: Cite to N.J. REV. STAT. if therein.

New Jersey Revised Statutes (1937)		N.J. REV. STAT. § x (19xx)

New Jersey Statutes Annotated (West)		N.J. STAT. ANN. § x (West 19xx)

Session laws: Cite to N.J. Laws if therein.

Laws of New Jersey		19xx N.J. Laws xxx
New Jersey Session Law Service (West)		19xx N.J. Sess. Law Serv. xxx (West)

Administrative compilation

New Jersey Administrative Code		N.J. ADMIN. CODE tit. x, § x (19xx)

Administrative register

New Jersey Register		N.J. Admin. Reg.

New Mexico

Supreme Court (N.M.): Cite to N.M. and to P. or P.2d.

New Mexico Reports		
5 N.M. to date	1890–date	N.M.
Gildersleeve Reports, E.W.S. ed. (Gild., B.-W. ed. and John. are unofficial reports and are not preferred.)	1883–1889	e.g., 3 N.M. (Gild., E.W.S. ed.)
Pacific Reporter	1883–date	P., P.2d

Court of Appeal (N.M. Ct. App.): Cite to N.M. and to P.2d.

New Mexico Reports	1967–date	N.M.
Pacific Reporter	1967–date	P.2d

Statutory compilation

New Mexico Statutes Annotated		N.M. STAT. ANN. § x (19xx)

Session laws

Laws of New Mexico		19xx N.M. Laws xxx

New York

Court of Appeals (N.Y.) after 1847: Cite to N.Y. or N.Y.2d, to N.E. or N.E.2d, and to N.Y.S.2d if therein.

New York Reports	1847–date	N.Y., N.Y.2d
Northeastern Reporter	1885–date	N.E., N.E.2d
West's New York Supplement (The first series of N.Y. is reprinted in N.Y.S. and N.Y.S.2d without separate pagination. Do not include a parallel cite to N.Y.S. or N.Y.S.2d in citations to the first series of N.Y.)	1938–date	N.Y.S.2d

Supreme Court, Appellate Division (N.Y. App. Div.): Cite to A.D., A.D.2d, N.Y. Sup. Ct., Lans., or Barb. and to N.Y.S. or N.Y.S.2d if therein.

Appellate Division Reports	1896–date	A.D., A.D.2d
Supreme Court Reports	1873–1896	N.Y. Sup. Ct.
Lansing's Reports	1869–1873	Lans.
Barbour's Supreme Court Reports	1847–1877	Barb.
West's New York Supplement	1888–date	N.Y.S., N.Y.S.2d

Other lower courts (e.g., N.Y. App. Term., N.Y. Sup. Ct., N.Y. Ct. Cl., N.Y. Civ. Ct., N.Y. Crim. Ct., N.Y. Fam. Ct.): Cite to Misc. or Misc. 2d and to N.Y.S. or N.Y.S.2d.

New York Miscellaneous Reports	1892–date	Misc., Misc. 2d
West's New York Supplement	1888–date	N.Y.S., N.Y.S.2d

Court for the Correction of Errors (N.Y.) and **Supreme Court of Judicature** (N.Y. Sup. Ct.): Cite to one of the following reporters.

Lockwood's Reversed Cases	1799–1847	Lock. Rev. Cas.
Denio's Reports	1845–1848	Denio
Hill and Denio Supplement (Lalor)	1842–1844	Hill & Den.
Hill's Reports	1841–1844	Hill
Wendell's Reports	1828–1841	Wend.
Cowen's Reports	1823–1829	Cow.
Johnson's Reports	1806–1823	Johns.
Caines' Reports	1803–1805	Cai. R.
Caines' Cases in Error	1796–1805	Cai. Cas.
Coleman & Caines' Cases	1794–1805	Cole. & Cai. Cas.
Johnson's Cases	1799–1803	Johns. Cas.
Coleman's Cases	1791–1800	Cole. Cas.

Court of Chancery (N.Y. Ch.): Cite to one of the following reporters.

Edwards' Chancery Reports	1831–1850	Edw. Ch.
Barbour's Chancery Reports	1845–1848	Barb. Ch.
Sandford's Chancery Reports	1843–1847	Sand. Ch.
Saratoga Chancery Sentinel	1841–1847	Sarat. Ch. Sent.
Paige's Chancery Reports	1828–1845	Paige Ch.
Clarke's Chancery Reports	1839–1841	Cl. Ch.
Hoffman's Chancery Reports	1838–1840	Hoff. Ch.
Hopkins' Chancery Reports	1823–1826	Hopk. Ch.
Johnson's Chancery Reports	1814–1823	Johns. Ch.

Other lower courts before 1888: Cite to Abb. N. Cas., Abb. Pr., or How. Pr.

Abbott's New Cases	1876–1894	Abb. N. Cas.
Abbott's Practice Reports	1854–1875	Abb. Pr., Abb. Pr. (n.s.)
Howard's Practice Reports	1844–1886	How. Pr., How. Pr. (n.s.)

Statutory compilations: Cite to McKinney's if therein.

McKinney's Consolidated Laws of New York Annotated	N.Y. [subject] LAW § x (McKinney 19xx)

Consolidated Laws Service	N.Y. [subjcct] LAW § x (Consol. 19xx)
Abandoned Property	ABAND. PROP.
Agricultural Conservation and Adjustment	AGRIC. CONSERV. & ADJ.
Agriculture and Markets	AGRIC. & MKTS.
Alcoholic Beverage Control	ALCO. BEV. CONT.
Alternative County Government	ALT. COUNTY GOV'T
Banking	BANKING
Benevolent Orders	BEN. ORD.
Business Corporation	BUS. CORP.
Canal	CANAL
Civil Practice Law and Rules	
Laws	N.Y. CIV. PRAC. LAW § x (McKinney 19xx) or: N.Y. CIV. PRAC. LAW § x (Consol. 19xx)
Rules	N.Y. CIV. PRAC. R. x (McKinney 19xx) or: N.Y. CIV. PRAC. R. x (Consol. 19xx)
Civil Rights	CIV. RIGHTS
Civil Service	CIV. SERV.
Commerce	COM.
Condemnation	CONDEM.
Cooperative Corporations	COOP. CORP.
Correction	CORRECT.
County	COUNTY
Criminal Procedure	CRIM. PROC.
Debtor and Creditor	DEBT. & CRED.
Domestic Relations	DOM. REL.
Education	EDUC.
Election	ELEC.
Employers' Liability	EMPL'RS LIAB.
Environmental Conservation	ENVTL. CONSERV.
Estates, Powers and Trusts	EST. POWERS & TRUSTS
Executive	EXEC.
General Associations	GEN. ASS'NS
General Business	GEN. BUS.
General City	GEN. CITY
General Construction	GEN. CONSTR.
General Municipal	GEN. MUN.
General Obligations	GEN. OBLIG.
Highway	HIGH.
Indian	INDIAN
Insurance	INS.

Judiciary	JUD.
Labor	LAB.
Legislative	LEGIS.
Lien	LIEN
Local Finance	LOCAL FIN.
Mental Hygiene	MENTAL HYG.
Military	MIL.
Multiple Dwelling	MULT. DWELL.
Multiple Residence	MULT. RESID.
Municipal Home Rule	MUN. HOME RULE
Navigation	NAV.
Not-for-Profit Corporation	NOT-FOR-PROFIT CORP.
Optional County Government	OPT. COUNTY GOV'T
Parks and Recreation	PARKS & REC.
Partnership	PARTNERSHIP
Penal	PENAL
Personal Property	PERS. PROP.
Private Housing Finance	PRIV. HOUS. FIN.
Public Authorities	PUB. AUTH.
Public Buildings	PUB. BLDGS.
Public Health	PUB. HEALTH
Public Housing	PUB. HOUS.
Public Lands	PUB. LANDS
Public Officers	PUB. OFF.
Public Service	PUB. SERV.
Railroad	R.R.
Rapid Transit	RAPID TRANS.
Real Property	REAL PROP.
Real Property Actions and Proceedings	REAL PROP. ACTS.
Real Property Tax	REAL PROP. TAX
Religious Corporations	RELIG. CORP.
Retirement and Social Security	RETIRE. & SOC. SEC.
Rural Electric Cooperative	RURAL ELEC. COOP.
Salt Springs	SALT SPRINGS
Second Class Cities	SECOND CLASS CITIES
Social Services	SOC. SERV.
Soil and Water Conservation Districts	SOIL & WATER CONSERV. DIST.
State	STATE
State Finance	STATE FIN.
State Printing	STATE PRINT.
Statute of Local Governments	STAT. LOCAL GOV'TS
Tax	TAX
Town	TOWN

Transportation	TRANSP.
Transportation Corporations	TRANSP. CORP.
Vehicle and Traffic	VEH. & TRAF.
Village	VILLAGE
Volunteer Firemen's Benefit	VOL. FIRE. BEN.
Workmen's Compensation	WORK. COMP.

Uncompiled laws: Cite to McKinney's if therein. For the user's convenience, the McKinney's volume in which the law appears is indicated parenthetically below.

McKinney's Consolidated Laws	N.Y. [law] § x (McKinney 19xx)
Consolidated Laws Service	N.Y. [law] § x (Consol. 19xx)
Administrative Procedure Act (56A)	A.P.A
New York City Civil Court Act (29A)	CITY CIV. CT. ACT
New York City Criminal Court Act (29A)	CITY CRIM. CT. ACT
Code of Criminal Procedure (66)	CODE CRIM. PROC.
Court of Claims Act (29A)	CT. CL. ACT
Family Court Act (29A)	FAM. CT. ACT
Surrogate's Court Procedure Act (58A)	SURR. CT. PROC. ACT
Uniform Commercial Code (62½)	U.C.C.
Unconsolidated Laws (65)	UNCONSOL. LAWS
Uniform City Court Act (29A)	UNIFORM CITY CT. ACT
Uniform District Court Act (29A)	UNIFORM DIST. CT. ACT
[Uniform] Justice Court Act (29A)	[UNIFORM] JUST. CT. ACT

Session laws

Laws of New York	19xx N.Y. Laws xxx

Administrative compilation

Official Compilation of Codes, Rules & Regulations of the State of New York	N.Y. ADMIN. CODE tit. x, § x (19xx)

North Carolina

Supreme Court (N.C.): Cite to N.C. and to S.E. or S.E.2d.

North Carolina Reports

63 N.C. to date	1868–date	N.C.
Phillips' Equity	1866–1868	62 N.C. (Phil. Eq.)
Phillips' Law	1866–1868	61 N.C. (Phil. Law)
Winston	1863–1864	60 N.C. (Win.)
Jones' Equity (54–59)	1853–1863	e.g., 54 N.C. (1 Jones Eq.)
Jones' Law (46–53)	1853–1862	e.g., 46 N.C. (1 Jones)
Busbee's Equity	1852–1853	45 N.C. (Busb. Eq.)

Busbee's Law	1852–1853	44 N.C. (Busb.)
Iredell's Equity (36–43)	1840–1852	e.g., 36 N.C. (1 Ired. Eq.)
Iredell's Law (23–35)	1840–1852	e.g., 23 N.C. (1 Ired.)
Devereux & Battle's Equity (21–22)	1834–1839	e.g., 21 N.C. (1 Dev. & Bat. Eq.)
Devereux & Battle's Law (18–20)	1834–1839	e.g., 20 N.C. (3 & 4 Dev. & Bat.)
Devereux's Equity (16–17)	1826–1834	e.g., 16 N.C. (1 Dev. Eq.)
Devereux's Law (12–15)	1826–1834	e.g., 12 N.C. (1 Dev.)
Hawks (8–11)	1820–1826	e.g., 8 N.C. (1 Hawks)
Murphey (5–7)	1804–1813, 1818–1819	e.g., 5 N.C. (1 Mur.)
Taylor's North Carolina Term Reports	1816–1818	4 N.C. (Taylor)
Carolina Law Repository	1811–1816	4 N.C. (Car. L. Rep.)
Haywood (2-3)	1789–1806	e.g., 2 N.C. (1 Hayw.)
Conference by Cameron & Norwood	1800–1804	1 N.C. (Cam. & Nor.)
Taylor	1798–1802	1 N.C. (Tay.)
Martin	1778–1797	1 N.C. (Mart.)
Southeastern Reporter	1887–date	S.E., S.E.2d

Court of Appeals (N.C. Ct. App.): Cite to N.C. App. and to S.E.2d.

North Carolina Court of Appeals Reports	1968–date	N.C. App.
Southeastern Reporter	1968–date	S.E.2d

Statutory compilation

General Statutes of North Carolina (official compilation published by Michie)	N.C. GEN. STAT. § x (19xx)

Session laws: Cite to N.C. Sess. Laws if therein.

Session Laws of North Carolina	19xx N.C. Sess. Laws xxx
Advance Legislative Service to the General Statutes of North Carolina	19xx N.C. Adv. Legis. Serv. xxx

Administrative compilation

North Carolina Adminstrative Code	N.C. ADMIN. CODE

North Dakota

Supreme Court (N.D.): Cite to N.D. if therein and to N.W. or N.W.2d.

North Dakota Reports	1890–1953	N.D.
Northwestern Reporter	1890–date	N.W., N.W.2d

Supreme Court of Dakota (Dakota): Cite to Dakota and to N.W.

Dakota Reports	1867–1889	Dakota
Northwestern Reporter	1867–1889	N.W.

Statutory compilation

North Dakota Century Code	N.D. CENT. CODE § x (19xx)

Session Laws

Laws of North Dakota	19xx N.D. Sess. Laws xxx

Administrative compilation

North Dakota Administrative Code	N.D. ADMIN. CODE § x (19xx)

Ohio

Supreme Court (Ohio): Cite to Ohio St., Ohio St. 2d, or Ohio and to N.E. or N.E.2d.

Ohio State Reports	1852–date	Ohio St., Ohio St. 2d
Ohio Reports	1821–1851	Ohio
Northeastern Reporter	1885–date	N.E., N.E.2d

Court of Appeals (Ohio Ct. App.): Cite to Ohio App. or Ohio App. 2d and to N.E. or N.E.2d.

Ohio Appellate Reports	1913–date	Ohio App., Ohio App. 2d
Northeastern Reporter	1921–date	N.E., N.E.2d

Other law courts: Cite to Ohio Misc. if therein; otherwise cite to another reporter in the following order of preference.

Ohio Miscellaneous	1965–date	Ohio Misc.
Ohio Opinions	1934–date	Ohio Op., Ohio Op. 2d, Ohio Op. 3d
Ohio Nisi Prius Reports	1894–1934	Ohio N.P., Ohio N.P. (n.s.)
Ohio Decisions	1894–1920	Ohio Dec.
Ohio Decisions, Reprint	1840–1893	Ohio Dec. Reprint
Ohio Circuit Court Decisions	1902–1923	e.g., 13-23 Ohio C.C. Dec.
Ohio Circuit Court Reports (Jahn)	1885–1901	Ohio C.C.
Ohio Circuit Decisions	1885–1901	Ohio Cir. Dec.
Ohio Circuit Court Reports, New Series	1903–1917	Ohio C.C. (n.s.)

Statutory compilations: Cite to one of the following codes.

Ohio Revised Code Annotated (Page)	OHIO REV. CODE ANN. § x (Page 19xx)
Ohio Revised Code Annotated (Baldwin)	OHIO REV. CODE ANN. § x (Baldwin 19xx)

Session laws: Cite to Ohio Laws if therein.

State of Ohio: Legislative Acts Passed and Joint Resolutions Adopted	19xx Ohio Laws xxx

Ohio Legislative Bulletin (Anderson)		19xx Ohio Legis. Bull. xxx (Anderson)
Baldwin's Ohio Legislative Service		19xx Ohio Legis. Serv. xxx (Baldwin)

Administrative compilation

Ohio Administrative Code (official compilation published by Banks-Baldwin)	1977–date	OHIO ADMIN. CODE § x (19xx)

Administrative and executive registers

Ohio Monthly Record (Banks-Baldwin)	1977–date	Ohio Monthly Rec.
Ohio Government Reports	1965–date	Ohio Gov't
Ohio Department Reports	1914–1964	Ohio Dep't

Oklahoma

Supreme Court (Okla.): Cite to Okla. if therein and to P. or P.2d.

Oklahoma Reports	1890–1953	Okla.
Pacific Reporter	1890–date	P., P.2d

Court of Appeals of Indian Territory (Indian Terr.): Cite to Indian Terr. and to S.W.

Indian Territory Reports	1896–1907	Indian Terr.
Southwestern Reporter	1896–1907	S.W.

Court of Criminal Appeals (Okla. Crim. App.), before 1959 **Criminal Court of Appeals** (Okla. Crim. App.): Cite to Okla. Crim. if therein and to P. or P.2d.

Oklahoma Criminal Reports	1908–1953	Okla. Crim.
Pacific Reporter	1908–date	P., P.2d

Court of Appeals (Okla. Ct. App.): Cite to P.2d.

Pacific Reporter	1969–date	P.2d

Statutory compilations: Cite to OKLA. STAT. if therein.

Oklahoma Statutes (1971 & Supp. 1978)		OKLA. STAT. tit. x, § x (19xx)
Oklahoma Statutes Annotated (West)		OKLA. STAT. ANN. tit. x, § x (West 19xx)

Session laws: Cite to Okla. Sess. Laws if therein.

Oklahoma Session Laws		19xx Okla. Sess. Laws xxx
Oklahoma Session Law Service (West)		19xx Okla. Sess. Law Serv. xxx (West)

Administrative register

Oklahoma Gazette		Okla. Gaz.

Oregon

Supreme Court (Or.): Cite to Or. and to P. or P.2d.

Oregon Reports	1853–date	Or.
Pacific Reporter	1883–date	P., P.2d

Court of Appeals (Or. Ct. App.): Cite to Or. App. and to P.2d.

Oregon Reports, Court of Appeals	1969–date	Or. App.
Pacific Reports	1969–date	P.2d

Tax Court (Or. T.C.): Cite to Or. T.R.

Oregon Tax Reports	1962–date	Or. T.R.

Statutory compilation

Oregon Revised Statutes		OR. REV. STAT. § x (19xx)

Session laws: Cite to Or. Laws. In citing statutes repealed during or after 1953, indicate parenthetically the former OR. REV. STAT. sections.

Oregon Laws and Resolutions		19xx Or. Laws xxx, 19xx Or. Laws Spec. Sess. xxx, 19xx Or. Laws Adv. Sh. No. xxx

Administrative compilation

Oregon Administrative Rules		OR. ADMIN. R. x (19xx)

Administrative register

Administrative Rules Bulletin		Or. Admin. R. Bull.

Pennsylvania

Supreme Court (Pa.): Cite to one reporter (other than A. or A.2d) below and to A. or A.2d.

Pennsylvania State Reports	1845–date	Pa.
Watts and Sergeant	1841–1845	Watts & Serg.
Wharton	1835–1841	Whart.
Watts	1832–1840	Watts
Rawle	1828–1835	Rawle
Penrose and Watts	1829–1832	Pen. & W.
Sergeant and Rawle	1814–1828	Serg. & Rawle
Binney	1799–1814	Binn.
Yeates	1791–1808	Yeates
Addison	1793–1799	Add.
Dallas	1754–1806	Dall.
Atlantic Reporter	1885–date	A., A.2d

Superior Court (Pa. Super. Ct.): Cite to Pa. Super. and to A. or A.2d.

Pennsylvania Superior Court Reports	1895–date	Pa. Super.
Atlantic Reporter	1931–date	A., A.2d

Commonwealth Court (Pa. Commw. Ct.): Cite to Pa. Commw. and to A.2d.

Pennsylvania Commonwealth Court Reports	1970–date	Pa. Commw.
Atlantic Reporter	1970–date	A.2d

Other lower courts: Cite to the legal reporter for the county, if available, and to Pa. D. & C., Pa. D. & C.2d, or Pa. D. & C.3d, if therein. Otherwise cite to Pa. D., Pa. C., or Pa. Fiduc.

Pennsylvania District and County Reports	1921–date	Pa. D. & C., Pa. D. & C.2d, Pa. D. & C.3d
Pennsylvania District Reports	1892–1921	Pa. D.
Pennsylvania County Reports	1885–1921	Pa. C.
Pennsylvania Fiduciary Reporter	1951–date	Pa. Fiduc.

Statutory compilations: Pennsylvania is undertaking its first official codification, PA. CONS. STAT.; the old, unofficial compilation is Purdon's PA. STAT. ANN., which uses a different numbering system. Purdon is also reprinting the new, official codification as PA. CONS. STAT. ANN., which is currently bound with PA. STAT. ANN. Cite to PA. CONS. STAT. or PA. CONS. STAT. ANN., in that order of preference. If the statute is contained in neither source, cite to PA. STAT. ANN. (*see* rule 12.3 (h)). These publications should not be confused with Pennsylvania Code, which is a code of regulations, not of legislation.

Pennsylvania Consolidated Statutes	x PA. CONS. STAT. § x (19xx)
Pennsylvania Consolidated Statutes Annotated (Purdon)	x PA. CONS. STAT. ANN. § x (Purdon 19xx)
Purdon's Pennsylvania Statutes Annotated	PA. STAT. ANN. tit. x, § x (Purdon 19xx)

Session laws

Laws of the General Assembly of the Commonwealth of Pennsylvania	19xx Pa. Laws xxx
Pennsylvania Legislative Service (Purdon)	19xx Pa. Legis. Serv. xxx (Purdon)

Administrative compilation

Pennsylvania Code (Shepard's)	x PA. ADMIN. CODE § x (Shepard's 19xx)

Administrative register

Pennsylvania Bulletin	Pa. Admin. Bull.

Puerto Rico

Supreme Court (P.R.): Cite to P.R. if therein and to P.R. Dec. or P.R. Sent., in that order of preference.

Puerto Rico Reports	1899–1972	P.R.
Decisiones de Puerto Rico	1899–date	P.R. Dec.
Sentencias del Tribunal Supremo de Puerto Rico	1899–1902	P.R. Sent.

Statutory compilation

Puerto Rico Laws Annotated		P.R. LAWS ANN. tit. x, § x (19xx)

Session laws

Laws of Puerto Rico		19xx P.R. Laws xxx

Administrative compilation

Commonwealth of Puerto Rico Rules and Regulations		P.R.R. & REGS. tit. x, § x (19xx)

Rhode Island

Supreme Court (R.I.): Cite to R.I. and to A. or A.2d.

Rhode Island Reports	1828–date	R.I.
Atlantic Reporter	1885–date	A., A.2d

Statutory compilation

General Laws of Rhode Island		R.I. GEN. LAWS § x (19xx)

Session laws

Public Laws of Rhode Island		19xx R.I. Pub. Laws xxx

South Carolina

Supreme Court after 1868 (S.C.): Cite to S.C. and to S.E. or S.E.2d.

South Carolina Reports	1868–date	S.C.
Southeastern Reporter	1886–date	S.E., S.E.2d

Courts of law before 1868: Cite to S.C.L.

South Carolina Law Reports		
Richardson (37–49)	1850–1868	e.g., 37 S.C.L. (4 Rich.)
Strobhart (32–36)	1846–1850	e.g., 32 S.C.L. (1 Strob.)
Richardson (30–31)	1844–1846	e.g., 30 S.C.L. (1 Rich.)
Speers (28–29)	1842–1844	e.g., 28 S.C.L. (1 Speers)
McMullan (26–27)	1840–1842	e.g., 26 S.C.L. (1 McMul.)

G

Cheves	1839–1840	25 S.C.L. (Chev.)
Rice	1838–1839	24 S.C.L. (Rice)
Dudley	1837–1838	23 S.C.L. (Dud.)
Riley	1836–1387	22 S.C.L. (Ril.)
Hill (19–21)	1833–1837	e.g., 19 S.C.L. (1 Hill)
Richardson (18)	1832	18 S.C.L. (3 Rich.)
Bailey (17–18)	1828–1832	e.g., 17 S.C.L. (1 Bail.)
Harper	1823–1828, 1830–1831	16 S.C.L. (Harp.)
McCord (12–15)	1821–1828	e.g., 12 S.C.L. (1 McCord)
Nott and McCord (10–11)	1817–1820	e.g., 10 S.C.L. (1 Nott & McC.)
Mill's Constitutional Court Reports (8–9)	1817–1818	e.g., 8 S.C.L. (1 Mill)
Treadway (6–7)	1812–1816	e.g., 6 S.C.L. (1 Tread.)
Brevard (3–5)	1793–1816	e.g., 3 S.C.L. (1 Brev.)
Bay (1–2)	1783–1804	e.g., 1 S.C.L. (1 Bay)

Courts of equity before 1868: Cite to S.C. Eq.

South Carolina Equity Reports

Richardson's Equity (24–35)	1850–1868	e.g., 24 S.C. Eq. (3 Rich. Eq.)
Strobhart's Equity (20–23)	1846–1850	e.g., 20 S.C. Eq. (1 Strob. Eq.)
Richardson's Equity (18–19)	1844–1846	e.g., 18 S.C. Eq. (1 Rich. Eq.)
Speers' Equity	1842–1844	17 S.C. Eq. (Speers Eq.)
McMullan's Equity	1840–1842	16 S.C. Eq. (McMul. Eq.)
Cheves' Equity	1839–1840	15 S.C. Eq. (Chev. Eq.)
Rice's Equity	1838–1839	14 S.C. Eq. (Rice Eq.)
Dudley's Equity	1837–1838	13 S.C. Eq. (Dud. Eq.)
Riley's Chancery	1836–1837	12 S.C. Eq. (Ril.)
Hill's Chancery (10–11)	1833–1837	e.g., 10 S.C. Eq. (1 Hill Eq.)
Richardson's Cases	1831–1832	9 S.C. Eq. (Rich. Cas.)
Bailey's Equity	1830–1831	8 S.C. Eq. (Bail. Eq.)
McCord's Chancery (6–7)	1825–1827	e.g., 6 S.C. Eq. (1 McCord Eq.)
Harper's Equity	1824	5 S.C. Eq. (Harp. Eq.)
Desaussure's Equity (1–4)	1784–1817	e.g., 1 S.C. Eq. (1 Des.)

Statutory compilation

Code of Laws of South Carolina 1976 Annotated (Law. Co-op.)	S.C. CODE ANN. § x (Law. Co-op. 19xx)

Session laws

Acts and Joint Resolutions, South Carolina	19xx S.C. Acts xxx

Administrative compilation: Cite to volumes 23–26 of S.C. CODE ANN.

South Dakota

Supreme Court (S.D.): Cite to S.D. if therein and to N.W. or N.W.2d.

South Dakota Reports	1890–1976	S.D.
Northwestern Reporter	1890–date	N.W., N.W.2d

Supreme Court of Dakota (Dakota): Cite to Dakota and to N.W.

Dakota Reports	1867–1889	Dakota
Northwestern Reporter	1867–1889	N.W.

Statutory compilations: Cite to S.D. CODIFIED LAWS ANN. if therein.

South Dakota Codified Laws Annotated	S.D. CODIFIED LAWS ANN. § x (19xx)
South Dakota Compiled Laws Annotated	S.D. COMP. LAWS ANN. § x (19xx)

Session laws

Laws of South Dakota	19xx S.D. Sess. Laws xxx

Administrative compilation

Administrative Rules of South Dakota	S.D. ADMIN. R. x (19xx)

Administrative register

South Dakota Register	S.D. Admin. Reg.

Tennessee

Supreme Court (Tenn.): Cite to Tenn. if therein and to S.W. or S.W.2d.

Tennessee Reports		
60 Tenn. to 225 Tenn.	1870–1971	Tenn.
Heiskell	1870–1876	e.g., 48 Tenn. (1 Heisk.)
Coldwell	1860–1870	e.g., 41 Tenn. (1 Cold.)
Head	1858–1859	e.g., 38 Tenn. (1 Head)
Sneed	1853–1858	e.g., 33 Tenn. (1 Sneed)
Swan	1851–1853	e.g., 31 Tenn. (1 Swan)
Humphreys	1839–1851	e.g., 20 Tenn. (1 Hum.)
Meigs	1838–1839	19 Tenn. (Meigs)
Yerger	1828–1837	e.g., 9 Tenn. (1 Yer.)
Martin & Yerger	1825–1828	8 Tenn. (Mart. & Yer.)
Peck	1821–1824	7 Tenn. (Peck)
Haywood	1816–1818	e.g., 4 Tenn. (1 Hayw.)
Cooke	1811–1814	3 Tenn. (Cooke)
Overton	1791–1816	e.g., 1 Tenn. (1 Overt.)
Southwestern Reporter	1886–date	S.W., S.W.2d

Court of Appeals (Tenn. Ct. App.): Cite to Tenn. App. if therein and to S.W.2d.

Tennessee Appeals	1925–1971	Tenn. App.
Southwestern Reporter	1932–date	S.W.2d

G

Court of Chancery Appeals (Tenn. Ch. App.) and **Court of Criminal Appeals** (Tenn. Crim. App.): Cite to Tenn. Crim. App. if therein and to S.W.2d.

Tennessee Criminal Appeals Reports	1967–1971	Tenn. Crim. App.
Southwestern Reporter	1967–date	S.W.2d

Statutory compilation

Tennessee Code Annotated	TENN. CODE ANN. § x (19xx)

Session laws

Public Acts of the State of Tennessee	19xx Tenn. Pub. Acts xxx
Private Acts of the State of Tennessee	19xx Tenn. Priv. Acts xxx

Administrative compilation

Official Compilation Rules & Regulations of the State of Tennessee	TENN. ADMIN. COMP.

Administrative register

Tennessee Administrative Register	Tenn. Admin. Reg.

Texas

Supreme Court (Tex.): Cite to Tex. or Dallam if therein and to S.W. or S.W.2d.

Texas Reports	1846–1962	Tex.
Dallam's Opinions	1840–1844	Dallam
Southwestern Reporter	1886–date	S.W., S.W.2d

Court of Appeals (Tex. Ct. App.), previously **Court of Civil Appeals** (Tex. Civ. App.): Cite to Tex. Civ. App. or Tex. Civ. Cas., if therein, and to S.W.2d.

Texas Civil Appeals Reports	1892–1911	Tex. Civ. App.
Texas Court of Appeals Decisions, Civil Cases (White & Willson)	1876–1892	Tex. Civ. Cas.
Southwestern Reporter	1932–date	S.W.2d

Court of Criminal Appeals (Tex. Crim. App.): Cite to Tex. Crim. if therein and to S.W. or S.W.2d.

Texas Criminal Reports (Texas Court of Appeals Reports)	1876–1963	Tex. Crim.
Southwestern Reporter	1892–date	S.W., S.W.2d

Texas Court of Appeals (Tex. Ct. App.): Cite to Tex. App. and to S.W.

Texas Appeals Reports	1873–1892	Tex. App.
Southwestern Reporter	1886–1892	S.W.

Statutory compilations: Texas is undertaking a recodification of its laws. Cite to the new subject-matter TEX. CODE ANN. if therein; otherwise cite to TEX. STAT. ANN. Note that the older codification contains several independent codes; these are not part of the new subject-matter TEX. CODE ANN. Volumes of the new code available as of March 1982 are followed by their year of publication.

Texas Codes Annotated (Vernon)	TEX. [subject] CODE ANN. § x (Vernon 19xx)
Agriculture	AGRIC.
Alcoholic Beverage (1978)	ALCO. BEV.
Business and Commerce (1968)	BUS. & COM.
Civil	CIV.
Corporations and Associations	CORPS. & ASS'NS
Criminal Procedure	CRIM. PROC.
Education (1972)	EDUC.
Election	ELEC.
Family (1975)	FAM.
Financial	FIN.
Government	GOV'T
Health and Safety	HEALTH & SAFETY
Highway	HIGH.
Human Resources (1980)	HUM. RES.
Insurance	INS.
Labor	LAB.
Natural Resources (1978)	NAT. RES.
Occupations	OCC.
Parks and Wildlife (1976)	PARKS & WILD.
Penal (1974)	PENAL
Probate	PROB.
Property	PROP.
Resources	RES.
Tax (1979)	TAX
Utilities	UTIL.
Vehicles	VEH.
Water (1972)	WATER
Welfare	WELF.
Texas Statutes Annotated (Vernon)	TEX. STAT. ANN. art. x (Vernon 19xx)
Texas Revised Civil Statutes Annotated (Vernon)	TEX. REV. CIV. STAT. ANN. art. x (Vernon 19xx)
Texas Business Corporation Act Annotated (Vernon)	TEX. BUS. CORP. ACT ANN. art. x (Vernon 19xx)
Texas Code of Criminal Procedure of 1965 Annotated (Vernon)	TEX. CODE CRIM. PROC. ANN. art. x (Vernon 19xx)
Texas Election Code of 1951 Annotated (Vernon)	TEX. ELEC. CODE ANN. art. x (Vernon 19xx)
Texas Insurance Code of 1951 (Vernon)	TEX. INS. CODE ANN. art. x (Vernon 19xx)

G

Texas Probate Code of 1955 Annotated (Vernon)		TEX. PROB. CODE ANN. art. x (Vernon 19xx)
Texas Taxation-General Annotated (Vernon)		TEX. TAX.-GEN. ANN. art. x (Vernon 19xx)
Texas Rules Annotated (Vernon)		TEX. [subject] RULES ANN. R. x (Vernon 19xx)
Civil Procedure (1979)		CIV. PROC.

Session laws: Cite to Tex. Gen. Laws if therein.

General and Special Laws of the State of Texas		19xx Tex. Gen. Laws xxx
Texas Session Law Service (Vernon)		19xx Tex. Sess. Law Serv. xxx (Vernon)

Administrative compilation

Texas Administrative Code		TEX. ADMIN. CODE tit. x, § x (19xx)

Administrative register

Texas Register		Tex. Admin. Reg.

Utah

Supreme Court (Utah): Cite to Utah or Utah 2d if therein and to P. or P.2d.

Utah Reports	1855–1974	Utah, Utah 2d
Pacific Reporter	1881–date	P., P.2d

Statutory compilation

Utah Code Annotated		UTAH CODE ANN. § x (19xx)

Session laws

Laws of Utah		19xx Utah Laws xxx

Administrative compilation

Administrative Rules of the State of Utah		UTAH ADMIN. R. x (19xx)

Administrative register

State of Utah Bulletin		Utah Admin. Bull.

Vermont

Supreme Court (Vt.): Cite to one of the following reporters (other than A. and A.2d) and to A. or A.2d.

Vermont Reports	1826–date	Vt.
Aikens	1825–1828	Aik.
Chipman, D.	1789–1824	D. Chip.

Brayton	1815–1819	Brayt.
Tyler	1800–1803	Tyl.
Chipman, N.	1789–1791	N. Chip.
Atlantic Reporter	1885–date	A., A.2d

Statutory compilation

Vermont Statutes Annotated	VT. STAT. ANN. tit. x, § x (19xx)

Session laws

Laws of Vermont	19xx Vt. Acts xxx

Administrative compilation

Vermont Administrative Procedures Compilation	VT. ADMIN. COMP. [agency name] R. [or §] x (19xx)

Administrative register

Vermont Administrative Procedures Bulletin	Vt. Admin. Bull.

Virgin Islands

All courts

Virgin Island Reports	1917–date	V.I.

Statutory compilation

Virgin Islands Code Annotated	V.I. CODE ANN. tit. x, § x (19xx)

Session laws

Virgin Islands Session Laws	19xx V.I. Acts xxx

Administrative compilation

Virgin Islands Rules and Regulations	V.I.R. & REGS. tit. x, § x (19xx)

Virginia

Supreme Court (Va.), previously **Supreme Court of Appeals** (Va.): Cite to Va. and to S.E. or S.E.2d.

Virginia Reports		
75 Va. to date	1881–date	Va.
Grattan	1844–1880	e.g., 42 Va. (1 Gratt.)
Robinson	1842–1843	e.g., 40 Va. (1 Rob.)
Leigh	1829–1842	e.g., 28 Va. (1 Leigh)
Randolph	1821–1828	e.g., 22 Va. (1 Rand.)

G

Gilmer	1820–1821	21 Va. (Gilmer)
Munford	1810–1820	e.g., 15 Va. (1 Munf.)
Henning & Munford	1806–1810	e.g., 11 Va. (1 Hen. & M.)
Call	1797–1825	e.g., 5 Va. (1 Call)
Virginia Cases, Criminal	1789–1826	e.g., 3 Va. (1 Va. Cas.)
Washington	1790–1796	e.g., 1 Va. (1 Wash.)
Southeastern Reporter	1887–date	S.E., S.E.2d

Statutory compilation

Code of Virginia — VA. CODE § x (19xx)

Session laws

Acts of the General Assembly of the Commonwealth of Virginia — 19xx Va. Acts xxx

Washington

Supreme Court (Wash.): Cite to Wash., Wash. 2d, or Wash. Terr. and to P. or P.2d.

Washington Reports	1889–date	Wash., Wash. 2d
Washington Territory Reports	1854–1888	Wash. Terr.
Pacific Reporter	1880–date	P., P.2d

Court of Appeals (Wash. Ct. App.): Cite to Wash. App. and to P.2d.

Washington Appellate Reports	1969–date	Wash. App.
Pacific Reporter	1969–date	P.2d

Statutory compilations: Cite to WASH. REV. CODE if therein.

Revised Code of Washington (1974) — WASH. REV. CODE § x (1974)

Revised Code of Washington Annotated — WASH. REV. CODE ANN. § x (19xx)

Session laws: Cite to Wash. Laws if therein.

Laws of Washington — 19xx Wash. Laws xxx

Washington Legislative Service (West) — 19xx Wash. Legis. Serv. xxx (West)

Administrative compilation

Washington Administrative Code — WASH. ADMIN. CODE R. x (19xx)

Administrative register

Washington State Register — Wash. Admin. Reg.

West Virginia

Supreme Court of Appeals (W. Va.): Cite to W. Va. if therein and to S.E. or S.E.2d.

West Virginia Reports	1863–1973	W. Va.
Southeastern Reporter	1886–date	S.E., S.E.2d

Statutory compilation

West Virginia Code	W. VA. CODE § x (19xx)

Session laws

Acts of the Legislature of West Virginia	19xx W. Va. Acts xxx

Wisconsin

Supreme Court (Wis.): Cite to Wis., Wis. 2d, Pin., Chand., or Bur. and to N.W. or N.W.2d.

Wisconsin Reports	1853–date	Wis., Wis. 2d
Pinney	1839–1852	Pin.
Chandler	1849–1852	Chand.
Burnett	1842–1843	Bur.
Burnett (bound with session laws for Dec. 1841)	1841	Bur.
Northwestern Reporter	1879–date	N.W., N.W.2d

Court of Appeals (Wis. Ct. App.): Cite to Wis. 2d and to N.W.2d.

Wisconsin Reports	1978–date	Wis. 2d
Northwestern Reporter	1978–date	N.W.2d

Statutory compilations: Cite to WIS. STAT. if therein.

Wisconsin Statutes (1975 and biannually)	WIS. STAT. § x (19xx)
West's Wisconsin Statutes Annotated	WIS. STAT. ANN. § x (West 19xx)

Session laws: Cite to Wis. Laws if therein.

Laws of Wisconsin	19xx Wis. Laws xxx
Wisconsin Legislative Service (West)	19xx Wis. Legis. Serv. xxx (West)

Administrative compilation

Wisconsin Administrative Code	WIS. ADMIN. CODE § [agency name as abbreviated in Code] x (19xx)

Administrative register

Wisconsin Administrative Register	Wis. Admin. Reg.

G

Wyoming

Supreme Court (Wyo.): Cite to Wyo. if therein and to P. or P.2d.

Wyoming Reports	1870–1959	Wyo.
Pacific Reporter	1883–date	P., P.2d

Statutory compilation

Wyoming Statutes	WYO. STAT. § x (19xx)

Session laws

Session Laws of Wyoming	19xx Wyo. Sess. Laws xxx

G

H Tables: Foreign

Common Law Jurisdictions 179

Other Jurisdictions 190

Common Law Jurisdictions

Australia

Privy Council (P.C.) and **High Court of Australia** (Austl.): Cite to reports listed under **United Kingdom** if therein; otherwise cite to a report below, in the following order of preference.

Commonwealth Law Reports	1903–date	C.L.R.
Australian Law Reports	1973–date	Austl. L.R.
Argus Law Reports	1895–1959	Argus L.R.
Australian Argus Law Reports	1960–date	Austl. Argus L.R.

Other federal courts: Cite to one report below, in the following order of preference. Begin the parenthetical phrase after the report citation with "Austl."

Federal Law Reports	1956–date	F.L.R.
Commonwealth Arbitration Reports	1905–date	C.A.R.
Australasian Tax Reports	1970–date	A.T.R.
Australian and New Zealand Income Tax Reports	1951–1969	A.N.Z.I.T.R.
Australian Income Tax Reports	1940–1948	I.T.R.

Statutory and regulatory compilations

Acts of the Australian Parliament	AUSTL. ACTS P.
Commonwealth Acts	AUSTL. C. ACTS
Statutory Rules, Consolidation	AUSTL. STAT. R. CONSOL.

Session laws and regulations

Acts of the Parliaments of the Commonwealth of Australia	Austl. Acts
Official Commonwealth Statutory Rules	Austl. Stat. R.

Digests

Australia Legal Monthly Digest	1947–1973	Austl. L.M.D.
Australian Annual Digest	1897–1939	Austl. A.D.
The Australian Digest	1925–1947	Austl. D.
The Australian Digest, Second Edition	1966	Austl. D.2d

Australian States and Territories

Courts: Cite to a report below, in the following order of preference; otherwise cite to an Argus report.

Federal Law Reports	1956–date	F.L.R.
New South Wales State Reports	1901–date	N.S.W. St. R.
New South Wales Law Reports	1880–1900	N.S.W.L.R.
New South Wales Supreme Court Reports	1862–1880	N.S.W.S. Ct. R.
New South Wales Supreme Court Cases	1825–1862	N.S.W.S. Ct. Cas.

New South Wales Weekly Notes	1884–date	N.S.W.W.N.
New South Wales Reports	1960–date	N.S.W.R.
New South Wales Industrial Arbitration Reports	1902–date	N.S.W. Indus. Arb. R.
New South Wales Local Government Reports	1913–1932	N.S.W. Local Gov't R.
New South Wales Land Appeal Court Cases	1890–1921	N.S.W. Land App.
New South Wales Worker's Compensation Reports	1926–date	N.S.W. Worker's Comp. R.
Queensland Reports	1958–date	Queensl. R.
Queensland State Reports	1902–1957	Queensl. St. R.
Queensland Law Journal and State Reports	1902–1907	Queensl. L.J. & St. R.
Queensland Law Journal and Reports	1879–1901	Queensl. L.J. & R.
Queensland Law Reports	1876–1878	Queensl. L.R.
Queensland Supreme Court Reports	1860–1881	Queensl. S. Ct. R.
Queensland Lawyer	1973–date	Queensl. Law.
Queensland Justice of the Peace Reports	1907–1972	Queensl. J.P.R.
Queensland Land Court Reports	1974–date	Queensl. Land Ct. R.
Crown Lands Law Report—Queensland	1859–1973	Queensl. Cr. Lands L.R.
South Australia State Reports	1922–date	S. Austl. St. R.
South Australia Law Reports	1867–1921	S. Austl. L.R.
South Australia Industrial Reports	1916–date	S. Austl. Indus. R.
Tasmania State Reports	1958–date	Tasm. St. R.
Tasmania Law Reports	1905–1957	Tasm. L.R.
Victorian Reports	1957–date	Vict. R.
Victorian Law Reports	1870–1956	Vict. L.R.
Australian Jurist Reports	1870–1874	Austl. Jur. R.
Reports of Cases . . . Supreme Court of Victoria	1861–1869	Vict. S. Ct.
Western Australia Reports	1960–date	W. Austl. R.
Western Australia Law Reports	1899–1959	W. Austl. L.R.

Statutory compilations

Laws of the Australian Capital Territory (in force on Jan. 1, 1960)	1911–1959	AUSTL. CAP. TERR. LAWS
Public Acts of New South Wales	1824–1957	N.S.W. PUB. ACTS
Public Acts of Queensland (Reprint)	1828–1936	QUEENSL. PUB. ACTS
Public General Acts of South Australia	1837–1936	S. AUSTL. PUB. GEN. ACTS
South Australian Statutes	1837–1975	S. AUSTL. STAT.
Tasmanian Statutes	1826–1959	TASM. STAT.
Victorian Statutes: the General Public Acts		VICT. STAT.
Reprinted Acts of Western Australia		W. AUSTL. REPR. ACTS

Session laws

Ordinances of The Australian Capital Territory		Austl. Cap. Terr. Ord.
Subsidiary Legislation of the Australian Capital Territory		Austl. Cap. Terr. Subs. Leg.
Statutes of New South Wales	1875–date	N.S.W. Stat.
New South Wales: Public Statutes	1824–1874	N.S.W. Pub. Stat.
New South Wales Rules, Regulations, and By-Laws	1899–date	N.S.W.R. Regs. & B.
New South Wales Incorporated Acts	1944–date	N.S.W. Inc. Acts
Northern Territorial Ordinances	1917–date	N. Terr. Austl. Ord.
Queensland Statutes	1941–date	Queensl. Stat.
Queensland Acts	1896–1940	Queensl. Acts
South Australia Statutes	1936–date	S. Austl. Sess. Stat.
South Australia Acts	1866–1936	S. Austl. Acts
Acts and Ordinances of South Australia	1837–1866	S. Austl. Acts & Ord.
Tasmania Statutes	1960–date	Tasm. Sess. Stat.
Tasmania Acts of Parliament	1901–1959	Tasm. Acts
Tasmanian Statutory Rules, with Tables		Tasm. Stat. R.
Acts of Van Dieman's Land		Van Diem. L. Acts
Victoria Acts of Parliament	1890–date	Vict. Acts
Victoria Statutory Rules, Regulations, and By-Laws		Vict. Stat. R. Regs. & B.
Statutes of Western Australia	1918–date	W. Austl. Stat.
Western Australia Acts	1896–1917	W. Austl. Acts
Western Australia Statutes	1832–1895	W. Austl. Stat.

Canada

Privy Council (P.C.) (criminal appeals until 1935, civil appeals until 1949): Cite to reports listed under **United Kingdom** if therein; otherwise cite to Olms.

Decisions of the Judicial Committee of the Privy Council re the British North American Act, 1867, and the Canadian Constitution		Olms.

Supreme Court of Canada (Can.): Cite to D.L.R. if therein; otherwise cite to S.C.R.

Dominion Law Reports	1969–date	e.g., 1 D.L.R.3d
	1956–1968	e.g., 1 D.L.R.2d
	1923–1955	e.g., [1923] 1 D.L.R.
	1912–1922	e.g., 1 D.L.R.
Canada Law Reports, Supreme Court	1923–date	e.g., 1972 S.C.R.
Canada Supreme Court Reports	1876–1922	e.g., 52 S.C.R.

Exchequer Court (Can. Ex.): Cite to D.L.R. if therein; otherwise cite to Can. Exch.

Canada Law Reports, Exchequer	1923–date	Can. Exch.
Canada Exchequer Court Reports	1875–1922	Can. Exch.

Tax Appeal Board (Can. T.A.B.): Cite to D.L.R. if therein; otherwise cite to Can. Tax App. Bd., Can. Tax App. Bd. (n.s.), or D. Tax.

Canada Tax Appeal Board Cases	1949–date	Can. Tax App. Bd., Can. Tax App. Bd. (n.s.)
Dominion Tax Cases	1920–date	D. Tax

Statutory and regulatory compilations

Revised Statutes of Canada	CAN. REV. STAT.
Statutory Orders and Regulations	CAN. STAT. O. & REGS.

Session laws and regulations

Statutes of Canada	Can. Stat.
Statutes of the Province of Canada	Prov. Can. Stat.
Canada Gazette (regulations)	Can. Gaz.

Canadian Provinces and Territories

Courts: Cite to D.L.R., W.W.R., Atl. Prov., E.L.R., Mar. Prov., or W.L.R., in that order of preference; otherwise cite to the province reporter.

Dominion Law Reports—*see* **Canada**

Western Weekly Reports	1971–date	e.g., [1971] 1 W.W.R.
	1951–1970	e.g., 8 W.W.R. (n.s.)
	1917–1950	e.g., [1917] 1 W.W.R.
	1911–1916	e.g., 6 W.W.R.
Atlantic Provinces Reports	1975–date	Atl. Prov.
Eastern Law Reporter	1906–1914	E.L.R.
Maritime Provinces Reports	1929–1968	Mar. Prov.
Western Law Reporter	1905–1916	W.L.R.
Alberta Law Reports	1907–1932	Alta.
	1977–date	Alta. 2d
British Columbia Reports	1867–1947	B.C.
	1977–date	B.C.L.R.
Manitoba Law Reports	1883–date	Man., Man. 2d
New Brunswick Reports	1825–date	N.B., N.B.2d
Newfoundland Supreme Court Decisions	1817–1828, 1846–1946	Nfld.
Newfoundland and Prince Edward Island Reports	1971–date	Nfld. & P.E.I.
Newfoundland Law Reports	1829–1895	Nfld. L.R.
Nova Scotia Reports	1834–1929, 1965–date	N.S.R., N.S.R.2d
Ontario Reports and Ontario Weekly Notes	1960–date	Ont. R. & W.N.

Ontario Reports	1931–date	Ont., Ont. 2d
	1882–1900	Ont.
Ontario Law Reports	1901–1931	Ont. L.R.
Ontario Weekly Notes	1910–1962	Ont. W.N.
Prince Edward Island Reports	1850–1882	P.E.I.
Rapports Judiciaires Officiels, Cour du Banc du Roi [de la Reine], Cour d'Appel (Quebec)	1892–date	Que. C.B.R., Que. C.A.
Rapports Judiciaires Officiels, Cour Supérieure (Quebec)	1892–date	Que. C.S.
Saskatchewan Law Reports	1980–date	Sask. R.
	1907–1931	Sask.
Northwest Territories Law Reports	1885–1907	N.W.T.L.R.

Statutory compilations

Alberta Revised Statutes	ALTA. REV. STAT.
British Columbia Revised Statutes	B.C. REV. STAT.
Manitoba Revised Statutes	MAN. REV. STAT.
New Brunswick Revised Statutes	N.B. REV. STAT.
Newfoundland Revised Statutes	NFLD. REV. STAT.
Northwest Territories Revised Ordinances	N.W.T. REV. ORD.
Nova Scotia Revised Statutes	N.S. REV. STAT.
Ontario Revised Statutes	ONT. REV. STAT.
Ontario Revised Regulations	ONT. REV. REGS.
Prince Edward Island Revised Statutes	P.E.I. REV. STAT.
Quebec Revised Statutes	QUE. REV. STAT.
Saskatchewan Revised Statutes	SASK. REV. STAT.
Yukon Territory Revised Ordinances	YUK. REV. ORD.

Session laws

Alberta Statutes	Alta. Stat.
Alberta Gazette	Alta. Gaz.
British Columbia Statutes	B.C. Stat.
British Columbia Gazette	B.C. Gaz.
Manitoba Statutes	Man. Stat.
Manitoba Gazette	Man. Gaz.
New Brunswick Statutes	N.B. Stat.
Newfoundland Statutes	Nfld. Stat.
Northwest Territories Ordinances	N.W.T. Ord.
Nova Scotia Statutes	N.S. Stat.
Ontario Statutes	Ont. Stat.
Ontario Regulations	Ont. Regs.
Prince Edward Island Statutes	P.E.I. Stat.
Quebec Statutes	Que. Stat.
Saskatchewan Statutes	Sask. Stat.
Saskatchewan Gazette	Sask. Gaz.
Yukon Territory Ordinances	Yuk. Ord.

India

Privy Council (P.C.) until 1949: Cite to reports listed under **United Kingdom**, to I.A., Indian App., or I. App., or to A.I.R. or Indian Cas., in that order of preference.

Law Reports, Privy Council, Indian Appeals	1875–1950 1873–1875 1836–1872	I.A. Indian App. I. App.
All India Reporter	1914–date	A.I.R.
Indian Cases	1909–1947	Indian Cas.

Supreme Court (India) and **Federal Court** (India Fed.), 1937–1950: Cite to A.I.R. if therein; otherwise cite to one of the other reporters listed below in the following order of preference:

All India Reporter	1914–date	e.g., 1967 A.I.R. (S.C.)
Supreme Court Reports	1950–date	e.g., [1963] 3 S.C.R.
Federal Court Reports	1939–1950	F.C.R.
Supreme Court Journal	1950–date	e.g., [1974] 1 S.C.J.
Federal Law Journal	1937–1949	F.L.J.
Indian Cases	1909–1947	Indian Cas.

High Court (e.g., Madras H.C.), **Supreme Court** (e.g., Calcutta S.C.) until 1860, **Court of the Judicial Commissioner** (e.g., C.J.C. Manipur), **Sadar Dewani Adalats** (e.g., S.D.A. Agra) until 1860: Cite to A.I.R., Indian Dec., or Indian L.R., in that order of preference.

All India Reporter	1914–date	e.g., 1954 A.I.R.
Indian Decisions	1774–date	Indian Dec.
Indian Law Reports (different series for each region)	1876–date	e.g., Indian L.R. Allahabad

Statutory and regulatory compilations: Cite to A.I.R. only if material does not appear in one of the compilations listed below.

India Code	INDIA CODE
Code of Civil Procedure	INDIA CODE CIV. PROC.
Code of Criminal Procedure	INDIA CODE CRIM. PROC.
Hindu Code	HINDU CODE
Indian Penal Code	INDIA PEN. CODE
General Rules and Orders	INDIA GEN. R. & O.
A.I.R. Manual: Unrepealed Central Acts (2d ed.)	INDIA A.I.R. MANUAL

Session laws and regulations

Central Acts	India Cen. Acts
Subsidiary Legislation	India Subs. Leg.

New Zealand

Privy Council (P.C.): Cite to reporters listed under **United Kingdom** if therein; otherwise cite to N.Z.L.R. or N.Z.P.C. Cas.

New Zealand Law Reports	1883–date	e.g., [1974] 1 N.Z.L.R.
New Zealand Privy Council Cases	1840–1932	N.Z.P.C. Cas.

Court of Appeals (N.Z. Ct. App.) and **Supreme Court** (N.Z.S.C.): Cite to N.Z.L.R. if therein; otherwise cite to N.Z.G.L.R.

New Zealand Law Reports	1883–date	e.g., [1974] 1 N.Z.L.R.
Gazette Law Reports	1898–1953	N.Z.G.L.R.

Court of Arbitration (N.Z. Ct. Arb.): Cite to N.Z. Awards if therein; otherwise cite to N.Z.G.L.R.

Awards, Recommendations, Agreements, etc.	1894–date	N.Z. Awards
Gazette Law Reports	1898–1953	N.Z.G.L.R.

Industrial Court (N.Z. Indus. Ct.) and **Compensation Court** (N.Z. Comp. Ct.): Cite to N.Z.L.R.

New Zealand Law Reports	1883–date	e.g., [1974] 1 N.Z.L.R.

Statutory compilation

Reprint of the Statutes of New Zealand	N.Z. REPR. STAT.

Session laws and regulations

Statutes of New Zealand	N.Z. Stat.
Ordinances of the Legislative Council of New Zealand	N.Z. Ords.
Statutory Regulations	N.Z. Stat. Regs.
Rules, Regulations and By-Laws under New Zealand Statutes	N.Z.R. Regs. & B.

United Kingdom

Judicial Committee of the Privy Council (P.C.) (matters referred by the Crown; appeals concerning certain constitutional questions from Northern Ireland; and appeals from the English Ecclesiastical Courts on certain matters, from the Probate, Divorce, and Admiralty Division in prize cases, and from the courts of the Channel Islands, the Isle of Man, the colonies, and those dominions that permit appeals from their highest courts): Cite to a Law Report or to Eng. Rep.

Law Reports		
Appeal Cases	1891–date	e.g., 1891 A.C.
	1875–1890	1 App. Cas. to 15 App. Cas.
Privy Council	1865–1875	1 L.R.-P.C. to 6 L.R.-P.C.
English Reports—Full Reprint	1094–1865	Eng. Rep.

House of Lords (H.L.) (appeals from the English Court of Appeals, from the Scottish Court of Session, Inner House, in civil cases, from the Scottish Court-Martial Appeal Court, and from the North Ireland Court of Appeal): Cite to a

Law Report, to Eng. Rep., or to House of Lords section of Session Cases, listed under **Scotland**, in that order of preference.

Law Reports		
Appeal Cases	1891–date	e.g., 1891 A.C.
	1876–1890	1 App. Cas. to 15 App. Cas.
English and Irish Appeals	1866–1875	1 L.R.-E. & I. App. to 7 L.R.-E. & I. App.
Scotch and Divorce Appeals	1866–1875	1 L.R.-S. & D. App. to 2 L.R.-S. & D. App.

Statutory compilations and sessions laws: The compilation listed below includes statutes of the Commonwealth (Interregnum). For other statutes, see rule 12.8.7(a).

Acts and Ordinances of the Interregnum	1642–1660	ACTS & ORDS. INTERREGNUM

Administrative materials

The Statutory Rules and Orders and Statutory Instruments Revised	to 1949	STAT. R. & O. & STAT. INST. REV.
Statutory Instruments	1948–date	STAT. INST.
Statutory Rules and Orders	1890–1947	STAT. R. & O.

Parliamentary debates

House of Lords, 5th series	1909–date	e.g., 218 PARL. DEB., H.L. (5th ser.) 260 (1959)
House of Commons, 5th series	1909–date	e.g., 525 PARL. DEB., H.C. (5th ser.) 300 (1954)
Parliamentary Debates, 1st to 4th series	1803–1908	e.g., 14 PARL. DEB. (2d ser.) 20 (1826)
Parliamentary History of England	pre-1803	e.g., 13 PARL. HIST. ENG. 417 (1644)
Journals		H.L. JOUR., H.C. JOUR.

Command Papers

Command Papers ("Command" is abbreviated as "CMD." and is followed by the series number, the paper number, the page, and the date)		e.g., LAW REFORM COMMITTEE, FIRST REPORT, CMD. 4, NO. 8809, at 4 (1953)

England and Wales

Cases before 1865: Cite to Eng. Rep. if therein; otherwise cite to Rev. Rep. A preceding parallel citation to the original report may be given. In citing the Year Books, include law term, regnal year, folio, and plea number; include a parallel citation to a nineteenth or twentieth century reprint if possible.

English Reports—Full Reprint	1693–1867	Eng. Rep.
Revised Reports	1785–1866	Rev. Rep.

Year Books		e.g., Y.B. Pasch. 17 Edw. 4, f. 2a, pl. 3 (1477)
Year Books in reprint		e.g., Y.B. Trin. 13 Rich. 2, pl. 7 (1389), *reprinted in* 7 AMES FOUNDATION 20 (1926)

Cases after 1864: Cite to Law Reports if therein. (Series and abbreviations of Law Reports are given under the separate court listings below.) Otherwise cite to W.L.R., to All E.R., L.T.R., Law Journal Reports, or T.L.R., or to W.N. or another report, in that order of preference.

Law Reports—*see* listings under separate court designations below		
Weekly Law Reports	1953–date	e.g., [1953] 1 W.L.R.
All England Law Reports	1936–date	e.g., [1954] 2 All E.R.
Law Times Reports	1859–1947	L.T.R. (n.s.)
Law Journal Reports, e.g., King's Bench, New Series	1822–1949	e.g., L.J.K.B. (n.s.)
Times Law Reports	1950–1952	e.g., [1951] 1 T.L.R.
	1884–1949	T.L.R.
Weekly Notes	1866–1952	e.g., 1950 W.N.
Annotated Tax Cases	1922–date	Ann. Tax Cas.
Commercial Cases	1895–date	Com. Cas.
De-Rating Appeals	1930–date	D.R.A.
Industrial Cases Reports	1919–date	e.g., 1980 Indus. Cas. R.
Justice of the Peace	1837–date	J.P.
Knight's Local Government Reports	1903–date	Knight's Local Gov't R.
Lawson's Registration Cases	1895–date	Lawson's Reg. Cas.
Lloyd's Law Reports	1968–date	e.g., [1969] 1 Lloyd's L.R.
Lloyd's List Law Reports	1951–1967	e.g., [1951] 1 Lloyd's List L.R.
	1919–1950	e.g., 84 Lloyd's List L.R.
Magisterial Cases	1896–1947	Mag. Cas.
Property and Compensation Reports	1968–date	e.g., 30 P. & C.R.
Planning and Compensation Reports	1949–1967	Plan. & Comp.
Rating and Valuation Reporter	1961–date	R. & V.R.
Rating Appeals	1965–date	e.g., 1969 R.A.
Reports of Patent Cases	1875–date	Pat. Cas.
Reports of Patent, Design and Trade Mark Cases	1884–date	e.g., 1978 R.P.D. & T.M. Cas.
Reports of Tax Cases	1875–date	e.g., 1 T.C.
Road Haulage Cases	1950–1955	R.H.C.
Road Traffic Reports	1970–date	e.g., 1970 R.T.R.
Simon's Tax Cases	1973–date	Simon's T.C.
Solicitor's Journal	1856–date	Sol. J.
Taxation Reports	1940–date	e.g., 1947 T.R.

Supreme Court of Judicature (consists of the **Court of Appeal** and the **High Court of Justice** listed below).

H

Court of Appeal, Civil Division (C.A.) (civil appeals from divisions and divisional courts of the High Court, and from the county courts), prior to 1875 **Court of Exchequer Chamber** (Ex. Ch.): There is no Court of Appeal series of reports; cases are reported in the series of the courts below. Thus, for example, cite an appeal from Queen's Bench to Queen's Bench reports.

Court of Appeal, Criminal Division (C.A.), 1907–1966 **Court of Criminal Appeal** (Crim. App.), previously **Court of Crown Cases Reserved** (Cr. Cas. Res.) (appeals from Assizes and Quarter Sessions): Cite to Queen's (King's) Bench, listed below, or to Cr. Cas. Res. if therein; otherwise cite to Crim. App. if therein.

Law Reports		
Crown Cases Reserved	1865–1875	1 L.R.-Cr. Cas. Res. to 2 L.R.-Cr. Cas. Res.
Criminal Appeal Reports	1908–date	Crim. App.

High Court of Justice (consists of three parts, which sit both as courts of first instance, in which case they are known as the **Queen's (King's) Bench Division**, the **Chancery Division**, and the **Family Division**, and as courts of limited appellate jurisdiction, in which case they are known as divisional courts (e.g., the Queen's Bench Divisional Court)).

Queen's (King's) Bench Division (Q.B., K.B.) (trials in tort and contract and other commercial claims) and **Queen's (King's) Bench Divisional Court** (Q.B. Div'l Ct., K.B. Div'l Ct.) (appeals from magistrate's courts and Quarter Sessions), prior to 1875 **Court of Queen's (King's) Bench** (Q.B., K.B.); incorporated in 1880 **Common Pleas Division** (C.P.D.) 1875–1880, previously **Court of Common Pleas** (C.P.) and **Exchequer Division** (Ex. D.) 1875–1880, previously **Court of Exchequer** (Ex.); also incorporated all nonfamily jurisdiction of Probate, Divorce, and Admiralty Division in 1971: Cite to Q.B., K.B., C.P., or Ex. if therein.

Law Reports		
Queen's and King's Bench	1952–date	e.g., [1952] 2 Q.B.
	1901–1951	[1901] 1 K.B. to [1952] 1 K.B.
	1891–1900	[1891] 1 Q.B. to [1900] 2 Q.B.
	1875–1890	1 Q.B.D. to 25 Q.B.D.
	1865–1875	1 L.R.-Q.B. to 10 L.R.-Q.B.
Common Pleas	1875–1880	1 C.P.D. to 5 C.P.D.
	1865–1875	1 L.R.-C.P. to 10 L.R.-C.P.
Exchequer	1875–1880	1 Ex. D. to 5 Ex. D.
	1865–1875	1 L.R.-Ex. to 10 L.R.-Ex.

Chancery Division (Ch.) (original equity jurisdiction: e.g., trusts, estates, wardship, mortgages, tax, partnership, and company law) and **Chancery Divisional Court** (Ch. Div'l Ct.) (appeals from, e.g., county court in bankruptcy,

Industrial Injuries Commissioner, Chief Land Registrar), prior to 1875 the **Chancellor's Court** (Ch.), **Rolls Court** (M.R.), **Vice-Chancellors' Courts** (V.C.), and **Court of Appeal in Chancery** (Ch. App.): Cite to Ch. or Eq. if therein.

Law Reports		
Chancery	1891–date	e.g., [1891] 1 Ch.
	1875–1890	1 Ch. D. to 45 Ch. D.
	1865–1875	1 L.R.-Ch. to 10 L.R.-Ch.
Equity	1865–1875	1 L.R.-Eq. to 20 L.R.-Eq.

Family Division (Fam.) and **Family Divisional Court** (Fam. Div'l Ct.); 1875–1971 **Probate, Divorce, and Admiralty Division** (P.)and **Probate Divisional Court** (P. Div'l Ct.); previously **Court of Probate** (P.), **Court of Divorce and Matrimonial Causes** (D.), and **High Court of Admiralty** (Adm.); all nonfamily jurisdiction was removed to Queen's Bench in 1971: Cite to Fam., P., or Adm. & Eccl. if therein.

Law Reports		
Family	1972–date	e.g., 1972 Fam.
Probate	1891–1971	e.g., 1891 P.
	1875–1890	1 P.D. to 15 P.D.
	1865–1875	1 L.R.-P. & D. to 3 L.R.-P. & D.
Admiralty and Ecclesiastical Cases	1865–1875	1 L.R.-Adm. & Eccl. to 4 L.R.-Adm. & Eccl.

Ecclesiastical courts: Cite to P. or Adm. & Eccl., listed above, if therein.

County Courts (sixty-four circuits geographically unrelated to the counties; original jurisdiction of most civil cases under a given amount in controversy): Cite according to **Cases after 1864** above.

Assizes (seven circuits), **Crown Courts** (Liverpool and Manchester), and the **Central Criminal Court**, previously **Old Bailey** (London) (original jurisdiction of most serious indictable offenses); **Quarter Sessions** (original jurisdiction of most indictable offenses; de novo review of magistrates' courts); **Magistrates' courts**, previously **Justices of the Peace** (trials of minor offenses): Cite according to **Cases after 1864** above.

Northern Ireland (and Ireland until 1924)

All courts (The court structure is similar to the English, except that the High Court of Justice is divided into two rather than three divisions: a Chancery Division and a Queen's Bench Division, the latter of which has jurisdiction over cases that in England would be under the Queen's Bench or Family Divisions.): Cite to N. Ir., Ir. R., L.R. Ir., Ir. R.-C.L., or Ir. Jur., if therein; otherwise cite to Ir. L.T.R.

Northern Ireland Law Reports	1924–date	e.g., 1924 N. Ir.
Irish Reports	1823–1924	e.g., 1922 Ir. R.

Law Reports, Ireland	1877–1893	L.R. Ir.
Irish Reports, Common Law Series	1867–1878	e.g., 7 Ir. R.-C.L.
Irish Jurist Reports	1849–1866	Ir. Jur.
Irish Law Times Reports	1874–date	Ir. L.T.R.

Statutory compilations and session laws: *See* rule 12.8.7.

Northern Ireland Statutes	1972–date	N. Ir. Stat.
Northern Ireland Public General Acts	1921–1971	N. Ir. Pub. Gen. Acts

Regulations

Statutory Rules and Orders of Northern Ireland	1922–date	STAT. R. & O.N. IR.

Scotland

Court of Session (Sess.) (general original and appellate jurisdiction of civil cases): Cite to Sess. Cas.

Session Cases, Court of Session section	1907–date	e.g., 1907 Sess. Cas.
Fifth Series	1898–1906	Fr.
Fourth Series	1873–1898	R.
Third Series	1862–1873	M.
Second Series	1832–1862	D.
First Series	1821–1838	S.

High Court of Justiciary (H.C.J.) (criminal appeals and trials of the most serious crimes): Cite to J.C. or to Sess. Cas. (J.)

Justiciary Cases (sometimes bound with Session Cases)	1917–date	e.g., 1917 J.C.
Session Cases, High Court of Justiciary section	1906–1916	e.g., 1907 Sess. Cas. (J.)
Fifth Series	1898–1906	Fr. (J.)
Fourth Series	1873–1898	R. (J.)

Statutes

The Acts of the Parliaments of Scotland	1124–1707 (1814–1875)	Scot. Parl. Acts

Other Jurisdictions

Argentina

Corte Suprema de Justicia (Argen.): Cite to Fallos and to J.A. or La Ley.

Fallos de la Corte Suprema de Justicia de la Nación	1863–date	Fallos

Foreign-language reporters, codes, and statutory collections should not be abbreviated the first time they are cited. *See* rule 6.2.

Jurisprudencia Argentina	1969–date	J.A.
	1918–1968	e.g., [1964] 3 J.A.
Revista Jurídica Argentina—La Ley	1936–date	La Ley

Other courts: Cite to one reporter, preferably J.A. or La Ley.

Statutes and decrees: Cite to either of the following.

Anales de Legislación Argentina	e.g., [1974] C Anales
Anuario de Legislación	e.g., [1974] A Anuario

Brazil

All courts: Cite to one reporter, in the following order of preference.

Archivo Judiciario	1934–date	Archivo
Diario da Justicia	1925–date	e.g., 1925 D. Just.
Revista Forense	1904–date	R. For.
Revista dos Tribunais	1912–date	R. Trib.

Statutes and decrees

Coleção das Leis, Atos do Poder Legislativo	Coleção

France

Ordinary jurisdiction: Cour de cassation, the highest court of ordinary jurisdiction, sits in sections, which are abbreviated as follows:

Assemblée plénière		Cass. ass. plén.
Chambres réunies		Cass. ch. réun.
Première section civile		Cass. civ. 1re
Deuxième section civile		Cass. civ. 2e
Troisième section civile		Cass. civ. 3e
Commerciale	to 1948	Cass. com.
	1948–date	Cass. civ. com.
Criminelle		Cass. crim.
Requêtes		Cass. req.
Sociale	to 1948	Cass. soc.
	1948–date	Cass. civ. soc.

Also **Cours d'appel** (regional courts of appeal; do not abbreviate); **Tribunaux de grand instance** (Trib. gr. inst.), prior to 1958 **Tribunaux de premier instance** (Trib. pr. inst.) (ordinary courts of original jurisdiction); and **Tribunaux d'instance statuant à juge unique** (Trib. inst.), prior to 1958 **Juges de paix** (J.P.) (courts of petty jurisdiction): Cite to one reporter, in the following order of preference.

Recueil Dalloz

Dalloz-Sirey, *Jurisprudence*	1955–1956, 1965–date	e.g., 1965 D.S. Jur.

Foreign-language reporters, codes, and statutory collections should not be abbreviated the first time they are cited. *See* rule 6.2.

Dalloz, *Jurisprudence*	1945–1955, 1956–1964	e.g., 1950 D. Jur.
Analytique, *Jurisprudence*	1941–1944	e.g., 1944 D.A. Jur.
Critique, *Jurisprudence*	1941–1944	e.g., 1943 D.C. Jur.
Périodique et critique	1825–1940	
I. Cour de cassation		e.g., 1878 D.P. I
II. Cours royales, cours impériales, cours d'appel		e.g., 1840 D.P. II
III. Conseil d'état		e.g., 1902 D.P. III
Recueil Sirey (entitled *Recueil Général de Lois et des Arrêts* until 1950)		
Sirey, *Jurisprudence*	1956–1964	e.g., 1957 S. Jur.
Sirey, *Jurisprudence*	1791–1955	
I. Cour de cassation		e.g., 1900 S. Jur. I
II. Other courts		e.g., 1927 S. Jur. II
III. Jurisprudence administrative		e.g., 1905 S. Jur. III
Juris-Classeur périodique, la semaine juridique	1942–date	e.g., 1943 J.C.P. II No. 23
	1927–1942	e.g., 1934 J.C.P. No. 23
Bulletin des ârrets de la Cour de cassation, chambres civiles	1792–date	
I. Première section civile		e.g., 1898 Bull. Civ. I
II. Deuxième section civile		e.g., 1954 Bull. Civ. II
III. Troisième section civile		e.g., 1971 Bull. Civ. III
IV. Commerciale et financière		e.g., 1933 Bull. Civ. IV
V. Expropriations		e.g., 1965 Bull. Civ. V
VI. Sociale		e.g., 1945 Bull. Civ. VI
Bulletin des arrêts de la Cour de cassation, chambre criminelle	1798–date	e.g., 1856 Bull. Crim.

Administrative jurisdiction: Tribunal des conflits (Trib. con.) (reconciles disputes between the Conseil d'état and the Cour de cassation); **Conseil d'état** (highest administrative court; do not abbreviate); and **Tribunaux administratifs** (Trib. admin.) (regional administrative courts of first instance): Cite to Lebon if therein; otherwise cite to Dalloz or Sirey.

Recueil des décisions [arrêts] du Conseil d'état	1821–date	e.g., 1821 Lebon

Constitutional jurisdiction: Conseil constitutionel (Con. const.) (constitutional court): Cite to Dalloz or Sirey.

Constitution

Constitution	CONST.

Codes

Code administratif	C. ADM.

Foreign language reporters, codes, and statutory collections should not be abbreviated the first time they are cited. *See* rule 6.2.

Code civil	C. CIV.
Code de commerce	C. COM.
Code pénal	C. PÉN.
Code de procédure civile	C. PR. CIV.
Code de procédure pénale	C. PR. PÉN.
Code de travaille	C. TRAV.

Statutes and decrees: Cite to two sources, in the following order of preference.

Journal Officiel de la République Française		e.g., 1972 J.O.
Recueil Dalloz		
Dalloz-Sirey, *Législation*	1955–1956, 1965–date	e.g., 1965 D.S.L.
Dalloz, *Législation*	1945–1955, 1956–1964	e.g., 1956 D.L.
Analytique, *Législation*	1941–1944	e.g., 1941 D.A.L.
Critique, *Législation*	1941–1944	e.g., 1941 D.C.L.
Périodique et critique	1848–1940, 1825–1847	e.g., 1848 D.P. IV e.g., 1825 D.P. III
Bulletin législatif Dalloz	1918–date	e.g., 1918 B.L.D.
Juris-classeur périodique, la semaine juridique	1942–date 1927–1942	e.g., 1942 J.C.P. III No. 5 e.g., 1927 J.C.P. No. 5
Collection complète, décrets, ordonnances, règlements et avis du conseil d'état (Duvergier & Bocquet)	1788–1949	e.g., 1788 Duv. & Boc.

German Democratic Republic (East Germany)

Supreme Court

Entscheidungen des Obersten Gerichts	
in Strafsachen	OGSt.DDR
in Zivilsachen	OGZ.DDR

Other courts

Neue Justiz	NJ.DDR

Constitution

Die Verfassung der DDR	VERF.DDR

Codes: Use editions published by Deutscher Zentralverlag (Berlin).

Bürgerliches Gesetzbuch	BGB.DDR
Strafgesetzbuch	STGB.DDR
Strafprozessordnung	STPO.DDR
Zivilprozessordnung	ZPO.DDR

Foreign-language reporters, codes, and statutory collections should not be abbreviated the first time they are cited. *See* rule 6.2.

Statutes and decrees: Cite to GBl.DDR or ZBl.DDR; a parallel citation to KBG.DDR may be given.

Gesetzblatt der DDR	GBl.DDR
Zentralblatt der DDR	ZBl.DDR
Karteibuch der Gesetze der DDR	KBG.DDR

Germany, Federal Republic of (West Germany)

Ordinary jurisdiction: Bundesgerichtshof, Vereinigte Grosse Senate (Bundesgerichtshof, Ver. Gr. Sen.), previously **Reichsgericht** (do not abbreviate) (resolves conflicts among the Senate and Grosse Senate); **Bundesgerichtshof, Grosse Senate für Zivilsachen** (Bundesgerichtshof, Gr. Sen. Z.) (en banc panels for civil cases); **Bundesgerichtshof, Grosse Senate für Strafsachen** (Bundesgerichtshof, Gr. Sen. St.) (en banc panels for criminal cases); and **Bundesgerichtshof, Senate** (Bundesgerichtshof) (ordinary panels of the highest court); 1945–1951 **Oberste Gerichtshof für die Britische Zone** (do not abbreviate); the lower courts of ordinary jurisdiction are those of the Länder: Cite to the Entscheidungen of the court.

Bundesgerichtshof	
in Strafsachen	BGHSt
in Zivilsachen	BGHZ
Oberster Gerichtshof für die Britische Zone	OGHBrZ
Reichsgericht	
in Strafsachen	RGSt
in Zivilsachen	RGZ

Administrative jurisdiction: Bundesverwaltungsgericht (highest administrative court), **Verwaltungsgerichtshof** (appellate administrative court in the former American Zone), **Oberverwaltungsgericht** (appellate administrative court in the former British Zone), **Verwaltungsgericht** (administrative court of first instance in the former American Zone), **Landesverwaltungsgericht** (administrative court of first instance in the former British Zone): Cite to the Entscheidungen of the court.

Bundesverwaltungsgericht	BVerwG
Verwaltungsgerichtshof	VerwGH
Oberverwaltungsgericht	OVerwG
Verwaltungsgericht	VerwG
Landesverwaltungsgericht	LVerwG

Constitutional jurisdiction: Bundesverfassungsgericht (highest constitutional court): Cite to BVerfG.

Bundesverfassungsgericht	BVerfG

Foreign language reporters, codes, and statutory collections should not be abbreviated the first time they are cited. *See* rule 6.2.

Special jurisdiction: Bundesarbeitsgericht (high court for labor matters), **Bundessozialgericht** (high court for social matters), **Bundesfinanzhof** (high court for fiscal matters): Cite to the Entscheidungen of the court.

Bundesarbeitsgericht	BAG
Bundessozialgericht	BSG
Bundesfinanzhof	BFH

Constitution

Grundgesetz	GG

Codes

Bürgerliches Gesetzbuch	BGB
Gerichtsverfassungsgesetz	GVERFG
Handelsgesetzbuch	HGB
Strafgesetzbuch	STGB
Strafprozessordnung	STPO
Zivilprozessordnung	ZPO

Statutes and decrees: Cite to BGBl or RGBl; a parallel citiation to BAnz may be added.

Bundesgesetzblatt, Teil I	1949–date	BGBl
Reichsgesetzblatt	1871–1945	RGBl
Bundesanzeiger		BAnz

Länder (West German States)

Ordinary jurisdiction: **Oberlandesgericht** (e.g., Oberlandesgericht, Hamm) (appellate court of the Land), **Landgericht** (e.g., Landgericht, Frankfurt) (ordinary court of first instance), and **Amtsgericht** (e.g., Amtsgericht, Bonn) (court of petty jurisdiction): Cite to OLGZ if therein; otherwise cite to a newspaper or periodical (the most common is *Neue Juristische Wochenschrift*, abbreviated NJW). Always include the city or town as part of the court designation.

Entscheidungen der Oberlandesgerichte in Zivilsachen	OLGZ

Constitutional jurisdiction: Verfassungsgerichtshof (constitutional court of the Land): Cite to the Entscheidungen of the court; add the name of the Land.

Verfassungsgerichtshof	e.g., VerfGH Bayern

Constitutions: Add the name of the Land.

Verfassung	e.g., VERF. BAYERN

Statutes and decrees: Cite to the official gazette of the Land or to SaBl.

Sammelblatt für Rechtsvorschriften des Bundes und der Länder	1950–date	SaBl

Foreign-language reporters, codes, and statutory collections should not be abbreviated the first time they are cited. *See* rule 6.2.

Italy

Ordinary jurisdiction: Corte de cassazione (Corte cass.) (court of last appeal in civil and criminal matters), **Corte d'appello** (Corte app.) (regional court of appeal), **Tribunale** (Trib.) (ordinary court of first instance), and **Conciliatore** (Concil.) and **Pretore** (Pret.) (courts of petty jurisdiction): Cite to Foro It. and Giur. Ital. if therein.

Foro Italiano	1876–date	
I. Corte cost., Corte cass.		Foro It. I
II. Criminal cases		Foro It. II
III. Administrative courts		Foro It. III
IV. EEC and foreign cases		Foro It. IV
V. Miscellaneous		Foro It. V
Giurisprudenza Italiana	1849–date	e.g., Giur. Ital. II
Giurisprudenza Completa della Corte Suprema di Cassazione	1944–1955	Giur. Compl. Cass. Civ., Giur. Compl. Cass. Crim.
Giurisprudenza delle Imposte Dirette di Registro e di Negoziazione	1928–date	Giur. Imp. Reg. Negoz.
Giustizia Civile (indicate section)	1951–date	e.g., Giust. Civ. II

Administrative jurisdiction: Consiglio di Stato (Cons. Stato) (court of last appeal in administrative matters), **Corte dei conti** (Corte cont.) (high court for fiscal matters), and **Giunte provinciale amministrative** (Giun. pro. ammin.) (administrative court of first instance): Cite to For. It. and Giur. Ital. if therein.

Foro Amministrativo	1925–date	Foro Amm. I, II, III
Giurisprudenza Italiana	1849–date	e.g., Giur. Ital. II

Constitutional jurisdiction: Corte costituzionale (Corte cost.) (highest court for constitutional matters): Cite to Rac. uff. corte cost. and to either Foro It. or Giur. Ital.

Raccolta ufficiale delle sentenze e ordinanze delle Corte costitutionale	1956–date	Rac. uff. corte cost.

Constitution

Costituzione	COST.

Codes

Codice civile	C.C.
Codice penale	C.P.
Codice di procedura civile	C.P.C.
Codice di procedura penale	C.P.P.

Statutes and decrees: Cite to Rac. Uff. or Gaz. Uff.; give a parallel citation to Leg. Ital. Cite by designation (e.g., Law, Royal Decree, Royal Decree-Law, Presidential Decree-Law, Decree-Law, or Ministerial Decree-Law) and exact date.

Foreign-language reporters, codes, and statutory collections should not be abbreviated the first time they are cited. *See* rule 6.2.

Raccolta Ufficiale delle Leggi e dei Decreti della Repubblica Italiana	Rac. Uff.
Gazetta Ufficiale della Repubblica Italiana	Gaz. Uff.
Legislazione Italiana (Giuffrè)	
I. National legislation	Leg. Ital. I
II. Parliamentary reports	Leg. Ital. II
III. Regional legislation	Leg. Ital. III

Japan

Great Court of Judicature

Daishin'in keiji hanreishū	1922–1947	Dai-han keishū
Daishin'in minji hanreishū	1922–1946	Dai-han minshū
Daishin'in minji hanketsu roku	1895–1921	Dai-han minroku
Daishin'in keiji hanketsu roku	1895–1921	Dai-han keiroku

Administrative Court

Gyōsei saibansho hanketsu roku	Gyō-han

Supreme Court

Saikō saibansho keiji hanrei shū	Sai-han keishū
Saikō saibansho minji hanrei shū	Sai-han minshū

Inferior courts

Kakyū saibansho keiji saiban reishū	Kakyū keishū
Kakyū saibansho minji saiban reishū	Kakyū minshū

Constitution

Kenpō	KENPŌ

Codes

Minpō (Civil Code), Law No. 89 of 1896 and Law No. 9 of 1898	MINPŌ
Shōhō (Commercial Code), Law No. 48 of 1899	SHŌHŌ
Minji soshō hō (Code of Civil Procedure), Law No. 29 of 1890	MINJI SOSHŌ HŌ
Keiji soshō hō (Code of Criminal Procedure), Law No. 131 of 1948	KEIJI SOSHŌ HŌ
Keihō (Penal Code), Law No. 45 of 1907	KEIHŌ

Statutes and decrees: Cite early Meiji statutes no longer in force to Hōrei zensho. Cite all other statutes by name, number, and year, as the codes are cited above. Decrees are cited like statutes (e.g., Seirei (Ministerial Order) No. 275 of July 1978).

Hōrei zensho (Complete Laws and Orders)	Hōrei zensho

Foreign-language reporters, codes, and statutory collections should not be abbreviated the first time they are cited. *See* rule 6.2.

Mexico

All courts: Cite to one of the following sources.

Anales de Jurisprudencia	1933–date	e.g., 1975 Anales Jur.
Boletín de Información Judicial	1945–1965	e.g., 1956 Bol. Info. Jud.
Semanario Judicial de la Federación	1870–date	Semanario

Statutes and decrees: Cite to D.O.; a parallel citation to Reportorio may be given.

Diario Oficial	D.O.
Reportorio Anual de Legislación	e.g., 1975 Reportorio

Netherlands, Kingdom of the

Hoge Raad der Nederlanden (highest court), **Gerechtshof** (regional court of appeal), **Arondissementsrechtbank** (ordinary court of first instance), and **Kantongerecht** (court of petty jurisdiction): Cite to N.J. if therein.

Nederlandse Jurisprudentie	e.g., 1975 N.J.
Nederlands Juristenblad	e.g., 1975 N.J.B.
Weekblad van het Recht (by issue number)	e.g., W. No. 12,627

Constitutions

Statuut voor het Koninkrijk der Nederlanden (constitution of the federation, superior to the constitution of the Kingdom)	STATUUT NED.
Grondwet (constitution of the Kingdom)	GRW. NED.

Codes

Burgerlijk Wetboek	B.W.
Wetboek van burgerlijke Rechtsvordering	Rv.
Wetboek van Koophandel	W.v.K.
Wetboek van Strafrecht	W.v.S.
Wetboek van Strafvordering	Sv.

Statutes and decrees: Cite to Stb.; a parallel citation to Alg. Med. or Ned. Staats. may be given.

Staatsblad voor het Koninkrijk der Nederlanden	Stb.
Algemene Mededelingen	Alg. Med.
Nederlandse Staatswetten editie Schuurman & Jordens	Ned. Staats.

Roman Law

Code of Justinian	e.g., CODE JUST. 2.45.2
Digest of Justinian	e.g., DIG. JUST. 9.2.23.8
Institutes of Justinian	e.g., INST. JUST. 2.23.pr.

Foreign-language reporters, codes, and statutory collections should not be abbreviated the first time they are cited. *See* rule 6.2.

Code of Theodosius	e.g., CODE THEOD. 8.4.14
Novels	e.g., NOV. 15.pr.

Switzerland

Whenever possible, give parallel German, French, and Italian citations for all federal materials; give court names in German.

Bundesgericht (**Tribunal fédéral, Tribunale federale**) (highest court); lower courts are those of the cantons: Cite to BG and ATF.

Entscheidungen des Schweizerischen Bundesgerichts, Amtliche Sammlung	
I. Administrative and constitutional	BG I
II. Civil	BG II
III. Debt and bankruptcy	BG III
IV. Criminal	BG IV
V. Social	BG V
Arrêts du Tribunal fédéral suisse, Recueil officiel (parts as in BG)	e.g., ATF II

Constitution

Bundesverfassung, Constitution fédérale, Costituzione federale	B.VERF., CONST., COST. FED.

Codes

Schweizerisches Zivilgesetzbuch, Code civil suisse, Codice civile svizzero	ZGB, C.C., COD. CIV.
Schweizerisches Obligationenrecht, Code des obligations, Codice delle obligazioni	OR, C.O., COD. OBL.
Schweizerisches Strafgesetzbuch, Code pénal suisse, Codice penale svizzero	STGB, C.P., COD. PÉN.

Statutes and decrees: Cite to A.S., ROLF, and RULF if therein; otherwise cite to SS and RS or to BBl, FF, and Fog.

Sammlung der Eidgenössischen Gesetze (entitled *Eidgenössische Gesetzessammlung*, 1927–1948; entitled *Amtliche Sammlung der Bundesgesetze und Verordnungen der schweizerischen Eidgenossenschaft*, 1848–1926)	1848–date	A.S.
Recueil officiel des lois et ordonnances de la Confédération suisse	1948–date	ROLF
Raccolta ufficiale delle leggi, decreti e regolamente della Confederazione svizzera	1948–date	RULF
Systematische Sammlung der Bundesgesetze und Verordnungen	1970–date	SSBGV
Recueil systematique des lois et ordonnances	1970–date	RSLO

Foreign-language reporters, codes, and statutory collections should not be abbreviated the first time they are cited. *See* rule 6.2.

Bundesblatt	BBl
Feuille fédérale	FF
Foglio federale svizzero	Fog.

Swiss Cantons

Cite cantonal material in the official language or languages of the canton; give court names in an official language in the following order of preference—German, French, Italian.

Obergericht (**Cour de cassation**) (cantonal court of appeal), **Bezirksgericht** (**Tribunal cantonal**) (ordinary court of first instance), and **Friedenrichter** (**Juge de Paix**) (court of petty jurisdiction): Cite to one of the following sources.

Basler Juristische Mitteilungen	BJM
Blätter für Zürcherische Rechtsprechung	BLZR
Journal des Tribunaux	
I. Federal administrative, constitutional, and civil	J.T. I
II. Debt and bankruptcy	J.T. II
III. Cantonal	J.T. III
IV. Criminal	J.T. IV
Die Praxis des Schweizerischen Bundesgerichts	Prax.
Schweizerische Juristenzeitung	SJZ
La Semaine Judiciaire	Sem. Jud.
Zeitschrift des Bernischen Juristenvereins	ZBJV

Statutes and decrees: Cite to the official gazette of the canton.

I

Index

Page references in regular type are to INSTRUCTIONS; page references in *italics* are to EXAMPLES.

Abbreviations
adjacent, spacing, 28–29
administrative reporters, 135–36
administrative reports, 77
agencies, *29*, 77
American reporters, 44, 133–76
"and," in case names, 38
Argentinian material, 190–91
authors, 81–82
bound services, 108–14
Brazilian material, 191
business firms, 38, 40
case history, 50–51
case names, 36–43
case names, in footnotes, 41–42
case names, international, 121
citations, repeating, 21–23
closing up of, 28–29
codes, 29
(*see also* name of jurisdiction)
codes, statutory, 60
commissions, 135–36
commonly abbreviated names, 29, 38, 40–41
congressional reports and documents, 73–74
corporate authors, 82
countries, 119
court of decision, 29, 44–48
dollar symbol, 30
editions of books, 83–85
English *Law Report* series, 187
English materials, 186–89
English periodicals, 91–103
English sovereigns, 70
English statutes, 70
explanatory phrases, 50–51
foreign countries, *inside back cover,* 29–30, 53–54
foreign courts, 53–54
foreign materials, 29–30
foreign periodicals, 103–04
foreign words in case names, 122
French materials, 191–93
generally, 28–30
geographical words in railroad names, 42
German materials, E. Ger., 193–94
German materials, W. Ger., 194–95
government agencies, 82
government reports, 73–74
"hereinafter," use of, 22–23
history of cases, 50–51
Indian materials, 184
initials, commonly recognized, 29, 38, 40–41
institutional authors, 29, 77, 82
international agreements, names of, shortened, 118–19
international and world organization materials, 124–30
Italian materials, 196–97
Japanese materials, 197
judges, titles, 33
law journals and reviews, *28,* 91–103
looseleaf services, 108–14
Mexican materials, 198
model codes, 68
months, *inside back cover*
multiple citations of same work, 21–25
multiple editions and printings, 83–85
municipal ordinances, 67
names, commonly abbreviated, 29, 38
Netherlands materials, 198
newspapers, 104
no date, 84
no place, 84
officials, titles, 33
ordinances, municipal, 67
other foreign, 71
paragraph symbols, 30
parliamentary materials, British, 186
parties to treaties, 119
percent symbols, 30
periodicals, 87, 91–103
periodicals, American, 91–103
periodicals, Commonwealth and common law, 91–103
periodicals, foreign, 103–04
periods, 29
pluralization of, 41
prepositions in periodical names, 91
prior case history, 50–51
publishers of services, 108
punctuation of, 29
railroads, 40, 42
repeating citations, 21–23
reporters, 29
(*see also* name of jurisdiction)
reporters, American, 44, 133–35
reporters, foreign, 54
restatements, 68
section symbols, 30
services, 108–14
session laws, 63
(*see also* name of jurisdiction)

Page references in regular type are to INSTRUCTIONS; page references in *italics* are to EXAMPLES.

spacing of, 28–29
standards, 68
statutes, 57–71
(*see also* name of jurisdiction)
subdivisions (e.g., section, article, chapter), 14–15, *18, 19*
subsequent case history, 50–51
Swiss materials, 199–200
taxation materials, 78
titles of books and pamphlets, 82
titles of individuals, 33
treaties, names of, shortened, 118–19
treaty series, 120–21
unambiguous, must be, 28, 41, 82, 91
unilateral, spacing, 28–29
unions, 40–41
"United States," 29, 41, 82, 102
use of abbreviations not listed in this book, 28, 41, 91

Abstracts, in law reviews, 89
***"Accord,"* as signal,** 8
***"Acquiescing,"* in case history,** 51
"Act," capitalization of, 31–32
Acts
(*see* Codes, Session laws, Statutes)
Addenda, 20
Addresses (speeches), *85*
Administrative agencies
abbreviation of, 77
adjudications, 43, *75*, 77
official releases, 43
reporters, 135–36
reports, 77
Administrative cases
citation of, 135–36
exact date, when required, 43
number of case, when required, 43
omission of procedural phrases, 37–38
parallel citation, *43*
recent, 43
services, when cited, 43
"*sub nom.*," use on appeal, 51–52
Administrative law judge, 33
Administrative materials
adjudications, *75*, 77
agency publications, *83*
basic citation forms, 75–76
British, 186
cases, 42–43, 51–52
citation order, 12
civil law countries, 190–200
Code of Federal Regulations, 75
compilations of regulations, 76–77
court administrative orders, 79
England, 186
executive orders, *76*, 78
Federal Register, 75, 76–77
federal rules and regulations, *75*
foreign, 76
generally, 75–79
Internal Revenue Service, 77–78
names of rules and regulations, 76
notices, 76–77
opinions, formal advisory, *75*, 77
order within signal, 12
orders, regulations, and rules, 76–77
popular names of rules and regulations, 76
presidential orders, *76*
presidential proclamations, 78
proposed rules and regulations, 76
regulations, rules, and orders, *75*, 76–77
reorganization plans, 78
revenue materials, 77–78
revenue rulings, 78
rules, *75*
rules, regulations, and orders, 76–77
state, 76, 136–76
tax materials, 77–78
Treasury decisions, *78*
Treasury materials, 77–78
Treasury regulations, *75*, 77–78
UN Administrative Tribunal, 128
United Kingdom, 186
United States Code, 76
varieties of, 76

Administrative Procedure Act, *24*, 75
Advance sheets, 43–44, 52, 77, 78
Advisory committee notes, 20
***"Affirmed"* and *"affirming,"* in case history,** 51
Agencies, administrative
(*see* Administrative agencies)
Agreement series (E.A.S.), 120
Agreements
executive, 118–21
international, 118–21
Alabama
courts and statutes, 136–37
Alaska
courts, statutes, and administrative materials, *62*, 137
Alberta
courts and statutes, 181–82
All England Law Reports, 187
Alterations in quotations, 26

Page references in regular type are to INSTRUCTIONS; page references in *italics* are to EXAMPLES.

Alternative holding, indication of, 49
***"Amended by,"* in statute citation,** *65*
Amended statutes, 18, 59, 65
Amendments
  Canadian statutes, 71
  constitutional, 57
  model codes, 68–69
  restatements, 68–69
  standards, 68–69
  statutes, 65
  Treasury regulations, 77–78
  uniform acts, 68
"Amendment(s)," abbreviation of, 14
American Bar Association
  generally, 68–70
  publications, *70*, 87
  section reports, 88
***American Jurisprudence* (Am. Jur.),** *86*
American Law Institute
  generally, 68–69
  Proceedings, 87, 88
  publications, 87
***American Law Reports* (A.L.R.),** 90
American Samoa
  courts and statutes, 137
Ampersand
  authors' names, *81*
  books and pamphlets, *82*
  case names, *37*, 38
  footnote citation, 18
  titles, *82*
Annals of Congress
  citation to, *75*
  first volume, 75
Annexes, UN records, 124–25
Annotations
  A.L.R., L.R.A., 90
  generally, 20
Annual Digest and Reports of International Law Cases, 123
Annual reports
  corporations, *82*
  government agencies, 77
  Permanent Court of International Justice, *122*
***Annuals* (Canadian statutes),** 70–71
***"Appeal dismissed,"* in case history,** 51
Appeal docketed, *35, 49*
Appeals, *35, 36, 49*
Appendices
  codes, 61–62
  generally, 20, 81
  statutes reprinted in codes, *62*
"Appendix (ces)," abbreviation of, 14
Arabic numerals
  monarchs, 70
  volumes, 15
Arbitrations
  cases, citation of, 42–43
  international, *117*, 123–24
  Permanent Court of, 124
"Arbitrator," abbreviation of, 33
Arbitrators, indicated parenthetically, 42–43
Argentina
  courts, statutes, and decrees, 190–91
Arizona
  courts, statutes, and administrative materials, 137–38
Arkansas
  courts, statutes, and administrative materials, 138
Article (part of speech), capitalization of, 31
Articles
  appearing in two or more parts, 90–91
  basic citation forms, 87
  capitalization, 31
  citation order, 12
  collected essays, printed in, 91
  components of citation, 87
  essays in collection, 91
  foreign periodicals, 103–04
  italicization in briefs and legal memoranda, 3–4, *6*
  italicization in law review footnotes, *6*
  law reviews and journals, 88
  magazines, 88
  multipart, 90–91
  newspapers, 104–05
  no author given in source, 88
  order within signal, 12
  page citation, 16–18
  particular page, citation of, 17
  periodicals, 88
  titles, capitalization, 31
  titles in italic type, 3–6, 88
  typeface, 3–6, 88
"Article(s)," abbreviation of, 14, *118*
"Ass'n," in case names, 40
"At," used in citation of pages or sections, 13, 16–17, 82, 125–26
"Attorney General," abbreviation of, 33
Attorney General, opinions, *77*
Australia
  courts and statutes, 179–81

Page references in regular type are to INSTRUCTIONS; page references in *italics* are to EXAMPLES.

Australian materials
(*see* Commonwealth materials)
Authorities in text, identification of, 8
Authorities previously cited, 21–25
Authors
articles in periodicals, 88
book reviews, 89
books and pamphlets, 81–82
collected essays, 85
congressional documents and reports, 74
essays in collection, 85
forewords, *17, 82*
given names not used, in article citations, 88
initials not given in article citations, 88
institutional, 74
law reviews and journals, 88
model codes, 68–69
multiple, books and pamphlets, 81
multivolume works, 81
newspapers, 104
news reports and articles, 104
not given for articles, 88
omitted, when, 88
periodical materials, 88
periodicals, surveys and symposia in, 90
prefaces, *17,* 82
restatements, 68–69
reviewer of book, 89
standards, 68–69
student, name not given, 89
typeface used in footnotes, 81, 88
UN material, 124
Author's mistakes in quoted material, 26

Ballentine's Law Dictionary, *86*
Bankruptcy
appellate panels, 45, 134
cases, 37, *107*
courts, 45, *107*, 134
Bankruptcy Reporter, 134
Bar publications, 87
"Baron," abbreviation of, 33
Basic charters, international and world organizations, 128–29
Bible, 86
Bills
bills and resolutions, 72–73
congressional, 72–73
foreign, 73
state, 73
statutory, *71*
Black's Law Dictionary, *86*
Blackstone's *Commentaries,* *84*
Block quotations, 25
Board of Tax Appeals
citation of cases, 42, 134
Book notes, 89
Book reviews
citation order, 12–13
periodicals, 89
"Book(s)," abbreviation of, 14
Books and pamphlets
ABA publications, *70*, 87
abbreviation of title, 82
administrative agency records and reports, 77, 82
ALI publications, 87
author, 81–82
basic form of citation, 81
book reviews, 89
capitalization, 31
citation, basic forms of, *inside front cover, i,* 81
citation, components of, 81
citation order, 12–13
collected essays, 85, 91
components of citation, 81
congressional materials, 71–75
corporate author, 82
date, 81, 83–85
date in title, 82
date not given by source, 84
dictionaries, legal, *86*
edition, 81, 83–85
editor, when indicated, 81, 83
encyclopedias, legal, *86*
exact date, when required, 83
The Federalist, 87
first name of author, 81
footnote typefaces, 81–82
forewords, *17, 82*
generally, 81–87
given names and initials of authors, 81
government agencies as authors, 82
government agency reports, 77
initial of author, 81
institutional authors, 74, 77, 82
interviews, *85*
italicization, when referred to in text, 3–5
law reviews and journals, 87–104
legal dictionaries and encyclopedias, 86
letters, *85*
limited circulation, 85–86
manuscripts, typed, *86*
mimeographed materials, *86*

Page references in regular type are to INSTRUCTIONS; page references in *italics* are to EXAMPLES.

multiple authors, 81
multiple editions, 81, 83–85
multiple printings, 83
multivolume works, 81–83
name of author, 81–82
names and titles, capitalization, 31
number, serial, 83
offprints, 85
order within signal, 12–13
page citation, 16–18, 81
paragraphs, 81
periodicals, 87–104
photoduplicated reprints, 85
place of publication not given by source, 84
place of publication, when required, 84
pocket parts, 84
prefaces, *17*, 82
printings, 83
publication number, 83
published prior to 1870, 84
repagination, 84
repeated citation of, *21–22*
reprints, 85
restatements, 87
sections, 81
serial number, 81, 83
series of, 83
special citation forms, 83, 85–87
star pages, 84
subdivisions of, 15–20
subtitles, omitted, 82
supplements, 84
theses, unpublished, 86
titles, 81–82
translator, when given, 81
typed manuscripts, *86*
typeface, 82, 85
typeface, authors, 86
typeface in law review footnotes, 8
typeface in text, 3–5
unpublished works, 81
volume designations, 81
well-known works, 84
writer of, 81
year, 83

Bound services
abbreviations, 108–14
generally, 107–14
typeface, 107

Brackets
alterations in quotations, 26–27
establishing short citation, used in, 22–23, 29–30, 54, 71
quotations, used in, 26
volume designations, 16, 107
years, 16, *49*

Brazil
courts, statutes, and decrees, 191

Briefs and legal memoranda
abbreviations in case names cited in, 38
citations in, *i*, 3–4
cross-references in, 21
Internal Revenue Code, citations to, 66–67
short forms in, *23*
typeface of citations in, 3–4

Briefs and records, citation of
citation order, 12
generally, *35*, 53
typeface used in footnotes, 53

British Columbia
courts and statutes, 181–82

British materials
(*see* England)

"Bros.," in case name, 40

Bureau of National Affairs (BNA) services, 108

Business firms, in case names, 38, 40

***"But cf.,"* as signal,** 9

***"But see,"* as signal,** 9

***"But see, e.g.,"* as signal,** *8*

Byline, newspaper articles, 104

California
courts, statutes, and administrative materials, *61*, 138–40

Callaghan services, 108
(*see also* Services and topical reporters)

Canada
(*see also* services and topical reporters)
courts and statutes, 181–83
treaty series, 120

Canal Zone
courts, statutes, and administrative materials, 140

Canons of Professional Responsibility, *69*

Cantons, Swiss, 200

Capital letters in text hypotheticals, 31

Capitalization
change in quotation, indication of, 26
generally, 31–33
headings, 31
people or groups, words referring to, 31
titles of books and articles, 31

Page references in regular type are to INSTRUCTIONS; page references in *italics* are to EXAMPLES.

Case comments in periodicals, 89
Case history
(*see* History of cases)
Case names
abbreviations, 36–42
abbreviations, in law review footnotes, 23–24, 41–42
abbreviations, in text, 23–24, 38–41
administrative actions, 42, 51–52
"administrator," omission of, 38
ampersand, use of in text, 38
appeal, when different on, 51–52
"appellee," omission of, 38
arbitrations, 42–43
arbitrations, international, 123
bankruptcy, 37
briefs and legal memoranda, *inside front cover,* 3, *7,* 38
business firms, 38, 40
cite as in official report, 36
cite first listed party only, 37
"Co.," abbreviation in text, 38
Commissioner of Internal Revenue, as party, 41
Common Market cases, 122
consolidated actions, 37
"Corp.," abbreviation in text, 38
"d/b/a," omission of, *37*
descriptive terms, 38
different on appeal, 51–52
"estate of," 38
"et al.," 37
"*ex parte,*" *38*
"*ex rel.,*" 37
first word, retention in full, 37
foreign cases, 53
foreign names, 40
generally, 21–24, 35–43
geographical terms, 39
given names and initials of parties, 39–40
"*In re,*" 37–38
in rem actions, 38
"Inc.," abbreviation in text, 38
"Inc.," when omitted, 40
Internal Revenue Commissioner, as party, 41
"Internal Revenue," omitted in, 41
international arbitrations, 123
International Court of Justice, 121
"Judgment of," 36–37, 53
Latin words italicized, 37–38
law review footnotes, abbreviations, 23–24, 41–42
law review text, 3, 5, 23–24, 38–41
lengthy, 37
"Ltd.," abbreviation to in text, 38
"Ltd.," when omitted, 40
omissions in, 37–41
omitted in official reporter, 36–37
parenthetical, 37
parties, only first-listed named, 37
partnerships, 37
Permanent Court of International Justice, 121
popular names, 23–24, 38
procedural phrases, 37–38, 42
railroads as parties, 40, 42
running heads, words omitted in, 37
state as party in state court decision, 39
surnames, 39–40
"The," omission of, 38
typeface used in footnotes, 5
unions as parties, 40–41
"Will of," 38
World Court, 121
Case notes in periodicals, 89
Case number
administrative cases, 43
appeal or petition for certiorari, *36,* 53
citation of unreported cases, 1, *35,* 52
Federal Cases, 133, 134
pending cases, 1, *35,* 53
unreported cases, *35–36,* 52
Case writeups
citation of, 89
cited with case, 14
Cases
(*see also* individual jurisdiction or court)
administrative actions, 42–43, 51–52, 77
advance sheets, when cited, 44
appeal, disposition on, *35–36*
appeal docketed, *35*
arbitrations, 42–43
bankruptcy, 37, *107*
before decision, *35, 36*
briefs, citation of, *35,* 53
British, 186–89
certiorari, citation of petition for, *36*
citation, basic forms of, *inside front cover, i,* 35–36
citation, components of, 36
citation order, 10–11
citation to particular page, *inside front cover, i,* 17
civil law, 53–54
commentary on, cited with case, 14, 54
Commonwealth and common law, 46–47
components of citations, 36

Page references in regular type are to INSTRUCTIONS; page references in *italics* are to EXAMPLES.

computerized research service, 52
concurring opinion, 49
country, indication of, 53–54
court of decision, 36
court of decision, abbreviations, 44–48
court of decision, American, 44–46
court of decision, other jurisdictions, 46–48, 53–54
court, when indicated, 44
date, civil law, 53
dates, 36, 48–49, 52
denial of rehearing, 50
dictum, 49
dissenting opinion, 49
docket number, *35–36*, 53
dual citation of sources, 43
England, 186–89
federal court, 133–35
filed, *35*, 52
foreign, names of, 53
foreign, other jurisdictions, 53–54
history on remand, 50
history, prior and subsequent, 50–52
interim orders, *35*
international, *117*
international and world organization, 121–24
international arbitrations, 123–24
International Court of Justice, 121–22
italicization of names in footnotes, 6
italicization of names in text, 3, 5
italicized words in history of, 50–52
Judge or Justice writing opinion, 49
LEXIS, cited to, *52*
memoranda in, citations to, 53
memorandum decision, 49
motions, citation to, 53
name cited as in official report, 36
name of country needed, 53–54
named in text, initial and subsequent citation, 23–24
names, 36–43
newspapers, cited in, *35*, *44*, 105
newspapers, when cited, 43–44
no names, citation of, 36–37
non-common-law, *36*, 53–54
number of case, *35–36*, 53
official reporters, when cited, 43
order within signal, 10–11
page citations, 16–18
parallel citation of sources, *inside front cover*, *i*, 43
particular page, citation of, *inside front cover*, *i*, 17
pending, *35–36*, 48–49, 53
per curiam decisions, 49–50
periodicals, when cited, 43–44
Permanent International Court of Justice, 121–22
plurality opinion, 49
prior history, 50–52
published decision, *35*
recent, *35*, *49*
records, citation of, *35*, 53
releases of administrative agencies, cited to, 43
repeating citations of, 21–24
reporters, 36, 44
reporters cited, 43–44
reporters, defined, 44
reporters, reprinted, 44
services, appearing in, *inside front cover*, *i*, *35*
services, when cited, 43
slip opinions, reported in, *35*, 44, 52–53
sources cited, 43–44
state courts, 45–46
statutory material, cited with, 14
subsequent history, *35–36*, 50–52
transcript of record, citations to, *35*, 53
typeface used in footnotes, 5–6
typeface used in text, 3, 5
unofficial reporter, when cited, 43–44
unreported, *35*, 52
weight of authority, 49–50
WESTLAW, cited to, 52
World Court, 121–22
year of decision, 48–49
Centuries, 30
Certiorari
applied for, granted, denied, *49*, 51
indication in case history, 51
petition, citation of, *36*
"*sub nom.*" not used, 51
"*Cf.*," as signal, 9
C.F.R., *75*, 76, 78
"Chancellor," abbrevation of, 33
Chancery Division, English, 188–89
Chapters
codes, statutory, 60–61
number, when given for federal statute, 63
"Chapter(s)," abbreviation of, 15
Charters, international organizations, 117, 128–29
"Chief Baron," "Justice," "Judge," abbreviation of, 33
"Circuit," capitalization of, 32

Page references in regular type are to INSTRUCTIONS; page references in *italics* are to EXAMPLES.

Circuit courts of appeals
(*see* Courts)
Circuit courts, old federal, 45, 133
Circuit Justice, 45, 133
Citation of commentary with case or book, 14
Citation order, 7, 10–13
Citation sentences and clauses, 7–8, 10–13
Citations
(*see also* specific types of material)
authoritativeness, order within citation, 10
authorities, 9
basic forms, *inside front cover, i*
briefs and legal memoranda, *inside front cover,* 3–4, 7, *21, 86*
cases cited with statutory material, *14*
comparing authorities, 9
direct contradiction, 9
direct support, 8
footnotes, 17–18
law review text and footnotes, *8*
material cited more than once, 21–25
numerous authorities, *7–8*
opposing proposition, 9
order of, 7–13
pages, 16–18
parenthetical explanations, 13
placement, 7–8
placement after quotation, 25
punctuation of, 7–8, 19–20
quotations, 25–28
repeating citations, 21–23
sampling of authorities, 8
signals in, 7–10
statutory material cited with case, *14*
string citations, 7–8, 10–13
subdivisions, 14–15
supplementary material, 9–10
supporting proposition, 8–9
typeface used, 3–6
weight of, indicated parenthetically, 49–50
City and county ordinances, 67
"City of," when omitted in case names, 39
Civil law jurisdictions
administrative materials, 190–200
cases, *36,* 53–54
codes, *58,* 71, 190–200
constitutions, 190–200
courts, 190–200
session laws, 190–200
statutes, *58,* 71, 190–200
Civil Rights Act of 1964, 75
"Clause(s)," abbreviation of, 15
Clean Air Act, 75
Closing up of abbreviations, 28–29
"Co.," in case names, 38, 40
"Code," capitalization of, 32
Code, Internal Revenue
(*see* Internal Revenue Code)
Code of Federal Regulations (C.F.R.), *75,* 76, 78
Code of Justinian, 198
Code of Theodosius, 199
Codes
(*see also* Statutes)
abbreviations, 60
administrative compilations, 77–78
American, *57–58,* 60
appendices, 61–62
appendix with reprinted statute, *62*
Canadian, 70–71
chapters, 60–61
citation, basic forms, *inside front cover, i, 57–58*
city ordinances, 67
civil law countries, 190–200
Code of Federal Regulations, 75, 76
commonwealth and common law countries, 179–190
compilers of, 61
components of citation, 58
county ordinances, 67
date, 62
editors, 61
English, 70
ethics, 69–70
federal, 60–62
federal and state, *57–58*
foreign, *29–30, 58,* 70–71, 179–200
(*see also* name of individual country)
future location of statutes, 64
Internal Revenue, 66–67
legislative materials, 71–75
materially different from statute, 59
municipal ordinances, 67
official and unofficial, 58
ordinances, municipal, 67
parallel citation to, 63–64
pocket parts, 62
positive law, enacted into, 59
publishers of, 61
Roman law, 198–99
scattered sections, 59–60
secondary sources cited to, 58

Page references in regular type are to INSTRUCTIONS, page references in *italics* are to EXAMPLES.

sections cited, 59–60
state, 60–62, 136–76
statutes, when cited to, 58–59
subject-matter, 60–62
subject-matter title, 61
supplements, 58–59, 60, 61, 62
tax materials, 66–67
titles, 60–61
Treasury materials, 77–78
typeface used, 60
uncompiled laws, 61
uniform acts, 68–69
unofficial, differently numbered, 62
volumes, 60–61
which to cite, 58–59, 60–62

Codification
session laws, parenthetical indication of, 64

Collected essays
citation of works in, 85
editor, 85
parallel citation to, 91
typeface, 85

Colorado
courts, statutes, and administrative materials, 140–41

Column, newspaper material cited by, 104

"Column(s)," abbreviation of, 15

Comma
citing commentary with case or statute, 14
citing multiple sections of code, *19*
periodical names, 92
titles ending in dates, 82

Command number, English, 120

Command Papers (English), 186

"Comment," designating student work, 89

Commentary
citation of, 14
foreign cases, on, 54

Comments
model codes, 69
periodicals, 89
restatements, 69
rules of ethics, 69
standards, 69

Commerce Clearing House (CCH) services, 108
(*see also* Services and topical reporters)

Commerce Court, 133

"Commissioner," abbreviation of, 33

Commissioner of Internal Revenue, in case names, 41

Committee materials, UN, 124–25

Committee prints, *72*, 74

Committee records, UN, 124–25

Common Market Law Reports, 129

Common Market materials, 122–23, 129

Common Market Reporter, *117*, 122–23, 129

Commonwealth materials
administrative materials, 186
cases, 35–36, 46–47, 179–90
codes, 70–71
codes, statutory, 179–90
periodicals, 91–103
session laws, 70–71, 179–90
statutes, *58*, 70–71, 179–90
treaties, 120–21

"Commonwealth of," when omitted in case names, 39

***"Compare . . . with . . . ,"* as signal,** 9

Compilations
administrative regulations, 76–78
international agreements, *117*
treaties, *117*, 120–21

Compilations of statutes
(*see also* Codes, Statutes)
federal, 60–62
foreign, 70–71
state, 60–62

Compiler of codes, 61

Computerized research services, 52

Concurrent resolutions, 72–73

Concurring opinions, *17*, 49, 52

"Congress," capitalization of, *31*

Congressional Debates, *75*

Congressional Globe, *75*

Congressional materials
bills and resolutions, 72–73
committee prints, 74
concurrent resolutions, 72–73
debates, 74–75
documents, *72*, 73–74
hearings, *71*, 73
joint resolutions, 72–73
parallel citations, 75
reports, 73–74
resolutions, 72–73
secondary authority, 75
unnumbered documents, 74

Congressional Record
daily edition, *71*, *72*, *74*
debates, 74
permanent edition, *74*
resolutions cited to, 72–73

Connecticut

Page references in regular type are to INSTRUCTIONS; page references in *italics* are to EXAMPLES.

courts, statutes, and administrative materials, 141–42
Consecutive pages or footnotes, citation of, 17
Consecutive sections of codes, 19–20
Consolidated actions, case names, 37
Constitutions
capitalization of parts of, 32
citation, basic forms, *inside front cover, i*
citation order, 11
civil law countries, 190–200
federal and state, 57
foreign, 57, 190–200
generally, 57
League of Nations, 129
order within signal, 11
subdivision, 57
superseded, 57
typeface in footnotes, 57
UN charter, *117*, 128
"*Construed in*," use of, 14
"Construing," use of, 14
"*Contra*," as signal, 9
Conventions, international, 118
"Corp.," in case names, 38
Corporations
abbreviations, 38
authors, 82
case names, 38
***Corpus Juris Secundum* (C.J.S.),** *86*
Council of Europe materials, 130
Countries
(*see also* name of jurisdiction)
abbreviated in case names, 41
abbreviations of, *inside back cover,* 119
indication of, in international arbitrations, 123
County and city ordinances, 67
"Court," capitalization of, 32
Court of Appeal, English, 188
Court of Claims, 134
Court of Customs and Patent Appeals, 134
Court of decision
abbreviations, 44–48
American, 44–46
civil law jurisdictions, 45, 47, 53–54
Commonwealth and common law jurisdictions, 44–45, 46–47
international arbitrations, *117*, 124
international cases, 121–24
state, 45–46
when indicated, 36, 44–45, 52, 53
when omitted, 45
World Court cases, 121
Court of International Trade, 134
Court of Justice of the European Communities, 122–23
Court of Military Appeals, 135
Courts
(*see also* name of court or jurisdiction)
abbreviations, 44–48
administrative orders, 79
Appeals, District of Columbia Circuit, Court of, 45, 133
Appeals, District of Columbia Municipal Court of, 143
appeals, United States courts of, 45, 133
Arbitration, Permanent Court of, 124
bankruptcy, 45, *107*, 134
bankruptcy appellate panels, 45, 134
Board of Tax Appeals, 134
circuit courts, old federal, 45, 133
Circuit Justices, 133
civil law countries, 190–200
Claims, Court of, 134
Commerce Court, 133
Commonwealth and common law countries, 179–190
Customs and Patent Appeals, Court of, 134
district, federal, 45, 134
Emergency Court of Appeals, 133
English, 186–89
federal, 133–35
foreign countries, 179–200
foreign, language used in citation of, 53
international, 121–24
International Court of Justice, *117*, 121–22
International Justice, Permanent Court of, 121–22
International Trade, Court of, 134
Judicial Panel on Multi-District Litigation, 45, 134
Military Appeals, Court of, 134, 135
old circuit, federal, 45
Permanent Arbitration, Court of, *117*, 124
Permanent Court of International Justice, 121–22
Railroad Reorganization Court, 133
rules, 67
state, 136–76
Tax Court, 134
Temporary Emergency Court of Appeals, 133

Page references in regular type are to INSTRUCTIONS; page references in *italics* are to EXAMPLES.

terms, 33
U.S. Supreme (*see* U.S. Supreme Court)
World Court, *117*, 121–22
Courts of Military Review, 135
Cross-references
briefs and legal memoranda, 21, *22*
generally, 21
groups of authorities previously cited, *21*
previous footnotes, 21
textual material in same work, 21
Cumulative Bulletin, 78
Customs Court, 134
Cyclopedia of the Law of Private Corporations, *83*

Dash, used in citing sections of codes, 19–20
Dates
administrative compilations, 78
amended statutes, 65
bilateral and trilateral treaties, 119
books and pamphlets, 81, 83–85
case history, 49
cases, 36, 48–49
cases, cited to U.S.L.W., *49*
cases, English, bracketed date, *49*
cases, foreign, 53
cases, in looseleaf services, *inside front cover*, *35*, 48, *107*
cases, in newspapers, *44*, 48, *105*
cases, in periodicals, *35*, 48
cases, pending, 48–49
cases, unreported, *inside front cover*, *35*, 48
cases, World Court, *117*, 121
Code of Federal Regulations, *75*, 76
codifications of statutes, 62
constitutions, when used, 57
enactment, session laws, 63–64
ethical opinions, 69–70
ethical rules, 69
exact date, administrative cases, 43
exact date, books and pamphlets, 83
exact date, cases, 48–49
exact date, foreign cases, 53
exact date, international agreements, 119
exact date, letters, speeches, and interviews, 85
exact date, ordinances, 67
exact date, periodicals, 87
exact date, services, 108
exact date, statutes, 65
exact date, treaties, 119
exact date, unpublished works, 86
exact date, unreported cases, 48
exact date, World Court cases, 121
filing of appeal, *49*
filing of cases, 52
forewords, 82
Internal Revenue Code, 66
international agreements, *117*, 119
legislative materials, 72, 74
looseleaf statutory codifications, 62
model codes, 68
multilateral treaties, 119
multiple decisions in one year, 49
multivolume works, 83
municipal ordinances, 67
newspapers, 104–05
ordinances, municipal, 67
periodicals, 87
pocket parts, books, 84
prefaces, 82
prior to 1870, books, 84
regnal years, in English statutes, 70
repealed statutes, 65
restatements, 68
rules of court, 67
rules of procedure, 67
services, 107–08
session laws, 63–64
standards, 68
statutes, 66
statutes, amended, 65
statutes, cited to session laws, 63–64
statutes, foreign, 71
statutes, in current code, 62
statutes, in supplements to code, 62
statutes, not in current code, 63–65
statutes, repealed, 65
statutes, uniform acts, 68
supplements, books, 84
supplements, codes, 62
titles ending in, 82
treaties, *117*, 119
UN materials, 126–27
uniform acts, 68
unreported cases, *35*, 48
U.S. Supreme Court cases, *36*, 48
year of decision of case, 36, 48–49
"D/b/a," omission in case names, *37*
Debates
congressional, *72*, 74–75
English parliamentary, 186

Page references in regular type are to INSTRUCTIONS; page references in *italics* are to EXAMPLES.

European Parliamentary Assembly, 129
legislative, *72,* 74–75
United Kingdom, 180
U.S. congressional, 74–75
U.S. congressional, prior to 1873, 75
Decades, 30
Decimal point, 30
Decision by implication, indication of, 49
"Decision(s)," abbreviation of, 15
Declaration of Independence, *19*
Delaware
courts and statutes, *19, 61,* 142
Deletions from quotations, 26–28
Denial of certiorari, *3, 49,* 51
Denial of rehearing, when given, 50
Department of State publications, 120
Department, state court, 46
Descriptive terms, omitted in case names, 38
Development Programme, UN, 127–28
"Developments in the Law," *89*
Dictionaries, legal, *86*
Dictum, indication of, 49
Digest of Justinian, 198
Disciplinary rules, 69
Discussion draft, *69*
Dismissal of appeal, 51
Dissenting opinion
indication of, *17,* 49
slip opinion, 52
District court, federal
cases in, 45, 134
rules of, 67
District of Columbia
Circuit Court of Appeals for the, 45, 133
courts, statutes, and administrative materials, 143
Divided court, parenthetical indication of, 49
Division, federal courts, 45
Docket number
appeal or petition for certiorari, *35, 36,* 53
citation of unreported cases, *35,* 52
pending cases, 53
renumbering, 53
unreported cases, *35–36,* 52–53
Document number, UN publications, 124, 125
Documents
congressional, *72,* 73–74
legislative, *72*
other international organizations, 128–30
UN, 124–28
Dollar amounts
numerals used, 30
Dominion Law Reports, 181
Dual citation, reporters requiring, 43
East Germany
(*see* Germany)
Ecclesiastical courts, 189
Economic and Social Council, UN, records, 124, 127
Editions
abbreviation of, 83–85
books and pamphlets, 81–85
Code of Federal Regulations, 76
Congressional Record, 74
The Federalist, 87
first edition, when cited, 84
names of, 83–85
newspapers, 105
when indicated, books and pamphlets, 83
year, 81–82
Editors
books and pamphlets, 81–82, 85
codes, 61, 71
collected essays, 85
essays in collection, 85
reporters, 44
***"E.g.,"* as signal,** 8
Ellipsis, 26–27
Emergency Court of Appeals, 133
Emphasis in quotations, 20, 26
Emphasis, italics for, 31
"En banc," parenthetical indication of, 49
Encyclopedias, legal, *86*
***"Enforced,"* in case history,** *51, 52*
***"Enforcing,"* in case history,** 51
England
administrative material, 186
case reports, abbreviations, 186–89
cases, court of decision, 46–47
cases, date, 48–49
cases, generally, 186–89
cases, House of Lords and Privy Council, other than English appeals, 46–47
courts, 186–89
parliamentary material, 186
reports, 186–89
sovereigns, abbreviations, 70
treaties, 120
English *Law Reports* series
abbreviations of, 187–89
citation of, 187, 188

Page references in regular type are to INSTRUCTIONS; page references in italics are to EXAMPLES.

English Reports—Full Reprint, 186
Essays in collection
citation of material in, 85
editor, 85
parallel citation to, 91
typeface, 85
"Estate of," in case names, 38
"Et al.," omitted, 37, 81
"Et seq.," prohibition on use, 19
Ethical considerations, 69
Ethics, codes of, 69–70
European Commission on Human Rights, 130
European Community materials, 122–23, 129
European Parliament Working Document, 129
European Parliamentary Assembly, 129
Evidence, rules of, 67
"*Ex rel.*," in case names, *3*, 5, *6*, 37
Exact date
(*see* Dates)
Executive Agreement Series **(E.A.S.),** 120
Executive orders, 78
Explanation of cited authorities, use of parentheticals, iv, 13, 49–50, 66, 86
Explanatory phrases
amended statute, *65*
italicization of, briefs and legal memoranda, *inside front cover*, 3
repealed statute, *65*
typeface used in briefs and legal memoranda, 3
typeface used in law review footnotes, 6

Family Divisional Court, English, 189
Federal Cases, 133, 134, 137
Federal courts
(*see also* individual court name)
courts of appeals, cited to West only, 133
courts of decision, 45
district courts, cited to West only, 139
generally, 133–35
Supreme Court, official cite only, 133
Federal government
(*see* United States)
Federal Judicial Center
Manual for Complex Litigation, 86
Federal Practice and Procedure, *81*, *86*
Federal Register, *75*, 76–78
Federal Regulations, Code of, *75*, 76, *78*
Federal Reporter, *3*, *6*, *35*, *36*, 133–34
Federal Rules Decisions, 134
Federal Rules of Appellate Procedure, *67*
Federal Rules of Civil Procedure, *67*
Federal Rules of Criminal Procedure, *67*
Federal Rules of Evidence, *20*, 67
Federal Rules Service, 134
Federal statutes
(*see* Statutes, *Statutes at Large*)
Federal Supplement, *inside front cover*, *i*, *5*, *13*, *35*, 134
The Federalist, 87
Financial prospectus, *83*
Financial reports, *82*
First editions, when cited, 84
First listed relator, not omitted in case names, 37
First names and initials
authors of books and pamphlets, 81
case names, 39–40
Florida
courts, statutes, and administrative materials, 143–44
"Follo(s)," abbreviation of, 15
Footnotes
abbreviation of, 17, 18
citation of, 17–18
consecutive and nonconsecutive, 18
cross-reference to, 21
material previously cited in, 21–25
multipage, 17
multiple, 18
numbers in, 30
omission from quotation, indication of, 26
spanning several pages, 17
textual, typeface used, 6
typeface used for citations in, 5–6
"Footnote(s)," abbreviation of, 15
"For the use of," abbreviated to "*ex rel.*," 37
Foreign countries
(*see also* name of individual country)
abbreviation of, *inside back cover*, 53–54, 119
World Court cases, 21
Foreign derivation, italicization of words of, 31
Foreign language
abbreviation of words, 122
cite to English version where possible, international materials, 120, 122, 129
constitutions, 57
court name and location, give English version, 53
titles of treaties, 118

Page references in regular type are to INSTRUCTIONS; page references in *italics* are to EXAMPLES.

treaties, citations to English-language materials preferred, 120
UN materials, 126
words italicized, 31

Foreign materials
(*see also* name of individual country)
abbreviations, 29–30, 53
bills and resolutions, 70–71
cases, court of decision, 45, 53, 179–200
cases, generally, *36*, 45, 53–54
cases, jurisdiction, 46–47
cases, name, 53
cases, reporters, case comments in, 54
citation, basic forms of, *36*
codes, statutory, 179–200
constitutions, 57, 190–200
English used in naming courts, 53
establishing abbreviations in initial citation, 29–30
international
(*see* International agreements, International organization materials)
international agreements, *117*, 118–21
parliamentary materials, 186
periodicals, 103–04
session laws, 70–71, 179–200
statutes, *58*, 70–71, 179–200
treaties, 118–21

Foreign names, citation of, 40

Forewords, *17, 82, 88*

Formal opinions on professional responsibility, *69*

France
administrative materials, 192
codes, 192–93
constitutions, 192
courts, 191–92
statutes and decrees, 193

Frequently cited authorities, short forms for, 22–25

General Assembly, UN, records, *117*, 124, 126–27

Geographical terms
abbreviated in footnotes, 41
abbreviations, *inside back cover*
case names, 39
railroad names, 42

Georgia
courts, statutes, and administrative materials, *61*, 144

Germany
administrative materials, W. Ger., 194
codes, E. Ger., 193
codes, W. Ger., 195
constitution, E. Ger., 193
constitution, W. Ger., 194–95
courts, E. Ger., 193
courts, W. Ger., 194
statutes and decrees, E. Ger., 194
statutes and decrees, W. Ger., 195

Given names and initials
authors, 81
corporation, partnership, and business names, 39
individuals, 39–40

Government agencies
annual and regular reports, 77
authors, as, *74*, 82
books and numbered publications, 82
capitalization of, *31*
subdivisions, 82

Government Printing Office Style Manual, *iv*, 31

Government publications, U.S., 73–75, 82, 83, 133–36

Groups of authorities previously cited, reference to, *21*

Guam
courts, statutes, and administrative materials, 145

Hague Court Reports, 124

Hawaii
courts and statutes, *16*, 145

Headings, capitalization in, 31–32

Hearings, *23*
bills and resolutions cited to, 73
congressional, *inside front cover, i, 4, 13, 23, 71*, 73
italicization in briefs and legal memoranda, 4
titles of, printed in italic type, 4, *5*, 73
typeface used in briefs and legal memoranda, 4

"Hereinafter," used for shortened citation forms, 23, 81

High Court of Justice, English, 188

History of cases
both prior and subsequent, 51
dates of decisions, 49
explanatory words, abbreviations, 51
explanatory words italicized or underscored, *inside front cover, i, 3, 6, 35–36, 49*, 50–52
"mem.," opinions designated as, 51

Page references in regular type are to INSTRUCTIONS; page references in *italics* are to EXAMPLES.

multiple, 50
ordering within signal unaffected by, 10
"per curiam," opinions designated as, 51
position of parentheticals, 13
prior and subsequent, 36, 50–52
prior history indicated for memorandum decision, 50
remand, when given, 50
separate decisions of other issues, when cited, 50–52
subsequent history, *35–36, 49,* 50–52
subsequent history, appeal filed, granted, *35, 49,* 51
subsequent history, certiorari applied for, granted, denied, *36,* 50–51
subsequent history, names of parties, when different on appeal, 51
subsequent history, reason for subsequent disposition, 51
typeface, 50–52

History of statutes
amended statutes, 59, 65–66
parenthetically indicated, 65–66

Holdings
alternative, indication of, 49
concurring opinion, 49
contrary to citations, 9
dictum, 49
dissenting opinion, 49
implied, indication of, 49
plurality opinion, 49
unclear, indication of, 49

House of Commons
debates and Journal, 186

House of Lords
court, 185–86
debates and Journal, 186
decisions on other than English appeals, 46–47

House of Representatives
(*see* Congressional materials)

***"Id.,"* use of,** 21–22

Idaho
courts and statutes, 145

Illinois
courts, statutes, and administrative materials, 146
statutes, use of original name in citation of, *61,* 146

Implied holdings, indication of, 49

***"In re,"* in case names,** 37–38

"In the matter of," abbreviated to *"In re,"* 37–38

"In," use of, 13–14

"Inc.," in case names, 38, 40

Inclusive numbers, 17–20

Income tax materials
(*see* Tax materials)

India
courts and statutes, 184

Indiana
courts, statutes, and administrative materials, 146–47

Informal and mimeographed materials, 81, 86

Informal opinions on professional responsibility, *70*

***"Infra,"* use of,** 21

Initials
authors of books and pamphlets, 81
authors of periodicals, 88
closing up of, 28–29
commonly abbreviated names, 29
editors, 81–82
parties in case names, 29, *37,* 38, 39
punctuation of, 29
translators, 81–82

Insertions in quotations, 26

Institutes of Justinian, 198

Institutes, regular publications by, 88

Institutional authors, 74, 77, 82

Interim orders, *35*

Internal Revenue Code
briefs and legal memoranda, citations in, 66–67
citation to other than current code, 66–67
generally, 66–67
legislative history, 75
privately published source, 66
supplements, 66
year, 66

Internal Revenue Commissioner, in case names, 41

"Internal Revenue," omitted in case names, 41

Internal revenue regulations and rulings, 77–78

International agreements
American treaties, *inside front cover, i,* 120
basic citation forms, 117–118
bilateral, *117*
citation, basic form of, *inside front cover, i,* 117–18

I

Page references in regular type are to INSTRUCTIONS; page references in *italics* are to EXAMPLES.

citation order, 12
compilations of agreements, 120–21
components of citation, 118
country names, 119
date, 119
entry into force, 119
Executive Agreement Series (E.A.S.), 120
foreign countries, 119
foreign language, titles in, 118
international sources, 120
language of source, 120
League of Nations Treaty Series (L.N.T.S.), 120
multilateral, *117*, 120–21
name, 118–19
official sources, 120–21
opening for signature, 119
order within signal, 12
parallel citation, *inside front cover, i,* 120
parties to, 119
popular name, 118–19
sources, international, 120–21
sources, official, 120–21
State Department sources, 120
Statutes at Large (Stat.), 120
subject matter, 118–19
title, 118–19
Treaties and Other International Acts Series (T.I.A.S.), *inside front cover, i,* 120
treaty collections, 120–21
Treaty Series (T.S.), 120
trilateral, *117*
U.S. a party, *inside front cover, i, 117,* 120
U.S. not a party, *117,* 120–21
U.S. Treaties and Other International Agreements (U.S.T.), *inside front cover, i,* 120
year, 119

International Court of Justice, 121–22

International law
arbitrations, 123–24
cases, 121–24
Common Market, 129
Council of Europe, 130
courts, 121–24
European Community, 129
generally, 117–30
international agreements, 118–21
League of Nations, 129
treaties, 118–21
UN, 124–28
yearbooks, 130–31

International Law Cases, Annual Digest and Reports of, 123

International Law Commission, Yearbook, 128, 130

International Law Reports, 123

International materials
arbitrations, 123–24
basic citation forms, *117*
cases, 121–24
Common Market, 129
Council of Europe, 130
European Community, 129
generally, 117–30
international agreements, 118–21
League of Nations, 129
treaties, *inside front cover, i,* 118–21
treaty series, 120
UN, 124–28
yearbooks, 130–31

International organization materials
(*see also* UN materials)
arbitrations, 123–24
basic citation forms, 117
cases, 121–24
charters, 128, 129
Common Market, *117*, 129
Council of Europe, *117*, 130
Court of Justice of the European Communities, 122–23
courts, 121–24
debates, European Parliamentary Assembly, 129
document number of League of Nations materials, 129
document number of UN materials, *117,* 126
European Community, *117*, 129
foreign language version of UN materials, 126
generally, 121–30
International Court of Justice, *117,* 121–22
League of Nations, 129
League of Nations covenant, 129
League of Nations Official Journal, 129
number, League of Nations documents, 129
number, UN documents, *117*, 126
pages, UN materials, 125–26
paragraphs, UN materials, 125–26
Permanent Court of International Justice, 121–22
Reports of International Arbitral Awards, United Nations, 124

Page references in regular type are to INSTRUCTIONS; page references in *italics* are to EXAMPLES.

serial number, League of Nations documents, 129
United Nations Treaty Series (U.N.T.S.), 120
World Court, 121–22
yearbooks, 124, 130–31

Interviews
citation of, *85*
typeface of citations to, *85*

Introductory signals
(*see* Signals)

Iowa
courts, statutes, and administrative materials, *62,* 147

"I.R.C." replacing "26 U.S.C.," 66, 135

Ireland (before 1924), 189–90

Italicization
(*see also* Typeface)
foreign words, 31
hypothetical parties, 31

Italy
administrative materials, 196
codes, 196
constitution, 196
courts, 196
statutes and decrees, 196–97

Jackson, Howell, *43*, 203–37

Japan
administrative materials, 197
codes, 197
constitution, 197
courts, 197
statutes and decrees, 197

Joining citations
order of citations, 10–13
punctuation, 7–8

Joint resolutions, 72–73

Journal
House of Commons, 186
House of Lords, 186
League of Nations, Official, 129
periodical names, 97

Judge
indication of, in citation, 33, 49
used as title, 33

"Judge," capitalization of, 32

Judgements of the U.N. Administrative Tribunal, 128

"Judge(s)," abbreviation of, 33

Judges and Justices
order of listing, 33
titles, use of, 33

"Judgment of," use in citation, 36–37, 53

Judicial history of cases
(*see* History of cases)

Judicial Panel on Multi-District Litigation, 45, 134

Jump cites
(*see* Pinpoint citations)

Jurisdiction, indication of
American cases, 44–45
American statutes, 63
common law cases, 44–45
Commonwealth and common law jurisdictions, cases, 46–47
Commonwealth and common law jurisdictions, statutes, 71
municipal ordinances, 67
non-common-law citations, 53–54
ordinances, municipal, 67
session laws, 63

Justice
indication of, in citation, 49

"Justice," capitalization of, 32

"Justice(s)," abbreviation of, 33

Justinian, Institutes, Digest, and Code of, 198

Kansas
courts, statutes, and administrative materials, 147–48

Kentucky
courts, statutes, and administrative materials, 148–49

Kings Bench Division, 188

***"L"* as letter in subdivision,** 31

Labor unions, in case names, 40–41

Länder
(*see* Germany)

Large and small capitals
(*see* Typeface)

Latin words
citation forms, italicization in, 37–38
italicization of, 31
italicization in case names, 3, 5, 6, 38
procedural phrases in case names, 37–38
shortened citation forms, italicization in, *21–22*
use of, 20–22

Law Journal Reports, 187

Law journals and reviews
abbreviations, American, 91–103
abbreviations, Commonwealth and common law, 91–103
abbreviations, non-common-law, 103–04

Page references in regular type are to INSTRUCTIONS; page references in *italics* are to EXAMPLES.

abbreviations, spacing of, *28*
articles, 88
basic citation forms, *inside front cover, i, 4, 5, 6, 7, 8, 17,* 87
book reviews, 89
citation in, 6–7
citation order, 12–13
comment, 89
commentary cited with case, 14
components of citation, 87
generally, 87–104
new series (n.s.), 92
notes, 89
order within signal, 12–13
short commentary, 89
special projects, 89
student material, 89
typeface of citations in briefs and legal memoranda, 3–4
typeface of citations in law review text, 5
typeface of citations in law review footnotes, 5–6

Law Times Reports, 187
***Lawyer's Reports Annotated* (L.R.A.), annotations in,** 90
Leaflets, *83*
League of Nations materials
(*see* International organization materials)
League of Nations Treaty Series (L.N.T.S.), 120
Legal dictionaries, *86*
Legal encyclopedias, *86*
Legal newspapers
(*see* Newspapers)
Legal services, looseleaf
(*see* Services and topical reporters)
Legislation
(*see* Codes, Session laws, Statutes)
Legislative histories, 71–75
Legislative materials, 71–75
basic citation forms, *inside front cover, i,* 71–72
bills and resolutions, 72–73
citation order, 12
committee prints, 74
components of citation, 72
debates, 74–75
documents, 73–74
English, 186
foreign, 72
hearings, *inside front cover, i, 4, 5, 23,* 73
order within signal, 12
parallel citations, 75
presidential messages, *79*
reports, *inside front cover, i,* 73–74
secondary authorities, 75
state, 73
typeface used in briefs and legal memoranda, 4
United Kingdom, 186
unnumbered documents, 74

Letters
correspondence, citation of, *81, 85*
typeface in footnotes, 85

Letters of the alphabet, inserted or substituted in quotations, 26
LEXIS, *52*
Limited circulation, works of, 81, 85–86
Local court rules, 67
Location, phrases of
letters, speeches, and interviews, 86
omitted from case names, 39
railroad names, in, 42
unpublished works, 86
Long case names
"hereinafter" form, when used, 22, 37
Looseleaf services
(*see* Services and topical reporters)
Looseleaf statutory codifications, 62
"Lord Justice," abbreviation of, 33
Louisiana
courts, statutes, and administrative materials, 149–50
"Ltd.," in case names, 38, 40

Magazines, 87–104
"Magistrate," abbreviation of, 33
Maine
courts and statutes, 150
Manitoba
courts and statutes, 181–82
Manual for Complex Litigation, 86
Manuscripts, typed
citation of, 81, 86
Maritime provinces
courts and statutes, 182–83
Maryland
courts, statutes, and administrative materials, 150–51
Massachusetts
advance sheets, *43*
courts, statutes, and administrative materials, *62,* 152
"Master of the Rolls," abbreviation of, 33
Materially different language in code and statute, 59

Page references in regular type are to INSTRUCTIONS; page references in *italics* are to EXAMPLES.

Matthew Bender services (MB), 108
(*see also* Services and topical reporters)
"Mediator," abbreviation of, 33
Memoranda, 53
Memorandum decision
indication of, 49, 51
prior history must be given, 50
Mexico
courts, statutes, and decrees, 198
Michigan
courts, statutes, and administrative materials, 153
statutes cited to official or unofficial code, *67*
Microfiche, iv
Military cases, 134–35
Military Justice Reporter, 135
Mimeographed and other informally printed matter, 81, 86
Minnesota
courts, statutes, and administrative materials, 153–54
Mississippi
courts and statutes, 154
Missouri
courts, statutes, and administrative materials, 154–55
Mistakes in quotations, indicated by "[sic]," 26
Mixed arbitral tribunals, cases before, 123–24
Model Code of Professional Responsibility, 69
Model codes, 68–69
Model Penal Code, *69*
Model Rules of Professional Conduct, 69
"*Modified*" and "*modifying*," in case history, 51
Monarchs, English, 70
Monographs, *83,* 108
Montana
courts, statutes, and administrative materials, 155
Month used to indicate volume, *108*
Months, abbreviation of, *inside back cover*
Moore's Federal Practice, *18, 82*
Motions, 53
Multinational materials
arbitrations, 123–24
cases, 121–24
Common Market, 129
Council of Europe, 130
European Community, 129
generally, 117–30
international agreements, 118–21
League of Nations, 128–29
treaties, 118–21
treaty series, 120
UN, 124–28
yearbooks, 130
Multipart articles, 90–91
Multiple authors, *inside front cover, i, 7, 8, 20, 23,* 81
Multiple decisions within a single year, 49
Multiple editions and printings of book, 81–85
Multiple pages, citation of, 17–18
Multiple parties, words indicating, omitted in case names, 37
Multiple printings of books, 83
Municipal ordinances, 67

Name of state, when omitted in case name, 37
Names
authors, books and pamphlets, 81–82
book reviews, 90
bound services, abbreviated, 108–14
commonly abbreviated, 29, 38
editions of books and pamphlets, 83–85
editors, 81–82
looseleaf services, abbreviated, 108–14
newspaper sections, 104–05
newspapers, abbreviated, 104
parties, when different on appeal, 51–52
periodicals, abbreviated, English language, 91–103
periodicals, abbreviated, non-English language, 103–04
periodicals, abbreviation and typeface, 87
prepositions in periodical names, 91
rules and regulations, 76–77
services, 107
services, abbreviated, 108–14
state, when omitted, 37
statutes, 60
translators, 81–82
treaties, 118–19
Names of cases
(*see* Case names)
National Labor Relations Act, 75
National Reporter System
(*see* Unofficial reporters)
Nebraska
courts, statutes, and administrative materials, *62,* 155

Page references in regular type are to INSTRUCTIONS; page references in *italics* are to EXAMPLES.

Netherlands
codes, 198
constitutions, 198
courts, 198
statutes and decrees, 198
Nevada
courts, statutes, and administrative materials, 155–56
New Brunswick
courts and statutes, 181–82
New Hampshire
courts, statutes, and administrative materials, 156
New Jersey
courts, statutes, and administrative materials, *19*, 156–57
New Mexico
courts and statutes, *19*, 157
New series (n.s.) of periodical, 92
New York
courts, statutes, and administrative materials, *20*, *61*, 157–61
New Zealand
courts, 184–85
statutes, 185
treaty series, 120
Newfoundland
courts and statutes, 182–83
Newspapers
abbreviated names, 104
articles, 104–05
authors, 104
bylines of articles, 104
cases cited to, *35*, 43–44, 105
citation of, 104–05
citation order, 12
columns, 104
dates, 104–05
editions, 105
pages, 104
pinpoint citations, 104–05
sections, 104–05
statutes cited to, 58, 59, 64–65
titles of articles, 104–05
titles of, printed in italic type, 3, 5
typeface, 104
typeface in briefs and legal memoranda, *inside front cover*, 3–4
typeface in law reviews, *i*, 6
typeface of titles, *4*, 5
when cited, 43–44, 64–65
"No.," in case names, 38
"[No signal]" as signal, 8
Nonconsecutive pages, citation of, 18
Nonconsecutive sections, citation of, 19
North Carolina
courts, statutes, and administrative materials, 161–62
North Dakota
courts, statutes, and administrative materials, 162–63
Northern Ireland
courts, statutes, and administrative materials, 189–90
Northwest Territories
courts and statutes, 182–83
"Note," designating student work, cited in roman, *inside front cover*, *i*, *5*, *10*, *23*, 89
***"Noted in,"* use of,** 14
Notes
(*see also* Footnotes)
statutory, 20
Notes, in periodicals, 89
"Noting," use of, 14
Nouns, capitalization of, 31–33
Nova Scotia
courts and statutes, 182–83
Novels (Roman Law), 199
Number and series
League of Nations materials, 129
Permanent Court of International Justice, 121
UN materials, *117*, 126
Number of case
administrative cases, 43
appeal or petition for certiorari, *35*, *36*, 53
Federal Cases, 133, 134
pending case, *35*, *36*, 53
renumbered, 53
service citations, 108
unreported cases, *35*, *36*, 52
Numbers
Arabic numerals designating monarchs, 70
Arabic numerals designating volumes, 15
beginning sentence, 30
centuries, 30
commas, used to separate groups, 30
Congress and session, 72, 74
decades, 30
designating subdivision, spelled out, 30
docket
(*see* Number of case)
dollar amounts, numerals used, 30
English sovereigns, 70
ethical opinion, 69–70

Page references in regular type are to INSTRUCTIONS; page references in *italics* are to EXAMPLES.

five or more digits, 30
generally, 30
inclusive pages, 17
inclusive paragraphs, 20
inclusive sections of codes, 19
legislature, 74
ordinance, 67
percentages, numerals used, 30
round numbers spelled out, 30
Roman numerals, when not used, 15, 70
serial, of books and pamphlets, 83
serial, of publications, 83
series, consistency in, 30
spacing of, in abbreviations, 28–29
volumes designated by Arabic numerals, 15
"Number(s)," abbreviation of, 15

Occupational Safety and Health Act, 75
"Of America," in case names, 39
Office of Legal Counsel, opinions, *77*
Official and West reporters
generally, 43
U.S. Supreme Court, 133
Official codes
American, 60
Canadian, 70–71
Commonwealth and common law, 70–71
English, 70
other foreign jurisdictions, 71
***Official Journal of the European Community*,** 129
Official names of statutes, 60
Official records
(*see* Records)
Official records, UN, 124
Official releases of administrative agencies, 43
Official reporters
(*see also* name of individual jurisdiction)
abbreviations used, 36
administrative cases, 43
cite case as in, 36
England, 186–89
France, 191–92
Germany, E. Ger., 193
Germany, W. Ger., 194–95
Italy, 196
state cases, 43–44, 45–46, 136–37
Switzerland, 199–200
U.S. Supreme Court cases, 133
when to cite, 43
Official sources
international agreements, 120
international arbitrations, 123–24
statutes, France, 192–93
statutes, Germany, E. Ger., 194
statutes, Germany, W. Ger., 195
statutes, Italy, 196–97
statutes, Switzerland, 199–200
treaties, 120–21
Offprints
(*see* Photoduplicated reprints)
Ohio
courts, statutes, and administrative materials, 163–64
Oklahoma
courts, statutes, and administrative materials, *62,* 164
Omissions
book and pamphlet titles, 82
case names, 37–41
quotations, 26–28
"On the relation of," abbreviated to *"ex rel.,"* 37
Ontario
courts and statutes, 182–83
***"Opened for signature,"* use of,** *117,* 119
Opinion letters, 108
Opinions
administrative, 77
concurring and dissenting, *17,* 49
ethics, 69–70
formal advisory, 77
Opinions of Attorney General, *77*
Opposing citations, introductory signals to, 9, *10*
Order of citation, 7–9, 10–13
Orders, regulations, and rulings of administrative agencies, 76–77
Ordinances, municipal and county, 67
Oregon
courts, statutes, and administrative materials, 165
Original edition of books, citation to star pages, 84
Original source
identified after a quotation, 8, *14*

Pages
administrative compilations, 76
annotations, 90
"at," used in citations to particular pages, 13, 16, *18,* 82
books and pamphlets, 16–18, 81
bound services, 44, 108
Code of Federal Regulations, 76, 78
Common Market cases, 122

Page references in regular type are to INSTRUCTIONS; page references in *italics* are to EXAMPLES.

consecutive and nonconsecutive, 17–18
Federal Register, 76
first page of authority, citation to, 17
generally, 16–18
inclusive, 17
institutes, publications by, 88
International Court of Justice cases, 121
law journals and reviews, 87
legal newspapers, 104
legislative reports and documents, 74
looseleaf services, 108
multipart articles, 91
multiple, citation of, 17–18
newspapers, 104
particular, reference to, 17, 21
"*passim*," use of, 18
periodicals, 87
Permanent Court of International Justice cases, 14
reporters, 44
reprinted reporters with different pagination, 44
services, 108
session laws, 63
slip opinions, 52
star, in books and pamphlets, 84
statutes, 63
statutes, secondary sources, 64
UN materials, 124–26
unpublished opinion, 52
World Court cases, 121

"Page(s)," abbreviation of, 15, 16–17

Pamphlets
(*see* Books and Pamphlets)

Paragraph number, in services, 18, 108

Paragraphed reporters
(*see* Services and topical reporters)

Paragraphs
ABA section reports, 88
ALI proceedings, 88
books and pamphlets, 18, 81
citations to, 18–20, 30
consecutive and nonconsecutive, 20
indented but unnumbered, 18–19
institutes, publications by, 88
international agreements, 118
multiple, 20
omission of, in quotations, 27–28
proceedings, 88
services, *inside front cover, i,* 18, 108
treaties, 118
UN materials, 124–26
unnumbered, citation of, 18–19

"Paragraph(s)," abbreviation of, 15, 18–19, 30, *118*

Parallel citations
articles and collected essays, 91
cases, administrative, 43
cases, American, 43
cases, federal, 74, 133–35
cases, international, 123
cases, reprinted reporters, 44
cases, state, *inside front cover, i, 7, 8, 21,* 43, *46*
collected essays and articles, 91
European Community materials, 122–23, 129
international arbitration awards, 123–24
international law reports, 123
interviews, 86
letters, *86*
limited circulation, works of, 86
order of citations, generally, 43
repeating citations, *21*
services, 43, 122–23
speeches, 86
statutes, American, 63–64
statutes, foreign
(*see* name of individual country)
Treasury regulations, 77
treaties, 120
treaty collections, 120
unpublished works, 86
West reporters, 43

Parenthetical explanations of authorities, 13, 49–50, 66, *85*

Parenthetical indications
alterations in quotations, 26
alternative holding, 49
amended statutes, 65
amendment of statutes, 65
arbitration, international, 123
arbitrator, 42–43
author of opinion, 49
codification of session laws, 64
commentary, 14
computer services, *52*
concurring opinions, 49
court of decision, 36, 44–47
court of decision, American cases, 44
court of decision, common law cases, 44
court of decision, international cases, 124
dates, 44
dictum, 49
dissenting opinions, 49

Page references in regular type are to INSTRUCTIONS; page references in *italics* are to EXAMPLES.

divided court, 49
docket numbers, *36,* 53
editors of books, 81–82
editors of reports, 44
effective date of statute, 62
en banc decisions, 49
ethical opinions, 70
explanatory phrases, 50
implied holding, 49
International Court of Justice, 121
judge writing opinion, 49
jurisdiction, American cases, 44
jurisdiction, common law cases, 44
jurisdiction, Commonwealth and common law materials, 46–47, 71
jurisdiction, non-common-law citations, 53–54
Justice writing opinion, 49
letters, *85*
location of, 13, *14,* 49–50
location of letters, speeches, and interviews, 86
location of unpublished works, 86
memorandum decisions, 49
microfiche, iv
model codes, 68
multipart articles, 90–91
new series (n.s.), 92
number and series of books and pamphlets, 83
order, 13, *14,* 49–50
per curiam decision, 49–50
Permanent Court of International Justice, 121
plurality opinions, 49
popular name of statute, 63
prior history of statute, 65–66
proposed drafts, 68
repealed statutes, 65
restatements, 68
separate opinions, 49
serial number, books and pamphlets, 83
series and number in series publications, 83
services, later bound form, 107
session laws, 64
split decisions, 49
standards, 68
statutes, 66
statutes, amended, 65
statutes, history of, 65–66
statutes, prior history, 65–66
statutes, repealed, 65
tentative draft, 68
translators of books, 81–82
unclear holdings, 49
weight of citations, 49–50
World Court cases, 121
year, English statutes, 70

Parlement Européen Documents de Séance, **129**

Parliamentary materials, British, 72

Parties
appeal, under different names, 51–52
arbitrations, international, 123
citation in case names, 37, 38–41
hypothetical, 31
international agreements, *117,* 119
international arbitrations, *117,* 123
International Court of Justice, *117,* 121
omitted in case names, 37
Permanent Court of International Justice, *117,* 121
treaties, *117,* 119
World Court, *117,* 121

Partnership names in cases, 37, 39

"Part(s)," abbreviation of, 15

"*Passim,*" use of, 18

Pending cases, *35, 36,* 48–49, 53

Pennsylvania
courts, statutes, and administrative materials, *61,* 165–66

"People of," omitted in case names, 39

"Per curiam"
in case history, 51
parenthetical indication of, *inside front cover, i,* 49–50

Percentages, numerals used, 30

Periodicals
ABA section reports, 88
abbreviations, American, 91–103
abbreviations, Commonwealth and common law, 91–103
abbreviations, non-common-law, 29–30, 103–04
abstracts in, 89
ALI proceedings, 88
annotations, 90
articles, *inside front cover, i, 6, 7, 8, 14, 15, 17,* 88
basic citation forms, *inside front cover, i, 4, 5, 6, 7, 8, 14, 15, 17, 18, 22, 23,* 87
book notes, *89*
book reviews, *89*
case comments, *89*
case notes, *89*

Page references in regular type are to INSTRUCTIONS; page references in *italics* are to EXAMPLES.

cases, when cited to, *43–44*
citation order, 12–13
comments, law review, *4,* 89
components of citation, 87
date, 87
"Developments in the Law," *89*
generally, 87–104
institutes, regular publications by, 88
jump cites, 87
multipart articles, 90–91
names, abbreviation of, 87
names, typeface used, 87
new series (n.s.), 92
notes, law review, *inside front cover, i, 5, 17, 18,* 89
order within signal, 12–13
page citation, 16–18
pages, 87
pinpoint citations, 87
proceedings, 88
punctuation in titles, when omitted, 92
recent cases, 89
recent developments, 89
recent statutes, 89
special projects, law review, 89
statutes cited to, 58–59, 64–65
student-written material, 89
subdivisions in, 87–88
Supreme Court note, *89*
surveys of law, 90
symposia, 90
titles, 89
typeface used, authors and titles of articles, *inside front cover, i,* 3–6, 88
typeface used, names of periodicals, *inside front cover, i,* 3–6, 87
volume, 15–16, 87
when cited, 64–65
year, 87

Periods, to indicate omissions in quotations, 26–28
Permanent Court of Arbitration, 124
Permanent Court of International Justice, 121–22
Permanently bound services
abbreviations of, 108–14
generally, 107
Photoduplicated reprints, 85
Phrases of location
letters, speeches, and interviews, 86
omitted from case names, 39
railroad names, in, 42
unpublished works, 86

Pike & Fischer (P & F) services, 108
(*see also* Services and topical reporters)
Pinpoint citations
Common Market cases, 122
Federal Register, 76
generally, *inside front cover, iv,* 17
multipart articles, 90–91
newspapers, 104–05
opinions, formal advisory, 77
periodicals, 87
session laws, 63
statutes, 64
World Court cases, 122
Pleadings, Oral Arguments and Documents, 121
Pleadings, World Court cases, 121
Plenary materials, UN, 124–25
Plurality opinion, indication of, 49
Pluralization of abbreviations, 41
Pocket parts
books and pamphlets, 84
codes, 61
Popular names
cases, 36–37
international agreements, 118
statutes, 60, 63
treaties, 118
Positive law, codes enacted into, 59
Preamble, constitutional, *57*
Prefaces, *17,* 82
Prentice Hall (P-H) services, 108
(*see also* Services and topical reporters)
Prepositions
capitalization, 31
in periodical names, 91
Presidential messages, *79*
Presidential proclamations, 78
Previously cited authorities
cross-reference to, 21–25
short forms for, 21–25
Prince Edward Island
courts and statutes, 182–83
Printing, when indicated, 83
Prior history
(*see* History of cases, History of statutes)
Private laws, 59
Privy Council, 185
indicated in citation, 46–47
indication of jurisdiction, other than English appeal, 46–47
"Probable jurisdiction noted," **in case history,** 51

Page references in regular type are to INSTRUCTIONS; page references in *italics* are to EXAMPLES.

Procedural phrases, in case names, 3, 5, 6, 37–38
Procedure, rules of, 67
Proceedings, 88
Professional Responsibility, Code of, 69–70
Professionally written law review material, 88
Proposed administrative rules and regulations, 76
Proposed draft, restatements and model codes, 68
Prospectus, financial, *83*
Provinces, abbreviation of, *inside back cover*
Provisional editions, UN official records, 128
Public law number, when given for federal statutes, 63, 135
Public Papers of the Presidents, 79
Publication number
League of Nations publications, 129
series publications, 83
UN publications, *117,* 124, 126
Publication, place of, 84
Publications
ABA section reports, 88
ALI proceedings, 88
considered periodicals or reporters, 44
institutes, regular publications, 88
proceedings, 88
typeface in briefs and legal memoranda, *inside front cover,* 3–4
typeface in law review footnotes, *i,* 6, 81, 82, 85
typeface used for names, 87
Publisher
books, 82
codes, 61, 71
foreign codes, 71
services, 107–08
session laws, 64
statutes, 64
Puerto Rico
courts, statutes, and administrative materials, 167
Punctuation
between case and commentary, 13–14
between statute and case construing it, 13–14
citations, separated by semicolons, 7
initials, 29
periodical titles, 92
quotations, 25–28
subdivisions, 19–20
subsequent history of cases, 50–51
with introductory signals, 7, *8–10*

Quasi-statutory material, 72–77, 77–78
Quebec
courts and statutes, 182–83
Queen's Bench Division, 188
"*Questioned in,*" use of, 14
"Questioning," use of, 14
Quotation marks, 25–28
Quotations
alteration of, 26–28
generally, 25–28
identification of original source, 26
long and short, 25–28
mistakes in, indicated by "[sic]," 26
omissions in, 26–28
"*Quoted in,*" use of, 14
"Quoting," use of, *14*

Railroad Reorganization Court, 134
Railroads, in case names, 40, 42
Recent cases, citation of, *35,* 44, *49*
Recent cases, in law reviews, 89
Recent developments, in law reviews, 89
Recent statutes, 59, 63–64
Recent statutes, in law reviews, 89
Records
cases, 53
UN, 124–28
"Referee," abbreviation of, 33
References to previously cited authorities, 21–25
Regnal years, in English statutes, 70
Regulations of administrative agencies
generally, *75,* 76–77
Internal Revenue, 77–78
Treasury, *75,* 77–78
Rehearing
denial, when indicated, 50
"*sub. nom.*" not used, 51
"*Rehearing granted,*" in case history, 51
Related authority, 13–14
"Relation of," abbreviated to "*ex rel.,*" 37
Relator, first listed, not omitted, 37
Releases of administrative agencies, 43
Remand, history of case on, 50
Renumbered and reprinted reports, 44
Reorganization plans, 78

Page references in regular type are to INSTRUCTIONS; page references in *italics* are to EXAMPLES.

Repagination
books and pamphlets, 84
case reporters, 44
***"Repealed by"* in statute citation,** *65*
Repealed statutes, 65
Repeating citations, 21–25
Report of Judgments, Advisory Opinions and Orders, 121
Reporter editor, when given, 44
Reporters of cases
(*see also* Services and topical reporters)
abbreviations, 44
administrative cases, 43
American, 133–35
annotations of cases, 90
case notes in foreign reporters, 54
Common Market cases, 122
computer services, *52*
court administrative orders, 79
dual citations, 44
editor named, 44
federal cases, 133–35
foreign, generally, 54
generally, *35–36,* 43–44
international arbitrations, 123–24
jurisdiction named, 44, 45
official and West, when cited, 43
page citation, 44
publications considered as, 44
renumbered and reprinted, 44
requiring dual citation, 44
services, permanently bound, 107
state, 43, 45–46
typeface, *35–36*
unofficial, when cited, 43–44
volume citation, 15–16, 44
World Court, 121–22
Reports
(*see also* Reporters of cases)
administrative agencies, 77
congressional, *71,* 73–74
government agencies, 77
legislative, *71*
"Representative," abbreviation of, 33
Reprinted case reporters, 44, 186–89
***"Reprinted in,"* use of,** 13–14, *75, 78*
***"Reprinted in,"* with multiple sources,** *72, 78*
Reprints, photoduplicated, 85
Resolutions
congressional, 72–73
statutory, *71*
UN organs, 126–28
Restatements, *20,* 68–69
comments, 20
reporter's notes, 20
Reuben, Michael B., *43, 85*
Revenue Acts, 66–67
Revenue rulings, *78*
Reversals, in subsequent case history, 50
***"Reversed,"* in case history,** 51
Reversed names of parties, citation of on appeal, 51–52
***"Reversing,"* in case history,** 51
Review, cited with book reviewed, 14
***"Reviewed in,"* use of,** 14
Reviewer of book, 89–90
"Reviewing," use of in book review citation, 14, 89
Revised Reports, 186
***Revisions* (Canadian statutes),** 70–71
Rhode Island
courts and statutes, 167
Roman law references, 198–99
Roman numerals, when not used, 15, 70
Roman type
(*see* Typeface)
Rules
administrative, 76–77
court, 67
ethics, 69–70
evidence, 67
procedure, 67
Rules and regulations, proposed, 76

Sales number, UN, *117,* 124
Saskatchewan
courts and statutes, 182–83
Scattered sections of code, 59–60
"Schedule(s)," abbreviation of, 15
Scotland
courts and statutes, 190
SEC releases, *43*
Secondary authorities
administrative reporters, 43
books and pamphlets, 81–87
British materials, 186
citation order, 12–13
congressional materials, 73–75
law journals and reviews, 87–104
legislative histories, 75
letters, speeches, interviews, 86
limited circulation, 86
magazines, 87–104
order within signal, 12–13
periodicals, 87–104
periodicals, American, 91–103

periodicals, Commonwealth and common law, 91–92
periodicals, other foreign jurisdictions, 103–04
services, 107–14
statutes cited to, 58, 64–65
Treasury regulations, 77
unpublished works, 86
Section number
generally, 15, 18–20, 30
services, 108
Sections
ABA section reports, 88
administrative compilations, 76
ALI proceedings, 88
amending act, 18
books and pamphlets, 81
citation to, 30
Code of Federal Regulations, 76
codes, consecutive, 19–20
codes, statutory, 60
generally, 15, 18–20, 30
institutes, publications by, 88
international agreements, 118
model codes, 68–69
municipal ordinances, 67
newspapers, 104–05
ordinances, municipal, 67
proceedings, 88
restatements, 68–69
scattered, 59–60
services, 108
session laws, 63
standards, 68–69
statutes, 60
treaties, 118
"Section(s)," abbreviation of, 15, 18–19, 30
Security Council, UN, records, 124, 127
***"See also,"* as signal,** 8
***"See,"* as signal,** 8
***"See, e.g.,"* as signal,** *8*
***"See generally,"* as signal,** 9–10
Senate materials
(*see* Congressional materials)
"Senator," abbreviation of, 33
Separate decisions of other issues, in case history, 51
Separate opinions
indication of, *17,* 49
slip opinion, 52
Serial numbers
books and pamphlets, 81, 83
executive orders, *78*
leaflets, 83
League of Nations documents, 129
monographs, 83
pamphlets and books, 83
proclamations, *78*
publications in series, 83
reorganization plans, 78
UN documents, *117,* 126
World Court cases, 121
"Series" and "Serial(s)," abbreviation of, 15
Series, books and pamphlets in, 83
Series numbers
renumbered, 44, 92
Services and topical reporters
abbreviations, 108–14
abbreviations of publishers, 108
administrative rules and announcements, 77
basic citation form, *inside front cover, i, 35,* 107
cases, *35*
citation of cases, 43
Common Market materials, 129
components of citation, 107
dates, 107
dates of materials in, 108
European Community materials, 122–23, 129
generally, 107–14
looseleaf, citations of, 107
name, *inside front cover, i, 20, 35*, 107
pages, *20,* 107, 108
paragraphs, *20*, 107, 108
parallel citations, for administrative cases, 43
parenthetical indications of later bound form, 107
publishers, 107–108
sections, 107–108
state law services, 64–65
statutes, 58–59, 64–65
subdivisions, 107–08
title of service, 107
transfer binders, 107
typeface, *inside front cover, i,* 107
U.S. Law Week, *36,* 113, 133
volumes and editions, 15–16, 107
years, 107–08
Session laws
(*see also* Codes, Statutes)
abbreviations, 63
"Act of ___", 63
amendments cited to, *18,* 59, *65*

Page references in regular type are to INSTRUCTIONS; page references in *italics* are to EXAMPLES.

Canadian, 70–71
chapter numbers, 63, *135*
citation, basic forms, *inside front cover, 57–59*
cited by page, *18,* 63
civil law countries, 190–200
codification, future, 64
Commonwealth and common law countries, 179–90
dates, 63–64
effective date of statutes, 64
enactment, year or date, 63–64
English, 70
federal, 63–64
Federal Register, 76–77
foreign countries, 179–200
former version of statute, 59
jump cites, 63
jurisdiction, abbreviated name of, 63
municipal ordinances, 67
name of session law, 63
name of statute, 63
official and privately published, 58, 59
omission of words in title, 63
ordinances, uncodified, 67
pages, when cited to, 63
parallel citation of, 63–64
pinpoint cites, 63
printed in roman type, *inside front cover, i,* 63
private editor or compiler, 64
public law number, *inside front cover, i,* 63, 135
publishers, 64
recent statutes, 59, 63–64
scattered sections of code, 59–60
sections and subsections, 18–20, 63
short title of statute, 63
signature by executive, year of, 64
state, 63–64, 136–76
statute cited as historical fact, 59
statute, name of, 63
statute not in current code but in force, 59
statute not in force, 59, *65*
Statutes at Large, *inside front cover, i,* 59, 73, 78, 120, 135, 143
statutes, when cited to, 59
subsections and sections, 18–20, 63
typeface, 63
U.S. Code Congressional & Administrative News, cited to, 64
volume, 63
year as volume number, 63

Short citation forms
books and pamphlets, 81
cases, 23–24
constitutions, 25
generally, 23–25
repeating citations, 21–25, 67
statutes, 24
Short Titles Act, 70
"[Sic]," use of, 26
Signals
analogous support, 9, *10*
authority from different jurisdiction, 8
authority stating proposition, 8
background material, 9–10
comparison, 9
direct contradiction, 9, *10*
direct support, 8
generally, 7–10
identification, 8
italicization in briefs and legal memoranda, 3
italicization in law review footnotes, 6
joining citations, *7–8*
opposition, 9
order of citation, 10
order within signal, 10–13
sampling of authorities, 8
source of quotation, 8
string citations, 7, *10*
supplemental material, 9–10
support, 8–9
table of signals, 8–10
typeface used in briefs and legal memoranda, 3
typeface used in law review footnotes, 6
Slip opinions, *inside front cover, i, 35,* 44, 52
South Carolina
courts, statutes, and administrative materials, 167–68
South Dakota
courts, statutes, and administrative materials, 169
Spacing of abbreviations and initials, 28–29
Special concurrence, indication of, 49
Special Fund, UN, 127–28
"Special Project," designating student work, 89
Special projects in periodicals, 89
Special reports of government agencies, 77
Speeches, 85

Page references in regular type are to INSTRUCTIONS; page references in *italics* are to EXAMPLES.

Split decision
indication of, 49
Standards, 68–69
Star pages in books and pamphlets, 84
State administrative agencies
generally, 136–76
reports, 76
State cases
court of decision, abbreviations, 45–48, 136–76
courts of decision, indication of, 45–46
department or division of court, 46
identification of court of decision, 45–46
official and unofficial reporters, 43–44
parallel citations, 43, 136–76
reporters
(*see* name of individual state)
State courts
generally, 136–76
rules of court, *67*
State Department publications, 120
"State of," omitted in case names, 39
States
(*see also* name of individual jurisdiction)
abbreviated in case names, 41
abbreviation of, *inside back cover*
law services, *64,* 73
omitted in case names, 39
session laws, 63–64, 136–76
statutes, 57–69, 136–76
statutory codes, 136–76
Statute Law Revision Act, 70
Statutes
(*see also* Codes, Session laws)
administrative rules and regulations, 76–77
amended, 59
amended, uniform acts, 60
amendments, 65
amendments of Canadian, 71
American, *inside front cover, i, 57–58*
appendices to codes, appearing in, 61–62
basic forms of citation, *inside front cover, i,* 24, *57–58*
bills and resolutions, 72–73
Canadian, 70–71
case construing statute, cited with, 14
citation order, 11–12
citations in law review text, 24
cited by page, 63
city ordinances, 67
civil law countries, 190–200
code appendices, appearing in, 61–62
commentary on, cited with, 14
Commonwealth and common law countries, 70–71, 179–90
compilations, 60–62
components of citation, 58–59
concurrent resolutions, 72–73
county ordinances, 67
current code, *inside front cover, i,* 66
date, Internal Revenue Code, 66–67
dates, 65
dates of amendment, 65
effective date, 62, 64
English, 70
ethics, rules of, 69–70
exact date, 65
explanatory parenthetical phrases, 66
federal and state, *57–58*
foreign jurisdictions, *58,* 70–71, 179–200
future codification, 64–65
generally, 57–71
historical fact, cited as, 59
history of, as amended, 59, *60,* 65–66
Internal Revenue Code, 66–67
joint resolutions, 72–73
legislative history, 71–75
legislative materials, 71–75
materially different from code, 59
miscellaneous citation forms, 66–71
multiple sections and subsections, 19–20
municipal ordinances, 67
name of, in session laws, 63
names, 60
newspapers, cited to, 64–65
no longer in force, 65
not in current code, 59, 60, 65
order within signal, 11–12
ordinances, municipal and county, 67
original enactment, indication of, *66*
pages, when cited to, 63
parallel citations to, 63–64
parenthetical indications, 66
parenthetical indications of amendment, 65
periodicals, cited to, 64–65
present similar statute, indication of, *65*
prior history, 65–66
private editor or compiler, 64
private laws, 59
privately published, Internal Revenue Code, 66
publication of, 58–59
publisher, 64
recent, 63–65
related authority, 13–14

Page references in regular type are to INSTRUCTIONS; page references in *italics* are to EXAMPLES.

repealed, 59, 65
reprinted in appendix of code, *62*
resolutions, 72–73
revenue, 66–67
scattered sections of code, 19, 59–60
secondary sources, 58, 64–65
sections, citation to, 18, 60
services and topical reporters, 59, 64–65, *108*
signature by executive, year of, 64
source to cite, 58–60
special citation forms, 66–71
state, 136–76
state, uniform acts, 68
subsequent history, 65
substance, parenthetical indication of, *66*
superseded, 59
supplements, *20,* 58–59
tax materials, 66–67
Treasury regulations, 77–78
uncompiled, 61
uniform acts, 68–69
United States Code (U.S.C.), 60, 135
United States Code Annotated (U.S.C.A.), 60, 135
United States Code Service (U.S.C.S.), 60, 135
very recent, 65
withdrawn, uniform acts, 68

Statutes at Large, *inside front cover, i,* 63, 73, 78, 120, 135, 143
(*see also* Session laws)

Statutory Instruments Revised, The Statutory Rules and Orders and, 186

Statutory materials
American, *inside front cover, i, 57–58*
basic citation forms, *inside front cover, i, 57–58*
bills and resolutions, 72–73
city ordinances, 67
civil law countries, 190–200
components of citation, 58
constitutions, *inside front cover,* 57
county ordinances, 67
federal and state, *inside front cover, i, 57–58*
foreign jurisdictions, *58,* 70–71
generally, 57–71
international agreements, *117,* 118–21
legislative materials, *inside front cover, i,* 71–75
ordinances, municipal, 67
regulations, orders, and rulings, 76–79
Roman law references, 198–99
secondary sources, 58
Treasury regulations, 77–78
treaties, *117,* 118–21
uniform acts, 68–69

String citations, *7–8, 10*

Student work, in periodicals, 89

Style
abbreviations, 14–15, 28–30
capitalization, 31–33
quotations, 25–28
titles of officials, 33
typeface, 3–6, 31
U.S. Government Printing Office Manual, iv, 31

"Sub nom.," **in case history,** 52

Subdivisions in cited material
ABA section reports, 88
abbreviations, 14–15
administrative compilations, 76
ALI proceedings, 88
"at," used to indicate page citations, 13
books and pamphlets, 81
Code of Federal Regulations, 76
codes, statutory, 60–61
constitutions, 32, 57
English statutes, 70
footnotes, 17–18
generally, 14–21
"in," used to indicate location in an entire work, 13
institutes, publications by, 88
international agreements, 118
model codes, 68–69
multipart articles, 91
multiple pages, 17–18
multiple paragraphs, 20
multiple sections, 19–20
newspapers, 104–05
ordinances, municipal, 67
pages or sections, generally, 16–20
pages or sections, in books, 81
pages or sections, in codes, 19–20
pages or sections, in services, 108
pages or sections, in session laws, 63
"passim," use of, 18
proceedings, 88
restatements, 68–69
schedules, 15, 70
separately paginated, 16
services, 107, 108
session laws, 63
standards, 68–69
statutes, 60–61, 63
treaties, 118

Page references in regular type are to INSTRUCTIONS; page references in *italics* are to EXAMPLES.

UN materials, 124, 125
Subject-matter title of codes, 61
Subsections
multiple, in statutes, 19
session laws, 63
Subsequent citations, short forms, 21–25
Subsequent history
(*see* History of cases, History of statutes)
Subsidiary organs, UN, 127–28
Substitutions in quotations, 26
Subtitles of books, 82
Successive citations, short forms, 21–25
Supplementing citations
introductory signals to, 8–9
Supplements
books and pamphlets, 81, 84
codes, 61
Internal Revenue Code, 66
separately paginated, 16
statutory, 60
UN, 124–25
Supporting citation
introductory signals to, *7–8,* 8–9
"Supra"
briefs and legal memoranda, use in, *21,* 22
groups of authorities in work, *21*
previously cited authority, 22–23
textual material in work, 22
Supreme Court Justice sitting as Circuit Justice, 45, 133
Supreme Court note, *89*
Supreme Court Foreword, *88*
Supreme Court of Judicature, English, 187–89
Supreme Court Reporter, 133
Supreme Court Review, *87*
Supreme Court, U.S.
(*see* U.S. Supreme Court)
Surnames, composed of two words, 39–40
Surveys, in periodicals, 90
Switzerland
cantons, 200
codes, 199
constitution, 199
courts, 199–200
statutes and decrees, 199–200
Symbols, 30
Symposia in periodicals, 90

Tax Court, citation of cases, 42, 134
Tax materials
codes, 66–67
Cumulative Bulletin, 78
generally, 77–78
Internal Revenue Bulletin, 78
Internal Revenue Code, 66–67
revenue rulings, *78*
Treasury decisions, 78
Treasury regulations, 77–78
Telephone interviews, *85*
Temporary Emergency Court of Appeals, *48,* 133
Tennessee
courts, statutes, and administrative materials, 169–70
Tentative drafts, restatements, and model codes, 68
"Term," capitalization of, 33
Term of court, 33
Texas
courts, statutes, and administrative materials, *61,* 170–72
Text
abbreviation of case names in, 38
briefs and legal memoranda, typeface in, 3–4
numbers in, 30
typefaces, 5
Textual footnote materials
typeface used in, 6
Textual material in same work, cross reference to, 21
Textual reference to statutes, 24
"The," in case name, 38
Theses, unpublished, 81, *86*
Times Law Reports, 187
Titles
abbreviations, 82
articles in periodicals, 88
book reviews, 90
books and pamphlets, 81–82
capitalization of, 31–33
codes, statutory, 60–61
congressional documents and reports, 73–74
ending with date, 82
hearings, 73
international agreements, *117,* 118–19
multivolume works, 82
newspaper articles, 104–05
pamphlets and books, 82
parties, omitted in case names, 37
personal titles, 33
services, 107

Page references in regular type are to INSTRUCTIONS; page references in *italics* are to EXAMPLES.

student-written materials, 89
subtitles of books, 82
Supreme Court Justices, 33
surveys and symposia, 90
treaties, *117*, 118–19
typeface, 3–4, 5–6, 82, 85
UN materials, *117*, 124
unpublished works, 82
"Title(s)," abbreviation of, 15
"To be codified at," use of, *64, 76*
Topical reporters
(*see* Services and topical reporters)
Touton, Louis, *iv, 85*
Transcript of record, 53
Transfer binders, services, 107
Translators of books, 81–82
Treasury decisions, 78
Treasury Decisions Under Customs and Other Laws, 78, 136
Treasury Decisions Under Internal Revenue Laws, 78, 136
Treasury regulations, *75*, 77–78
Treaties
(*see* International agreements)
***Treaties and Other International Acts Series* (T.I.A.S.),** *inside front cover, i, 117*, 120
Treatises, *18*, 81, 82, 83
(*see also* Books and pamphlets)
Treaty collections, 120–21
***Treaty Series* (T.S.),** 120
Trusteeship Council Official Records, 124, 127
Typed manuscripts, 86
Typeface
articles, authors of, 88
articles, titles of, 88
authors, articles, 88
authors, books, 81, 85
authors, essays in collection, 85
bills and resolutions, *72–73*
books and pamphlets, 81, 82, 85
books, cited in briefs and legal memoranda, *inside front cover, 4*
books, cited in law review footnotes, 6
bound services, 107
briefs and legal memoranda, *inside front cover, i*, 3–4, 86
case history terms, 50–52
case names, in briefs and legal memoranda, *inside front cover*, 3
case names, in law review footnotes, *i*, 5
case names, mentioned in law review text, 5
citations in briefs, *inside front cover*, 3–4
codes, 60
collected essays, 85
commentary, indication of, 14
constitutions, 57
documents, legislative, *73–74*
explanatory phrases in briefs and legal memoranda, *inside front cover*, 3
explanatory phrases in law review footnotes, *i*, 6
footnotes, 5–6
generally, 3–6
hearings, *inside front cover, i, 4, 13, 23, 73*
international agreements, *117*
interviews, citations of, 85
italics, 3–6
italics, in footnote citations, 5–6, *13–14, 31*
italics, in law review text, 4–5
italics represented by underscoring, *inside front cover*, 3
italics showing style, 31
large and small capitals, 3–6, 81, 82, 85, 87, 104
large and small capitals, in footnote citations, 5–6
law review footnotes, *i*, 5–6
law review text, 4–5
letters, citation to, 85
looseleaf services, 107
manuscripts, typed, citations to, 86
mimeographed materials, citations to, 86
model codes, 68
newspapers, 104
ordinances, municipal, 67
ordinary roman, 3–6
periodicals, names of, 87
publications, cited in briefs and legal memoranda, 3–4
publications, cited in law review footnotes, 6
related authority, indication of, 13–14
reporters, *35–36*
reports, legislative, *73–74*
restatements, 68
roman type, in footnote citations, 5–6
roman type, in text, 6
rules of court procedure, 67
services, 107
session laws, 63
shortened citation form, 23–24
signals, 8–10
signals used as part of sentence, 10

Page references in regular type are to INSTRUCTIONS; page references in *italics* are to EXAMPLES.

speeches, citations to, 85
standards, 68
student-written materials, 89
subsequent and prior history of cases, 50–52
textual footnote material, 6
textual material in law reviews, 4–5
theses, unpublished, citations to, 86
titles, 82, 85
treaties and other international agreements, *117*
typed manuscripts, 86
underscoring, use of to represent italics, 3
uniform acts, 67

Unclear holdings, indication of, 49
Uncompiled laws, 61
Understandings, international, 118
Uniform acts, 68–69
Uniform Adoption Act, *68*
Uniform Commercial Code, *21, 68*
Uniform Laws Annotated **(U.L.A.),** 68
Unions, in case names, 40–41
United Kingdom
administrative materials, 186
command numbers, 120
courts and statutes, 185–86
parliamentary materials, 186
statutes, 186
treaty series, 120
United Nations materials
Administrative Tribunal, 128
basic citation forms, 124–26
charter, *117*, 126
citation, specific materials, 126–28
Development Programme, 127–28
document numbers, *117*, 124, 126
documents, 124–28
Economic and Social Council, 127
foreign language versions, 126
General Assembly, *117*, 126–27
generally, 124–28
International Law Commission, 128
official records, *117*, 124–28
organizational conference materials, 128
pages or paragraphs, 125–26
preparatory materials, 128
provisional editions, 128
publications, 124–28
sales number, *117*, 124
Security Council, 127
serial number, 126
Special Fund, 127–28
subdivisions, 125
subsidiary organs, 127–28
Treaty Series, *117*, 120
Trusteeship Council, 127
volume number, 125
yearbooks, 128
United Nations Reports of International Arbitration Awards, 124
United Nations Treaty Series **(U.N.T.S.),** *117*, 120
United States
administrative publications, 75–79, 133–36
bankruptcy appellate panels, 45, 134
bankruptcy courts, 45, *107*, 134
Board of Tax Appeals, 134
circuit courts, old federal, 45, 133
Circuit Justices, 45, 133
Commerce Court, 133
Court of Claims, 134
Court of Customs and Patent Appeals, 134
Court of International Trade, 134
Court of Military Appeals, 135
Court of Military Review, 135
courts of appeals, 45, 133
Customs Court, 134
district courts, 45, 134
Emergency Court of Appeals, 133
international agreements, 118–21
Judicial Panel on Multi-District Litigation, 45, 134
Railroad Reorganization Court, 133
session laws, 63–64, 133
statutory compilations, 60–62, 135
Supreme Court (*see* U.S. Supreme Court)
Tax Court, *42*, 134
Temporary Emergency Court of Appeals, *48*, 133
treaties, *117*, 118–21
"United States," abbreviation of, 29, 82, 121
United States Code **(U.S.C.)**
appendix, *20, 62, 76*
generally, *19*, 60, *61–62*, 66, 78, 135
supplement, 61
United States Code Annotated **(U.S.C.A.),** 60, *61*, 66, 78, 135
United States Code Congressional & Administrative News, 58–59, 64, 74, 79
United States Code Service **(U.S.C.S.),** 60, *61*, 66, 78, 135

Page references in regular type are to INSTRUCTIONS; page references in *italics* are to EXAMPLES.

United States Department of State publications, *83*
United States Law Week **(U.S.L.W.),** *36*, 45, 133
United States Reports, 133
United States Supreme Court
abbreviation of, 45
administrative orders, *79*
Circuit Justices, 45, 133
citation, *36,* 133
citation in subsequent history, *36,* 50
cite only to official reporter, 133
date of decision, 48
docket numbers, *36,* 53
Justice, sitting as Circuit Justice, 45, 133
recent decisions, *36,* 133
renumbered and reprinted reporters, 44, 133
rules, *67*
subsequent history, 50
Supreme Court Reporter, *36,* 133
U.S. Law Week, *36*, 133
U.S. Reports, 133
United States Treasury, decisions and regulations, 77–78
United States Treaties and Other International Agreements **(U.S.T.),** *inside front cover, i, 117,* 120
Unofficial codes, differently numbered, 62
Unofficial reporters
(*see also* name of individual jurisdiction)
administrative cases, 43
federal courts, 133–35
state courts, 43
U.S. Supreme Court, 133
when cited, 43
Unofficial sources
English, 186–89
international arbitration awards, 123–24
statutes, American, 58–60
statutes, foreign, generally, 71
Unpublished works, *inside front cover, i,* 81, 86
Unreported cases, *35,* 36, 52
"Use of," changed to "*ex rel.*" in case names, 37
Utah
courts, statutes, and administrative materials, 172

"*Vacated,*" in case history, 51
Vermont
courts, statutes, and administrative materials, *62,* 172–73
"Vice Chancellor," abbreviation of, 33
Virgin Islands
courts, statutes, and administrative materials, 173–74
Virginia
courts and statutes, 174
Volume number
administrative reports, *77*
ALI proceedings, 88
Arabic numerals, 15
books and pamphlets, 15, 81
case reports, 44
codes, statutory, 60–61
Common Market cases, 122
Cumulative Bulletin, 78
Federal Register, 76
generally, 15–16
institute publications, 88
law journals and reviews, 87
letter with year, *90*
location in citation, 15
looseleaf services, 15–16
month used to indicate, *108*
periodicals, 15–16, 87
proceedings, 88
renumbered reports, 44
services, 107
session laws, 63
UN materials, 124, 125
World Court cases, 121
year part of, 49
year with letter, *90*
"Volume(s)," abbreviation of, 15

Wales
(*see* England)
Washington
courts, statutes, and administrative materials, *19,* 174
Weekly Compilation of Presidential Documents, 79
Weekly Notes **and** ***Weekly Law Reports,*** 187
Weight of a citation
(*see* Parenthetical indications)
West Germany
(*see* Germany)
West reporters
(*see also* Unofficial reporters)
generally, 48
West Virginia
courts and statutes, 175

Page references in regular type are to INSTRUCTIONS; page references in *italics* are to EXAMPLES.

Western Weekly Reports, 182
WESTLAW, 52
West's Federal Practice Manual, *82*
"Will of," in case name, 38
Wisconsin
courts, statutes, and administrative materials, 175
Words
designating student work, 89
explaining case history, 50–52
foreign, abbreviation of, 122
foreign derivation, 31
inserted or substituted in quotations, 26
omission in name of session laws, 63
omitted in case names, 36–43
periodical names, 91
referring to a second source, 13–14
session laws, omission of in, 63
World Court, *117,* 121–22
Writers, indication of, 81–82
Wyoming
courts and statutes, 176

Years
(*see also* Dates)
administrative agency reports, *77*
administrative compilations, 76
books and pamphlets, 81, 83–85
Code of Federal Regulations, *75,* 76
codes, 66
Common Market cases, 122
enactment, session laws, 63–64
English statutes, 70
ethical opinions, 69–70
ethical rules, 69
Federal Register, *75,* 76
forewords, 82
Internal Revenue Code, 66
international agreements, 119
League of Nations materials, 129
legislative materials, 72, 74
model codes, 68
ordinances, municipal, 67
periodicals, 87
pocket parts, 84
prefaces, 82
regnal, in English statutes, 70
restatements, 68
rules of court, 67
rules of procedure, 67
services, 107, 108
session laws, 63–64
standards, 68
statutes not in current code, 63–64
statutes, uniform acts, 68
supplements, 16, 61, 84
Treasury regulations, *75,* 77
treaties, *117,* 119
uniform acts, 68
volume numbers, in administrative reports, 15–16
volume numbers, in Commonwealth and common law case reporters, 16
volume numbers, in looseleaf services, 15–16
volume numbers, in periodicals, 15–16, 87
volume numbers, in session laws, 63
Yearbooks
basic citation forms, 117
generally, *117,* 130–31
International Court of Justice, *117, 122,* 130
International Law Commission, 128, 130
sales number, cited to, 124
UN, *117,* 128, 130–31
Yukon Territory
statutes, 182–83

READER'S NOTES

READER'S NOTES

READER'S NOTES

READER'S NOTES

READER'S NOTES

READER'S NOTES

READER'S NOTES